Hoover Institution Publications 150

Amoral America

AMORAL AMERICA

George C. S. Benson

and

Thomas S. Engeman

with the collaboration of

Ellen L. S. Riley

and

Ruth Aura Ross

1975
Hoover Institution Press
Stanford University
Stanford, California

Hoover Institution Publications 150
International Standard Book Number 0-8179-1503-6
Library of Congress Catalog Card Number 75-18665
© 1975 by the Board of Trustees of the
    Leland Stanford Junior University
Printed in the United States of America

Contents

Preface

The authors have collaborated for several years on this project and agree on the major conclusions. Nevertheless, a division of labor has been necessary. Benson has had major responsibility for Chapters 2, 3, 4, 7, 8, 9, 10; Engeman for the Introduction, Epilogue, and Chapters 1, 5, 6, 11. Chapter 12 was written jointly. We are grateful to Ellen Riley for materials which have been used, especially in Chapters 7, 8, 9, and 10. We are also grateful to Dr. Ruth A. Ross for the appendices. Barbara Johnson has been perceptive, industrious, and very helpful in putting together the manuscript.

Our gratitude also includes our colleagues, Professors Steven Smith, Ward Elliott, and John Snortum, who read the manuscript for us, as well as many other of our colleagues who have suggested materials to us. Mr. Harris Seed, a trustee of Claremont Men's College, and Professors George Gibbs and Alfred Balitzer, both of Claremont Men's College, were especially helpful.

Our chief gratitude is to Mr. Henry Salvatori, donor of the Salvatori Center at Claremont Men's College. He originally suggested that we investigate the subject of ethics several years ago, and has been patient with our slowness in putting together the variety of information from many fields of knowledge which have entered into this book. We hope that he and our other readers will not be too disappointed with the results.

This book is the only serious effort we know of to appraise the sources of the ethical attitudes of a nation. We know that we must have made many errors in judgment. We hope for constructive criticisms.

Claremont, California   George C. S. Benson
April, 1975   Thomas S. Engeman

Introduction

This study will show that society in the United States ignores individual ethical instruction. As here understood, ethical instruction has two relatively distinct aspects: social ethics and individual ethics. Social ethics is concerned with social justice: helping minority groups achieve equality, maintaining a humanitarian foreign policy, improving the quality of the environment. Individual ethics, on the other hand, is concerned with the individual person's immediate responsibility over his own—as opposed to the society's—action toward other individuals. A person shows a high individual ethical conscience if he is honest, truthful, responsible, law-abiding, and non-violent.

Although social and individual ethics tend to be allied, there are many cases where they are not. To take two illustrative stereotypes: a revolutionary may have a clear perception of social injustice and strongly desire to eliminate it. His action toward others on an individual basis, however, either as a result of his tendency toward violence or because of an inability to fulfill personal commitments, may make him unethical in his personal responsibilities. On the other side, a businessman may be honest, truthful, and a good family man, but if he ignores the long-term interests of his employees, discriminates against minorities, or pollutes the environment, he is also deficient in his social ethics.

Social Ethics

It is the authors' belief that the United States—especially in this century—has emphasized the importance of social ethics at the expense of individual ethics. The change in direction from individual to social ethics may have been a healthy reaction against Puritanical moral standards—culminating in Prohibition—which demanded too much from individual conscience. Reactions themselves can go too

1

far. The events of the last two decades, including riots, assassina-
tions, and Watergate—in which the social end was used to excuse
criminal means—raise the legitimate question of whether or not
Americans relied too heavily on a social ethics ideology,
emphasizing institutional and mechanical solutions to problems,
while they ignored the habits and attitudes of the individual person.

Findings indicate that this is precisely what happened. A survey
of ethical instruction currently given in our society, including
television, the schools, and the churches, shows an almost total
emphasis on social ethics *to the near exclusion of individual ethics.*

An example of the prevalence of social ethics in our understanding of morality is "situation ethics."[1] This theory states that the
desirable social end—*agape* or love—shall be pursued, and that
ethical rules or codes are by nature inhibiting. Each situation is so
unique that to try to limit attainment of the social goal by rules—or,
as some ethicists say, by deontological restraints—will always limit
its successful achievement. In this view, it makes little difference
whether one steals, lies, or even murders if such action results in a
desirable social end.

There appear to be two major difficulties with social-situational
ethics. First, they place individual or group conscience over that of
the majority. Bullets or bombs replace ballots. Second, they destroy
the primary sense of ethical responsibility for one's actions toward
other individuals. The social cause replaces the concern for
particular people—one's friends, family, neighbors. The social
cause comes before one's conscience.

This is by no means a strictly theoretical danger: the emphasis on
social-situational ethics has brought many good results, but its evils
are increasingly clear. To a significant degree, the youth revolt of the
late Sixties, with literally thousands of bombings or bomb threats,
building seizures, and campus disturbances, was heavily influenced
by situational-social morality. War protestors rationalized their
actions with situation ethics. It was perhaps inevitable that when the
shoe was on the other foot, situation ethics was employed by the
elected representatives of U.S. democracy and by their agents. Jeb
Stuart Magruder testified before the Senate that he learned his
ethics from a leading situational ethicist, William Sloane Coffin. The
social end, the defense of lawful authority, and the political end, the
reelection of Richard Nixon (and so the Watergate break-in), would

best be obtained—so this reasoning went—by illegal means. The wheel had come full circle.

Teaching Individual Ethics

Can individual ethics be taught? Is it possible to change student attitudes and behavior? These questions will be discussed more fully in Chapter Five, but the conclusions are stated here. At a bare minimum, we believe that ethical standards can be improved if people learn to appreciate the ethical alternatives present in every human decision.

More significantly, we believe that ethical instruction can improve ethical attitudes, habits, and performance. Can these assertions be proven? By the strict standards of social science it seems unlikely that one will ever fully document the role which ethical education can play in human life because no reasonable experimental procedures could be devised to test it. Professor James Q. Wilson has argued that certain social-psychological phenomena are so complex that no test can ever be designed to measure them.[2] Ethical instruction, involving as it does literally hundreds of variables, seems to fit into this category.

Even without empirical data, a strong case can be made for the place of ethical instruction. Historically, it has been observed that the moral influences of various religions and philosophies have had a profound effect on peoples. In the last century England underwent an ethical reform described by one authority as "little short of miraculous." There are a number of other examples which could be cited. Also, it is generally accepted among comparative sociologists and criminologists that religious and philosophic views have enormous influence on shaping society, including its ethical habits.

Another intellectual tradition arguing the importance of ethics to public and to private behavior is that formed by the political philosophers from Plato to Heidegger. Aristotle, perhaps the most widely-read political philosopher, wrote in the *Nicomachean Ethics*: "The true student of politics, too, is thought to have studied virtue (morality) above all other things; for he wishes to make his fellow citizens good and obedient to the laws. By human virtue we mean not that of the body but that of the soul; and happiness also we call an activity of the soul. . . . The student of politics, then, must study the soul."[3]

In addition, in the *Nicomachean Ethics*, Aristotle gives a clear and comprehensive analysis of ethical education. The *Ethics*, it should be noted, is an exercise in ethical education; it is not a book about ethics or "how to teach it." Since it is a book designed to make the reader more ethical through reasonable discussion, it presumes a knowledge of ethical effects. Aristotle understands that you cannot teach ethical principles to the psychopathic, the emotionally disturbed, or the uncontrollable, for they are unable to understand them or to act in an ethically reasonable way. Moreover, someone who has not experienced ethical behavior in his parents or in those around him cannot understand the basis of ethical reasoning. For Aristotle, habits and experience (modeling) are of fundamental significance.

"Hence anyone who is to listen intelligently to lectures about what is noble and just and, generally, about the subjects of political science must have been brought up in good habits. For the fact is the starting point, and if this is sufficiently plain to him, he will not at the start need reason as well; and the man who has been well brought up has or can easily get starting points."[4]

John Dewey, no admirer of Aristotle, also speaks of the force of habit and experience in moral education. "The dynamic force of habit taken in connection with the continuity of habits with one another explains the unity of character and conduct, or speaking more concretely of motive and act, will and deed."[5]

Dewey belongs in the tradition of political philosophers through his understanding that individual habits are the consequences of social or political habit. The regime or society is the best or most important—not necessarily the sole—teacher of ethics. This is the reason why Aristotle says that the student of political science is concerned with virtue (the habits and attitudes of the individual). Political societies are best understood by the qualities which they tend to form in their members. Dewey's *Democracy and Education* is a good example of a study which associates the nature of the political regime with its educational goals.

In the last century, Alexis de Tocqueville, perhaps the finest student ever of American institutions, reiterated the importance of popular morality for political institutions.

I have said earlier that I considered mores to be one of the great general causes responsible for the maintenance of a democratic republic in the United States. I here mean the term 'mores' (*moeurs*) to have its original Latin meaning; I mean it to apply not only to '*moeurs*' in the strict sense, which might be called the habits of the heart, but also to the different notions possessed by men, the various opinions current among them, and the sum of ideas that shape mental habits. So I use the word to cover the whole moral and intellectual state of a people.

I am concerned that the luckiest of geographical circumstances and the best of laws cannot maintain a constitution despite mores, whereas the latter can turn even the most unfavorable of circumstances and the worst laws to advantage. The importance of mores is a universal truth to which study and experience continually bring us back. I find it occupies the central position in my thoughts; all my ideas come back to it in the end. . . .

One cannot, therefore, say that in the United States religion influences the laws or political opinions in detail, but it does direct mores, and by regulating domestic life it helps to regulate the state.[6]

Many of our greatest scholars and philosophers agree on the essential place of public morality and ethical education for the well being of society.

Role of Institutions in Teaching Individual Ethics

Given the apparent importance of individual ethical education, why are American institutions—the churches, schools, television, the media, and the home—not doing an adequate job of ethical education? Secondly, what can be done to improve ethical education in our society?

The most important single body influencing ethical education in our society are the intellectuals. Some of the intellectual and philosophical obstacles to ethical education will be discussed in later chapters. To a large extent, the absence of ethical education can be traced to the power of these intellectual criticisms of individual ethics.

Institutions have differing responsibilities and methods of operation. This study analyzes individual ethical instruction in the social institutions of the U.S. (e.g., television, public education, religious schools, the family). Complementing the analysis are recommendations for improvement or inclusion of ethical material. These recommendations are based on the uses and needs of the institutions involved. For example, television, which could have a profound ethical influence on our society, is limited in the kinds of programming it can provide because it is commercially financed and must compete for audiences. The public schools must tread lightly in the area of ethics related to religious faith. The proposals made, we hope, are applicable to all these institutions.

Although we emphasize the role which individual ethical instruction might play in improving American life, we do not wish to negate the other progressive steps which should be taken in the areas of improved educational opportunities, better housing and jobs, and police procedures. We vigorously support prudent social welfare policies and improved police functions. However, we believe that they in themselves are not enough to ensure a fundamental improvement in social attitudes. As we have just indicated, a nation may have the most desirable constitutional and economic system, and if the citizens are unconvinced of the benefits and justice of the system no institutional correctives will avail.

Does not increasing the emphasis on individual ethics pose grave dangers to either intellectual or political freedom, or lead to increased conformity? In general, we recognize that there may be some risk. However, we believe the real threat is that too little will be done, not that overnight we will be made into moral martinets. A possible hazard is that the persons given the responsibility of implementing ethical instruction will be professional educators who are themselves the leading spokesmen for increased social ethics and who will, in fact, push that view of morality regardless of their obligation. This objection has some merit, but it is unduly skeptical of the educational profession. In a study of teachers in California schools conducted in 1973 by the Salvatori Center (cited in Chapter Ten), the large majority (72 percent) believed that they should take the initiative in teaching individual ethics. In addition to these findings, the American Institute for Character Education noted similar reactions by teachers to the materials which emphasize individual ethics.

Another danger closely allied to the foregoing is a possibility that government may become active in this area, thereby increasing its role in our daily lives at the expense of religious, business, and private associations of all kinds. Needless to say, this is not our desire. While there is room for increased government action to encourage greater ethical instruction in the schools and on TV, especially in the Office of Education and in the Federal Communications Commission, it would be fruitless for the government to try to legislate in these matters as has been done in the areas of civil rights and ecology. In the long run, any reform as fundamental as we are recommending—to become effective—must be supported by an underlying popular consensus of many groups. The government would have little lasting influence, in fact, if the local schools, the churches, the press and other media, the bar associations, the chambers of commerce, the university, and others were not also fundamentally committed to the need for educational change.

An Appreciation

While our approach follows in a long tradition of philosophic and scholarly writings about democratic societies, particularly Alexis de Tocqueville's *Democracy in America*, we must acknowledge the help we received from contemporary social scientists. The late Professor Leonard D. White and Professor Paul Douglas, both of the University of Chicago, indicated their concern that America might have to reconsider its whole system of maintaining an adequate level of ethics in the population.[7] Professor Lawrence Kohlberg of Harvard published extensively on ethical instruction. Professor Edwin M. Schur expressed concern about the sources of our moral values.[8] Professor Carl J. Friedrich discussed the possible effect of corruption on the national "ideatic core."[9] Irving Kristol has written extensively on the morality basis of our society.[10] In addition, Professors Schafer and Polk proposed a course in law and order which would analyze the concept of a "rule of law."[11]

We are grateful to these colleagues, both living and dead, and hope that this book is a useful addition to their work. If it leads other scholars to include a consideration of the instruction of ethics in the United States, its purpose will have been served.

— 1 —

America's Ethical Malaise

Until Watergate it was unfashionable in many circles of our society to speak of individual virtues. Honesty, obedience to the law, truthfulness, moral courage were somehow outdated. It was no accident that these words and concepts went out of fashion while others—sociability, social justice, equal rights—came in. Henry Steele Commager, in *The American Mind*, speaks of the transition from an individual moral code found in the eighteenth and early nineteenth centuries—"a moral code in which good and evil were significant terms, and responsibility personal—to the complex, impersonal practices of the twentieth century."[1] To put it in philosophical terms, the individual Protestant conscience yielded to a scientific, mechanistic view of morality—which is the basis of what is called social ethics.

Increased understanding of the social origins of ethics has replaced to a certain extent the perceived need for individual ethics. The ideological belief that crime is caused by social forces alone prescribes a therapeutic treatment, while punishment of the criminal might be dictated if crime were an act of free will. If the criminal was free when he committed the crime, as Kant said, he then chose to be punished. Social ethics tend to universalize liability, and thus guilt, liberating the individual from responsibility for his actions.

In spite of the prevalence of social ethics, the need and the popular support for individual ethics is strong. We still believe that it is wrong for an individual to murder, rape, steal, or lie. A recent Gallup Poll reported that over 98 percent of Americans believe that criminals should be punished for their acts. This view implies a lingering belief in individual responsibility for ethical action.

A study of the social basis for individual ethics must examine the religious and philosophical movements whose teachings have most

8

affected our concepts of ethics. Except for sex standards, these differing religions and philosophies have almost identical messages about individual liability. It is important to appraise these sometimes contradictory approaches to similar ethical behavior, for in our pluralistic society different groups have different rationales for their ethics. For example, Catholics, Jews, Oriental-Americans, while all sharing reasonably similar views of ethical behavior, differ in their ways of understanding the basis of ethics.

In light of this continuing pluralism, what aspects of the American intellectual heritage maintain these conceptions of individual ethical responsibility? What forces have led to the reduction of training in individual responsibilities? This chapter addresses itself to analysis of the intellectual history of American individual ethics.

Influence of Religion on Ethics

Organized religion has perhaps played the greatest role in maintaining ethical views in the United States. Religious groups in America traditionally concentrated on individual ethical responsibilities as opposed to religious dogma, and they succeeded in involving a large percentage of the population in their activities. In 1900 Max Weber, the German sociologist, reported: "In the main the congregations [in America] refused entirely to listen to the preaching of 'dogma' and to confessional distinctions. . . . 'Ethics' alone could be offered."[2] Religion in this country focused on matters of practical concern—not on the life to come. "Religion became a matter of conduct, of good deeds, of works with only a vague background of faith. It became highly functional, highly pragmatic; it became a guarantee of success, moral and material."[3]

The success of religion in America has been remarkable by almost any standard. Census figures estimated that 92 percent of the population in 1890 and 91 percent in 1910 were linked to religious denominations. According to one authority, Professor Seymour Martin Lipset, these estimates are similar to those made by other analysts of American religion, extending with minor variations from the 1830s to 1957.[4] Alexis de Tocqueville said in the 1830s that "America is still the place where the Christian religion has kept the greatest real power over men's souls."[5] In the twentieth century, while Christianity continues to occupy a dominant, if diminished, status, Judaism is considerably more influential than it was in the last century.

The general agreement on the greater importance of ethics over dogma has helped to moderate sectarian friction. Except for the Mormon experience, actual warfare between religious sects never approached the level found in Europe, where such fighting continues into this century. Sectarian controversy, although comparatively moderate, nevertheless played a role in restricting ethical instruction in public education. School superintendents often found themselves in the midst of sectarian battles over ethical programs, and the nearly sacred principle of separation of church and state was used to eliminate all religious—and ethical—teachings.

Although the Judeo-Christian heritage is complex, it continues to serve as a source for our ethical beliefs. The values of both religions are very similar. Looking at the complexity, most authorities contrast the clarity of Jewish ethics, stemming from the Mosaic law, with the diffuseness of Christian ethics, stemming from the general commandment to love thy neighbor as thyself.[6]

Even among Christians there were differing ethical practices, although most sects preached the Ten Commandments as the basis of Christian social life until the Social Gospel overshadowed them in this century. From one point of view, the diffuseness and the perfectionism of Christianity has had a negative or antinomian effect on ethics. It demands impossible behavior: to love one's neighbor as oneself, to abandon the things of this world. What should one do in the majority of situations to which these general principles may not be applied? Also, one cannot discuss the import of Christian ethics without an analysis of the doctrine of forgiveness of sin. Considering these difficulties, the technical legalism of the Jewish tradition appears preferable. However, Christianity, precisely because it is general, offers a more historically adaptable ethical framework than the Mosaic law which was originally written for a pre-industrial, agricultural people.

In the United States the different theological approaches to individual ethics were harmonized around the "Protestant ethic" described by Max Weber, or the democratic ethos described by Tocqueville. Even the Jewish and Catholic immigrants tended to adopt similar social and ethical habits from their religions, such as personal industry, a sense of honesty, equality, and a prohibition of crime.

Although religion has had a constructive part in helping to maintain mores regarding individual action, it has sometimes gone off on tangential crusades, namely, Prohibition, blue laws, etc. Nevertheless, religion in this country has helped to foster the view that one best loves one's neighbor by acting toward him in an ethical manner. The religious view of immortality may have had a significant influence in teaching people to think of the consequences of their desires and actions which, as Tocqueville noted, is salutary for ethics in general.[7]

In spite of the great influence of organized religions, at the same time they have suffered from jealousies and competition. In many cases their contentiousness has eliminated ethical instruction from the schools because one group feared that another was gaining ascendency.[8] Even when religious denominations exerted influence over government policy they disagreed with each other. Prohibition was opposed by Catholics, Jews, and most Episcopalians. Many of the Social Gospel planks, including opposition to the war and some civil rights activities, were rejected by the fundamentalist denominations. One reason why America has high crime rates is because our institutions, including the churches, collectively have been ineffective in teaching the ethical principles contained in the religious and philosophical tradition of our country.

Chapter Eleven examines some of the other features of religion in our society. Although religion will have difficulties in an increasingly secular and technological society, it seems likely that it will continue to be an important part of our social institutions for many decades to come. However, organized religion's place in teaching individual ethics is becoming increasingly slight. The church is following in the modern intellectual movement toward social ethics. If it is not willing to revive its original interest in individual as well as social ethics, its usefulness in this field will be very limited.

Philosophic Movements and Ethics

As religion lost its grip on ethics, philosophical bases of ethics became more important to many educated Americans.

Kantianism

One major philosophical approach to ethics is idealism, based in large part on the thought of Immanuel Kant (1724 –1804). In early nineteenth century America, philosophic idealism was incorporated in transcendentalism, a partly religious movement. Given its American formulation by Emerson, transcendentalism emphasized the American virtues of self-reliance and social optimism, but it based its ethics upon *a priori* intuitions rather than on sensual experience.[9] Thus Kant's famous imperative, "Act only on that maxim which you can at the same time will to be a universal law," served as the ethical basis for transcendentalism.

The practical basis of the transcendentalist approach was the notion of "goodwill." What is important is not the consequence of the moral action, as it was for utilitarianism, but the intention of the individual. Although Kant did not seek to divorce judgment about possible consequences resulting from the goodwill, he emphasized the importance of intention.

Kant's theories are highly sophisticated, and comparatively few Americans have ever become his intellectual followers. However, the rather simple ethical teachings of Kant, as opposed to his intellectual reasons for them, have had some influence on popular understanding.[10] One authority argues that, on the whole, Kantianism penetrated more deeply than any other modern philosophy.[11] Indeed, Kantianism seems to be gaining in significance, as may be seen in the recent success of *A Theory of Justice*, Professor John Rawls's major reanalysis of the ethical basis of justice.[12] Rawls's work is "largely Kantian in nature," replacing utilitarianism, which he believes to have been the dominant ethical position of the last two centuries.

Obviously, other modes of thought have had an impact on American understanding of ethics. Professor Rawls, it is important to note, while discussing utilitarianism and Kantianism— philosophies that argue for ethical responsibility—only discusses social justice, ignoring individual ethics. Unfortunately, this is the prevalent attitude among the teachers of ethics in contemporary American colleges, which will be discussed later.

Utilitarianism

The English philosophy of utilitarianism—associated with Jeremy Bentham (*Principles of Morals and Legislation*, 1789), James Mill, and John Stuart Mill (*Utilitarianism*, 1863)—was influential in America in the last century. It also became tied with American religion. According to Harold Laski, "What begins as a theocratic principle (Puritanism) ends by becoming a tradition that is not very easy to distinguish from utilitarianism."[13] Although this philosophy is secular in orientation, its ethical goal of realizing the greatest good for the greatest number can be a powerful teaching force.

Utilitarianism is directly allied to the ethical principle of beneficence. In realizing the greatest good for the greatest number, one is expected not to injure or to interfere with others' liberty. Moreover, utilitarianism is usually associated with belief in the equality of men. Bentham's dictum that "everybody [is] to count for one, nobody for more than one" illustrates this equalitarianism.

Working jointly with organized religion, utilitarianism thus provided fairly high and thorough ethical training and concepts. One reason for its continuing popularity in the nineteenth century was its easy conversion to the ideas of social and technological progress. As the Industrial Revolution gathered momentum after the Civil War, this theory provided its ethical basis. William Frankena, a noted scholar of American ethics, has shown how it formed the ethical basis of Herbert Spencer's evolutionary doctrines.[14] Recently a former dean of St. Paul's Cathedral in Cincinnati and professor of Christian ethics, Joseph Fletcher, wrote extensively on the place of utilitarian considerations in Christian ethics.[15]

For a variety of reasons, utilitarianism has faded somewhat as an ethical force in this century. It tends to be "theoretical" and future-oriented. It has little appeal to the individual conscience so there is little sense of committing a morally satisfying act. There is instead a rational calculus about social and individual means and ends. Philosophically, utilitarianism has waned while philosophies of ethical determinism and of ethical doubt have waxed in the "American mind."[16] Utilitarianism has been negatively affected by this movement from natural rationally-based ethics to non-rationally based ethics.

Rousseau

In addition to Kantianism and utilitarianism, there have been many lesser philosophical movements which influenced American ethical views. Rousseau's *Social Contract* (1762) and *Émile* (1762) are both widely studied in the fields of political science and education, respectively. *Émile* is considered by many as the forerunner of the child-centered approach to education and ethical instruction. The profession of faith by the Savoyard Vicar in *Émile* outlines fundamental premises of civil religion and the central role which natural ethics can play in religious practice.

Hegel also had some minor influence. However, we believe the major intellectual influence of the nineteenth century upon ethics was supplied by utilitarianism and Kantianism.

The Law and Ethics

The American Constitution and our common law tradition maintain a legal and, to some extent, an ethical consistency in our society. As one analyst recently said:

> The common law thus comes to seem the very oracle experience, speaking in the accents of the settled daily life and judgement of the whole people. . . . Therefore, from the outset, Americans were accustomed to the emphasis on custom and precedent, as against arbitrary will, and the attention to regular procedure and regard for property and other rights which characterize common law.[17]

Judges often become moral guides and interpreters:

> In a democratic society like ours, where the law reflects many of the people's basic values, this overlap (between legal questions and moral questions) becomes all the more extensive and important. Under the official appearance of deciding legal issues presented to them, American judges are often required to assess moral interests and resolve problems of right and wrong.[18]

Of course, laws are legislated as well as adjudicated. Popular institutions responsive to popular opinion are able to change the definition of the ethical and unethical by changing the definition of the legal and illegal. Fifty years ago, many sexual acts which now escape censure were considered immoral and illegal. Abraham Lincoln, following the accepted precedent of his time, paid the expenses of some delegates to the Republican Convention of 1860;[19] today, he would probably be punished either by the courts or by his party, and he would likely fare ill at the polls. However, the basic ethical questions such as theft, assault, murder, perjury, and so on, have changed remarkably little over the years. Punishments and court procedures may have changed but the unethical and illegal qualities of most fundamental crimes have not.

It is interesting to inquire whether Americans have been a law-abiding people. Lee Coleman has shown that there is a strong inclination among them to disregard the law in favor of "direct action."[20] Tocqueville, on the other hand, believed that Americans are more inclined to obey the laws and to see them enforced than are Europeans because the former play a more direct role in the legislative process and in the execution of the law. A compromise solution is suggested by Arthur Schlesinger, Sr., who argues that Americans venerate the law in the abstract—as embodied in the Constitution—and also have a faith in the law as a solution to all types of social policies, as witnessed by our amazing number of laws and ordinances. On the other hand, Schlesinger thinks that Americans tend to see laws as restrictions to their freedom and seek to avoid them.[21] This confusion led Mark Twain to quip that in America "there is no end to the laws and no beginning to the execution of them." On balance, available evidence suggests that Americans have been somewhat less law-abiding than other nations.[22]

Although Americans may respect the idea of the rule of law, they have comparatively little respect for legislators. The Gallup Poll found that politicians have little prestige; therefore, the laws passed in the ethical area do not carry great weight. Also, laws tend to be abstract and removed from the average man. Thus they do not serve as an effective educational tool in contemporary society. Laws are, in fact, only the last appeal of social conscience, even if they are a frequent appeal. For example, many attempts are even now being made to improve ethics by legislation—e.g., campaign financing laws, and conflict of interest statutes—in fields where ethical instruction has failed.

One advantage of a legalistic system such as our own is that it creates a class of men who are trained in legal ethics. These are the lawyers and jurists. Tocqueville said that American lawyers had a "taste for formality and an instinctive love for a regular concatenation of ideas" gained from the study and exercise of the law.[23] This spirit appears helpful in maintaining ethical practices in the law as well as in business and politics, where lawyers have great influence.

Patriotism and Ethics

Finally, the consciousness of America as the great experiment and hope for mankind contributed in our first century and a quarter to a popular consensus regarding the need for individual ethics to maintain free democratic institutions. The Northwest Ordinance of 1787 calls for "extending the fundamental principles of civil and religious liberty, which form the basis whereon these republics, their laws, and constitutions are erected. . . . Religion, morality, and knowledge [are] necessary to good government." Daniel Webster, speaking in commemoration of John Adams and Thomas Jefferson, said: "This glorious liberty, these benign institutions, the dear purchases of our fathers are . . . ours to transmit . . . We can never, indeed, pay the debt which is upon us but by virtue, by morality, by religion, by the cultivation of every good principle and every good habit." Abraham Lincoln joined the Constitution, law-abidingness (public morality), and freedom in this famous statement:

> Let every American, every lover of liberty, swear . . . never to violate in the least particular, laws of the country; and never to tolerate their violation by others. . . . Let reverence for the laws be breathed by every American mother to the lisping babe. . . . Let it be taught in schools, in seminaries, and in colleges; let it be written in primers, spelling books, and in almanacs; . . . let it be preached from the pulpit, proclaimed in legislative halls, and enforced in courts of justice. And, in short, let it become the *political religion* of the nation.[24]

This catalogue of patriotic-ethical statements could easily be continued and could include those of leaders from ethnic and racial groups. The decline in patriotism and the sense of uniqueness of our institutions may be reasons why concern with individual morality has decreased in recent decades.

There is also a connection between morality and a free democratic society which has long been recognized by democratic theorists. Freedom is only possible in a society which is essentially democratic and whose government is non-theological (where one is free to choose one's own government and religion). But even in a society of this kind some consensual attitudes are necessary. For example, religious groups must tolerate the existence of opposing religious faiths. Similarly, divergent political opinions need to be recognized and protected. Standards of honesty are necessary for democratic electoral procedures. Property rights must be insured if economic life is not to become chaos.

In addition to respect for property rights, there must also be respect for persons. Can a society be free where persons cannot come and go as they wish, for fear of their personal safety? Needless to say, this list of essential values could be multiplied—but the point should be fairly clear. The freedom to choose one's lifestyle—one's career, religion, sexual habits, dress, politics—should not be confused with the freedom to cheat, rape, or kill others. In fact, freedom is only possible when ethical fundamentals are ensured.

Patriotism may be a dangerous stimulus to ethical behavior. It can easily degenerate into chauvinism—my country right or wrong. Patriotism is also only a general commandment; it does not tell one what to do in practical ethical situations. In this it resembles the Christian dispensation of *agapé*. Also, the ethical benefit of patriotism may disappear when a nation suffers a reversal and patriotism is decried.

Forces Opposed to Ethical Instruction

There are several factors which have helped to eliminate ethical consideration from our schools and from public life in general. As has been mentioned, religious sectarian controversies, fueled in part by the massive immigrations in the last century, made religiously-based ethical instruction in the schools even more difficult until the First Amendment's separation of church and state eliminated it altogether. More important, perhaps, has been the great success of science and its impact in every aspect of our lives.

The adverse effect of scientific positivism and the later movement, existentialism, on ethical instruction is obvious: "Positivism and existentialism deny that ethical and value judgements can be justified at all."[25] Positivism maintains that all values are conventional and so cannot be empirically tested, leading all values to become equally matters of individual choice. Existentialism sees the world as a dimension of total freedom where men must create their own values.[26] These views have helped to lead many intellectuals to a negative view of ethics.

To measure the impact of scientific positivism on American ethics, one could study several major figures, including Darwin, Huxley, Spencer, James, or Sumner, in addition to those already chosen—John Dewey and the psychologists, especially Sigmund Freud. The need for brevity and our judgment of the relative importance of the figures involved determined our choice of Dewey and Freud.

Psychology

One can summarize Freud's theory simplistically as follows: our so-called conscious actions are subtly controlled by unconscious sexual patterns originally formed by our reactions to the Oedipus complex.[27] Thus, according to Freud, all later events in a person's life are powerfully influenced by these early experiences, and the only way to change a person's behavior pattern is through complex psychoanalytic therapy.

Freud believed that libidinal energy is the basis of the human psyche; he also believed that power is the matrix of social relations. "The first requisite of civilization, therefore, is that of justice—that is, the assurance that a law once made will not be broken in favor of an individual. This implies nothing as to the ethical value of such a law."[28] On another occasion, Freud blandly said, "Ethics are remote from me. . . . I do not break my head much about good and evil." He felt that ethics were necessary to provide psychic control, but he did not think that science could determine what values were good or bad. To him, most existing forms of repression were unjust because they created neuroses. What was needed was a new source of authority.

In America, Freud's theories were frequently invoked to minimize punishment as a deterrent and to restrict any kind of ethical instruction. Seymour Halleck, in *Psychiatry and the Dilemma of Crime* charges:

> [Our] model of mental illness can be used to encourage the notion that people are not responsible for their own behavior. The equation of sickness with non-responsibility seems to have been generalized to other behaviors, including delinquency. In a society in which people do not feel responsible for their own actions, the criminal adaptation is more easily justified and supported.[29]

Paul Roazen, an authority on Freud, stated that in child rearing, "there was a time in the history of psychoanalytic doctrine when the inclination was to view all suppression as negative, all controls of the child as hindrances to his development."[30]

Nathan Hale, in *Freud in America*, makes the following observation:

> The popularization of psychoanalysis coincides with the long-term decline in interest in what has been called 'traditional Christianity,' a decline well underway among intellectuals but spreading to larger groups of Americans. One aspect of this is clear in the popularization—a rejection of absolute moral judgements and of asceticism, both associated with Protestantism.[31]

Freud has had direct effects on criminology, child rearing, marriage counseling, political science, and sociology, as well as on education.

Another significant development in psychology is behaviorism. J. B. Watson, its founder, attempted to make psychology more scientific. He rejected the introspective methods of the Freudians and turned to the more objective and quantitative methods of the biological sciences, arguing that human behavior is a result of conditioned responses to stimuli, e.g., on a simple level, Pavlov's famous dog. In this view, consciousness is either ignored or denied, so ethical choice is replaced by psychological adjustment. An organism must be able to function in its environment.

The behaviorists' view has been most fully represented in recent years in the work of B. F. Skinner. In his latest book, *Beyond*

Freedom and Dignity, Skinner argues that the earlier view of an autonomous man possessing a conscious freedom and dignity, who is ethically responsible for his acts, has been outmoded by advances in behavioral science. He believes that men are not free in the sense that they can control themselves and their environment; rather, they are controlled by their environment. Skinner further believes that by recognizing man's position and by applying the techniques of behavioral science to it, man can gain a new freedom through controlling his environment and so can produce better men. In this scheme, there is little need for ethical instruction since men are controlled by external conditions.[32] However, in apparent contradiction to his formally expressed view, Skinner has a small course in ethics in his behavioral Utopia, *Walden II*.[33]

While by and large psychologists have tended to oppose conventional ethics, there are some who have taken a positive position toward them. Abraham Maslow's third force psychology has been favorable toward ethics for the sake of individual self-fulfillment. The new school of "transactional analysis," discussed in Thomas Harris's *I'm OK . . . You're OK*, also argues on behalf of an objective moral order based on the universal importance of human relations—a view which is admittedly similar in many respects to that of Christianity.[34]

John Dewey: Democratic Pedagogy

John Dewey, a philosopher of pragmatism, also had a deep and long-lived influence on American ethical education. Pragmatism, according to Commager, is a way of thinking "that can properly be designated American."[35] Describing Dewey, Commager says:

> So faithfully did Dewey live up to his own philosophical creed, that he became the guide, the mentor, and the conscience of the American people: it is scarcely an exaggeration to say that for a generation no major issue was clarified until Dewey had spoken. Pioneer in educational reform, organizer of political parties, counsellor to statesmen. . . . He was the spearhead of a dozen movements, the leader of a score of crusades, the advocate of a hundred reforms.[36]

The essence of Dewey's philosophy was growth—democratic, scientific, and individual. New ideas being discovered in all three areas needed to be implemented as rapidly as possible in order to further mankind's progress. Not only the approach, but the method of science could be applied in all areas; "Ethical science is not distinct in its methods and conception from physical science." Religion, Dewey believed, was both traditional and static; frequently it supported aristocratic principles. Ethical training suffered many of the same disadvantages, and obsolete ethical principles—such as the Golden Rule—could be used as unwise "standards of judging the worth of new experiences."

Moreover, Dewey said that any education which did not depend primarily on the student's experience would be "merely symbolic; that is, largely conventional and verbal. In reality, working as distinct from professed standards depends upon what an individual has himself specifically appreciated to be deeply significant in concrete situations."[37]

To portray Dewey as an opponent of personal or individual ethics may appear paradoxical. The words morality, habit, ethics appear everywhere in his work. Moreover, he wished to promote what he considered new and just standards of ethical education.

The net effect of Dewey's philsophy and pedagogy, however, was to foster what we have described as social ethics at the expense of individual ethics. He thought that social and philosophical reconstruction would lead to better personal ethical standards, that individual ethics were dependent on social experience, and that social experience should be experimental, open to growth. The goals of the old moralists—courage, justice, truthfulness, and so on—were replaced in the Deweyan scheme by open-mindedness, single-mindedness, and creativity. These he believed could not be taught but were learned indirectly through the experience of the school. When Lawrence Kohlberg questions the efficacy of the "hidden curriculum" in moral education, he is describing the pedagogy of *Democracy and Education, School and Society,* and *Human Nature and Conduct*. Dewey did not teach moral principles because insofar as those principles exist Dewey believed they were changing, and therefore to teach them necessarily limited the individual experience of the child.

Effects of Intellectual Changes in Education

Freud and Dewey were both part of an early twentieth century intellectual milieu which reflected the general revulsion against

religious moralism already begun in the nineteenth century. Charles
Darwin (1809–1882), Thomas Henry Huxley (1825–1895), and
Herbert Spencer (1820–1903) were other major proponents of
science who had helped foster an intellectual rejection of religious
morality by 1900. The Marxian critique of private property based on
modern science had a profound anti-ethical impact on many
intellectuals, and the argument from democratic theory that each
child should form his own ethics was also influential.

The effect on the United States of this intellectual change in
attitude has been well documented. Henry Steele Commager
described the transition period of the 1890s as follows:

> The decade of the '90s is the watershed of American history. As with
> all watersheds, the topography is blurred but, in the perspective of
> half a century, the grand outlines emerge clearly . . . The problems
> which confronted the men of this transition generation were no longer
> the familiar ones, nor did they yield to the familiar solutions. . . .
> There was the ethical problem which arose from the attempt to apply
> the individualistic moral code of the eighteenth and nineteenth
> centuries—a moral code in which good and evil were significant
> terms, and responsibility personal—to the complex impersonal
> practices of a twentieth century economic order.[38]

There are other empirical or quasi-empirical studies which
support the view that ethical instruction suffered in the hands of
educators schooled in new ways of thought. Professors deCharms
and Moeller, in a study of values in fourth grade readers from 1800 to
1950 which seeks to prove or to disprove Riesman's thesis of the
change in America from inner-directed to outer-directed values,
noted a decline in moral concern.

Number of pages (out of 25) with moral teaching:[39]

1810	16	1890	4.19
1830	16.75	1910	4.50
1850	12.42	1930	1
1870	6	1950	0.06

Similar observations were made by Margaret Foster in a study of
third grade readers, 1900 to 1953. She found that non-fiction material
began to disappear after 1930, as did "obedience and thoughtful-
ness" and honesty. At the same time, "social activities" and
"winning friends" became increasingly important. "Learning and
cleverness" reached a low point in 1930 but a high point in 1953.
Foster concludes that success now depends upon group approval

and meeting group standards.[40]

Another study, made by Parkin of the moral and religious content of 1,291 American school readers from 1776 to 1920, found complete emphasis (100 percent) on moral and religious content in the period 1776 to 1786, approximately 50 percent emphasis from 1786 to 1825, 21 percent in 1825 to 1880, and only 5 percent from 1916 to 1920.[41]

In yet another study, this time of child rearing practices, it was observed that the change in the articles written on the subject reflected the change in general intellectual attitudes. The percentage of topics dealing with various aspects of character and/or personality training in three women's magazines was found to be as follows: 1880, 35 percent; 1900, 31 percent; 1910, 39 percent; 1920, 3 percent; 1930, 24 percent; 1940, 23 percent; 1948, 21 percent. Stindler discussed these findings as follows:

> Interest in character or personality development had revived, with twenty percent of the articles in 1930 devoted to this topic as compared with only three percent in 1920. Now for the first time, the emphasis in this area was on *personality* rather than *character* development. Emotional problems of adjustment rather than moral problems claimed the attention of writers. . . .
>
> The influence of J. B. Watson on child training had made tremendous gains in the '20s and continued to grow in popularity in the '30s. The popularity of this school of child rearing can best be understood in the light of two important cultural trends. One of these trends was the great increase in the prestige and importance of science during the '20s. . . . Psychology shared in this prestige. . . . The American mother of 1930 was ripe for bringing her baby up on a book written in accordance with the latest psychological theory. . . .
>
> The '20s had also seen widespread acceptance of Freudian theory and many extreme applications of it to the training of children.

The greater influence of Freudian over behavioral methods can be seen in the fact that by 1940 "33% of the articles in infant discipline followed a modified behavioralistic style, 66% were advocating self-regulatory, permissive procedures."[42]

Ethical Instruction in Colleges

Another indication of the change in religious and philosophical positions toward ethics can be seen in the change in college courses in ethics. Until the first World War, ethics was a required course (in addition to chapel attendance) for undergraduates in private liberal arts colleges of denominational background. The texts for these courses can still be found in college libraries: *Problems of Conduct* by Durant Drake, Vassar College; *Ethics in Natural Law: A Reconstructive View of Moral Philosophy Applied to the Rational Art of Living* by G. L. Raymond, Professor of Oratory and Aesthetics, Princeton University; *A Handbook of Moral Philosophy* by H. Calderwood, Professor of Moral Philosophy, Edinburgh University. These texts often had a religious as well as a philosophic basis.

Although these books vary in their approach to the true ground for ethics—emphasizing first natural law, then passion, then reason—they all share a common concern for improving the character of students. Durant Drake, for example, points up the need for individual ethical instruction:

> Give every man and woman a fair chance for happiness in normal ways, and the lure of crime will largely vanish. Yet human nature in its most favored individuals has its twists and anti-social impulses. For the potential criminal—and that means for every one of us—there must be elaborated also a system of moral or religious training which shall seek to develop the better nature of every man.[43]

In today's colleges and universities the number of students registered in ethics courses in departments of religion or philosophy is small. The method of teaching ethics has also changed since the beginning of the century. This change is partially a consequence of the success of positivism in philosophy. Professors like Rawls, who actually teach about what is ethically good, are rare. Often the professors follow such leaders as Wittgenstein, one of the major proponents of linguistic positivism, who has dismissed ethics as a nonsensical discipline.

> I see now that these nonsensical expressions [sc. moral judgements] were not nonsensical because I had not yet found the correct expressions, but that their nonsensicality was their very essence. . . . My whole tendency, and I believe the tendency of all men who ever tried to write or talk Ethics, . . . was to run against the boundaries of language.[44]

The linguistic or emotively-trained ethicists prevalent in our colleges today try to answer such questions as: in what kinds of statements are ethical terms used such as "good"? What do people mean when they use the term "good"? What emotions is one trying to elicit when ones uses ethical terms such as "good"? Little of this, in our judgment, is useful in helping students to appreciate the realities of ethical activity in their own lives. Other professors use a Kantian approach which, because of its intellectual difficulty, is also hard for students to use as a guide for their own ethical decisions.

The other major approach taken in modern ethics courses is the "problems" or case study. Selected readings chosen from philosophers are on ethical subjects such as "freedom of the individual," allowing students to see the possible problems and solutions.[45] The case study approach is a good one, and these cases are often thoughtfully chosen. With the exception of the very brightest student, however, it appears unlikely that such abstract philosophical discussion would affect their individual ethical choices.

Ethics in Europe

At the same time that the study of individual ethics was being removed from American schools, the Northwestern European countries experienced the same intellectual forces as those which drove the United States away from the religiously based ethics of the early nineteenth century. Kant, Freud, and the founders of existentialism were all Europeans. Even an American philosopher like Dewey was widely read in Europe.

However, the impact of these changes was less in Europe than in the United States. No European country followed Dewey's directive against teaching ethics only through the child's experience in school as fully as the U.S.; Freud was taken much less seriously in Europe than in America, as he himself noted. Since European countries had no First Amendment to eliminate religion from the schools, there was no excuse for tossing ethics out with religion. Perhaps because the European universities educated a smaller proportion of the population, university students were better selected and less likely to accept new doctrines as enthusiastically as did Americans.

The results of this different European attitude toward ethics are noticeable in several respects. Programs of "moral education" are being planned in European public schools. Courses in religion, including a large amount of ethics, survive in more Northwestern European public schools. Anti-ethical movements in university philosophy departments have not had an impact on the teaching of ethics in schools to the extent they have had in this country. These themes will be developed more fully in later chapters.

American Ethics in Perspective

Our review of existing scholarship has convinced us of the following generalizations:

First, the essential American view of ethical responsibility has endured relatively unchanged up to the present time. Such acts as murder, theft, and rape are moral evils which reasonable, good-hearted persons can condemn and punish in all but the most extremely extenuating circumstances. Our traditions—political, religious, and philosophical—support us in making these value judgments.

Second, it appears that the emphasis on individual ethics which was a strong part of American thought in the last century is being obscured by the increasing popularity of new ways of social thought, including pragmatism, psychological and philosophical positivism, existentialism, and a confused notion of democratic liberty.

The ethical foundations of our pluralistic society are strong. But pluralism itself creates problems for ethical instruction because of its very diffuseness. There remains, therefore, the difficulty of making a pluralistic society work to foster an ethical respect for other members of the society.

One approach to this question has been to wait for the scientists and intellectuals to determine what ethics should be taught. The wait has proven unrewarding. Too often intellectual theories have no correspondence with the actual conditions of society. As political scientists, we feel that a more sane approach to the ethical problem in the United States is to start from the existing belief pattern concerning ethics and to clarify and improve our commitments to them. This can be done if the various institutions of our society—the schools, television, the government, the family—can define and clarify their responsibilities for ethical instruction. This is not an easy task. Institutions have purposes, needs, and habits, like individuals. And yet everything changes. The purpose of education and intellectual reform is to change opinions and ways of doing things for the better.

Our thesis is that there is a severe and almost paralyzing ethical problem in this country. Many people dispute this. There are some who do not believe there is a major crime problem; there are some who deny that ethics and crime are related. The objections of the first group will be taken up in the following three chapters, which show a startling and ominous picture of crime and corruption. The objections of the second group are not subject to a similar quantitative analysis; however, we believe that we can demonstrate that unlawful behavior is in part a result of absence of instruction in individual ethics. In spite of a number of bad legal statutes, laws do represent society's way of identifying and prohibiting the most serious kinds of ethical offences. Crime is the negation of another person's integrity as well as the social compact. A nation's crime rate says a great deal about the ethical patterns of that society.

— 2 —

Crimes: Street and White Collar

A distinguished National Commission on the Causes and Prevention of Violence, under the chairmanship of Dr. Milton Eisenhower, reported in 1969:

> The United States is the clear leader among modern stable democratic nations in its rates of homicide, assault, rape, and robbery, and it is at least among the highest in incidence of group violence and assassination.[1]

In several years of work on the problem of America's high crime and corruption rates, the writers have talked to many educated people who are not aware of the extent of crime in America, or who rely on the uncertainty of crime statistics as a means of putting the unpleasant facts about crime out of their minds. Those readers who are seriously interested in crime statistics are referred to Appendix A and the publications cited there. It is enough to say here that *most of the weaknesses in crime statistics tend to make America look better than it is*. Unfortunately, the F.B.I., in its sincere effort to keep Americans informed about crime, has emphasized annual increases of crime in the United States (figures which are not altogether reliable because of inadequate reporting to the F.B.I. itself) and has ignored the shocking international comparisons.

In addition to failure to realize the size of America's crime problem, many Americans also fail to recognize how much crime is an ethical problem. Most sociological discussions of crime proceed on the assumption that everyone "knows the difference between right and wrong." According to this viewpoint crime comes from psychological perversity, and from some bad combination of family, social, or economic factors. While the writers do not disagree with the existence of psychological or sociological reasons for crime (see

Chapter Three), they do not believe in the validity of the criminologists' usual assumption that delinquents have had adequate instruction in ethics.

The impact of crime on ethical viewpoints also should be remembered as the reader studies this chapter. The large incidence of crime—especially of unpunished crime—in a central city slum detracts from the ethical education of the younger slum dwellers. Living in a world of crime lowers one's sense of indignation.

A striking feature of U.S. crime is the youth of participants. Forty percent of arrests made for FBI Index Crimes in 1973 were of persons 20 years of age or younger. Sixteen percent of the population is made up of persons 10 to 17 years of age, but this age group accounted for 31 percent of all Crime Index offenses which were solved. Seventy-four percent of those arrested for auto theft were under 21. Thirty-seven percent of larceny arrests and 54 percent of burglary arrests in the cities were of persons under 18. Persons under 25 accounted for 61 percent of rape arrests and for 45 percent of those arrested for murder.

Crime has always been a tendency of youth, but in this country it is becoming more so in recent years. This may be a sign of youthful precocity, but the writers suspect that it is rather a result of our failure to indicate to some of our youth that crime is undesirable. The tendency of some youth to violence is understandable in view of the frequency with which it is shown on television and of the failure of churches and schools in their teaching.

Street Crime

A few pages of crime statistics will indicate the extent of America's difficulty. The social and economic significance of these figures will subsequently be discussed. In reading about our crime rates, the reader should remember that until recently this was the wealthiest country in the world and that it is still the best educated, as measured by the proportion of high school and university graduates. A good case can be made for its leadership in international humanitarianism. But this wealth, education, or humanitarianism has not been used to keep crime to a reasonable minimum.

Murder

This crime is the easiest to classify. The FBI estimated that there were 19,510 murders in 1973. Translated into percentages, this is 9.3 per 100,000, while most countries which we consider comparable to ours range between 1.0 and 2.5. Statistics for England and Wales indicate 247 murders in 1971; they would have had approximately 1,000 had their population been equal to ours. We killed each other off at a rate 19.5 times as high as their rate.

Appalling as these figures are in themselves, even more so is the rate of increase between 1960 and 1973. The absolute number of murders rose by 116 percent in 13 years, and the rate per 100,000 rose 86 percent.

Aggravated Assault

This is defined by the FBI as intentional assault by one person upon another for the purpose of inflicting serious bodily damage. There were 416,720 aggravated assaults reported in the United States in 1973, approximately 26 percent with firearms.

British statistics are compiled quite differently, but "crimes against the person" (omitting murder, dangerous driving, transportation offenses, child stealing) totalled approximately 45,000 in 1971[2]—less than one-half of our rate of aggravated assault. The figures for the United States are probably a substantial underestimate.

Rape

This category includes only forcible rape. During 1973 this crime reached an estimated total of 51,000 in the United States. The total number increased by 62 percent between 1968 and 1973; the rate per 100,000 by 55 percent.

Some projected statistics are startling. The Uniform Crime Reports for 1973 estimate "a victim risk rate of 100 per 100,000 females in core cities, while rural areas have an estimated risk rate of 23." The same source admits that "forcible rape" figures are not very accurate. Many respectable women do not bring a case to court because court procedures are unfair to the victim, while in other cases the degree of force is questionable. The British figure for 1971 is 784, which indicates that 15 times as many women per capita are reported to have been forcibly raped in this country as in Great Britain.

Robbery

This is the use of force (or threats of force) to obtain something of value in the presence of the person concerned. The FBI received reports of 382,680 robberies in the United States in 1973. This figure may be low (polls have indicated a much higher rate). British robberies in 1971 were 7,465—about one-twelfth of our per capita rate. Sixty percent of the reported American robberies involved firearms.

Burglary

Burglaries—the unlawful entry of a building in order to commit a felony or theft—totalled 2,540,900 in 1973. In 1971 Great Britain reported 442,000 burglaries. Rates for this crime in the two countries are closer than are other crime rates; however, we may have a higher rate of unreported burglaries.

Larceny or Theft

This is defined as the unlawful taking of property without the use of force, fraud, or violence, and is a vague category. In 1973 the FBI received reports of 4,304,400 such offenses, a rate of 883 per 100,000 inhabitants.

The crimes mentioned in the FBI index are generally the type in which there is heavy participation by the poor. One exception is auto theft, which is increasingly a middle class crime, according to several studies. Other crimes in which the middle classes share heavily, like embezzlement and shoplifting, are not regularly reported in the FBI index but will be discussed later in this chapter.

Impact of Crime on American Life

The total number of crimes reported to the FBI for 1973 was 8,638,400. If the polls on unreported crimes are correct, the number was probably doubled to over 15 million crimes. Obviously, the psychological losses from 19,500 murders and 51,000 rapes are incalculable. In two years we murder about as many people as were lost in eight years of the Vietnam War.

A more serious loss from American crime is the impact on the quality of life. If—as a recent Gallup Poll indicated—one out of every three people in core city areas was robbed, burglarized, or had something taken in 1972 and one out of every five people in suburban areas was so treated,[3] this must have a very negative impact on ease of living. Some women do not dare go out alone in the evening; apartments have to be triple locked; all kinds of precautions must be taken. The psychological effect of these crimes on good living is much more important than their financial effect.

One fact should be specially noted. Crime weighs most heavily on the people who are least able to withstand it: the poor in the core city areas. A high proportion of crimes are by poor blacks and against poor blacks. The black woman who is struggling to hold her family together on a welfare payment or a low paid job is the one who is most likely to be held up for the $75 which she badly needs to pay for groceries and a part of the rent. Most studies of core city blacks, for example, indicate that they are as much or more interested in vigorous enforcement of the law as they are concerned about "police brutality."[4]

But the impact of crime is not only on the poor. Even the wealthy suburbs are showing the influence of America's high crime rate. New subdivisions are planned with walls to help keep out burglars. Expensive subdivisions maintain uniformed guards, as do lush retirement homes. Architects are now considering "security" in planning both apartment houses and individual homes. Heavy new locks and partly barred windows are urged by police departments. We are becoming a "fortress America."

The economic costs of crime are not easy to calculate but estimates have been made by the President's Commission on Law Enforcement and the Administration of Justice, reporting in 1967. Most of the cost estimates noted here should be trebled for 1974, as a result both of inflation and of the tremendous increase in crime. The major items are worth listing.[5]

Loss in economic capacity of workers or potential workers murdered was estimated at $750 million in 1965. Assault and other crimes against persons totalled $65 million in time lost, medical bills, and other expenses.

In crimes against property, the Commission staff used an arson cost of $65 million in 1965. There were no reliable figures on vandalism but a national survey came up with estimates of $210 million. Unrecovered robbery costs were estimated by the FBI to be $27 million. Burglary costs were estimated by the FBI at $251 million, although a National Opinion Research Center survey would have raised the sum to $450 or $500 million. Larceny net costs were estimated by the FBI at $196 million. Embezzlement costs, based on fidelity insurance company reports, were estimated at $200 million.

Retail trade losses due to dishonesty were estimated at $1.3 billion annually and auto theft net costs (after recovered vehicles) were estimated at $140 million. Fraud net costs were reckoned at $1.35 million. Motor vehicle damage from unlawful accidents was estimated at $1.816 million, including chiefly driving while under the influence.

The cost of illegal services, e.g., gambling, narcotics, loan sharking, prostitution, and illegal alcohol sales was estimated at $8 billion, twice the cost of other crimes. Most of this illegal income was secured by organized crime.

Another necessary expenditure was approximately $4 billion a year for the cost of law enforcement and criminal justice. The largest single item here was the police at $2.792 million. Private costs related to crime ran close to $2 billion.

This record of annual crime costs of $25 billion and the record of ineffective results is a cause for concern. Given increased crime and inflation since 1965, the annual crime cost has at least doubled to $50 billion and may have trebled to $75 billion.

Middle Class Crime

In Chapter Three is a summary of the sociological reasoning about the causes of delinquency and crime, most of it concerned with crimes committed by poorer people in poorer areas—an emphasis which is justified by the fact that a high proportion of crimes *are* committed in poorer areas. Criminological theory, however, overlooks a number of crimes and other evidences of criminal attitudes which exist in more prosperous strata of people. The crimes are sometimes called "middle class crimes," and sometimes "white collar" crime. Since most people in America who are not poor are "middle class," this term is used to denote non-poor people. This section is not intended as an attack on the middle classes but is an effort to indicate that our ethical problems include more people than those who are handicapped by poverty and by slum life.

In addition to the "middle class" crimes specifically mentioned in this chapter, there is corruption in government, business and unions, all to be discussed in the next chapter. Corruption, of course, affects poor people who are frequently its victims, but the organizers of corruption are normally members of the middle class. A surprising amount of corruption is initiated and supervised by university graduates, who are often active church members. The implication regarding their ethical training is all too clear.

"Middle class" crimes discussed in this section include shoplifting, embezzlement, auto theft, "professional stealing," fraudulent transactions, and professional derelictions. There is also a brief discussion of other evidence that criminal tendencies are not confined to the poor.

Shoplifting

Shoplifting is one of the clearest examples of a crime which is wide-spread in "middle class" life. The FBI reports for 1973 indicate that 10.8 percent of 4,304,400 offenses of larceny involved shoplifting. This represents 423,883 cases in the United States. It is generally admitted that a high proportion of shoplifting cases are not reported to the police, for reasons of public relations and the time required for prosecution. Different stores follow differing policies on reporting shoplifters. Executives of larger retail chains have told the authors that their security departments report less than a quarter of apprehended shoplifters. If this is generally true, the number of arrested shoplifters must be near two million a year. We do not know how many are not arrested.

Sociological studies indicate that shoplifters are likely to come from all classes of the population. A study of 93 arrested shoplifters in Honolulu in the mid-1960s found only 13.8 percent to be domestic and service workers, and 10.3 percent to be of farm laborer or laborer classes. Almost 13 percent were professional and technical, and 10.7 percent were managerial or proprietor classes.[6] The most thorough study of shoplifting, *The Booster and the Snitch*, a book concerning a large Chicago store in 1950 written by Mary Owen Cameron, concludes: "Socioeconomic data on pilferers showed them to be mainly 'respectable' employed persons or equally 'respectable' housewives."[7]

Shoplifting reported to the police in England and Wales in 1972 was about a quarter of the American rate. We do not know the extent to which the British store police report arrestees to the government. The English figures are for thefts above five pounds ($12.50); the American figures are for all reported thefts regardless of value.

The total value of goods shoplifted in the United States in 1966, including thefts by employees, was estimated by the Task Force of the President's Commission · on Law Enforcement and the Administration of Justice to be $1.318 billion, a figure which would be much larger today. The Commission's staff also stated that the consensus of experts was that the loss from employee thefts was greater than the loss from outsider shoplifting. Unfortunately, statistics do not separate employee theft from outside shoplifters.[8]

Mark Lipman's *Stealing* gives a number of dramatic examples of large scale stealing which he uncovered in his business as a private investigator. In one case two millionaire brothers were stealing from the company to which they had sold their business, and one brother was stealing from the other. Lipman attempts no overall estimates but clearly believes that substantial employee stealing is widespread.[9]

Auto Theft

Another crime which is frequently committed by non-poor people, especially young males, is auto theft. At least one sociological study in Detroit has indicated that this is not a poverty area crime nor one associated with blacks or a poor background. The amount of auto theft is staggeringly large, although much of it is simply taking a car for a "joyride." In 1973, 923,600 motor vehicles were reported stolen. As with other crimes, the rate is larger in large cities. There is increasing evidence of auto theft "rings" which eliminate engine numbers and other identification and then sell stolen cars through fence outlets in the United States or abroad.[10]

Embezzlement

Embezzlement is largely a middle class crime: few slum dwellers could secure a position from which they could embezzle.

Total figures in this field are not easily available. Even more than in shoplifting, there is a tendency to "cover up" for a variety of reasons. The FBI received reports of 3,157 cases in 1967—these, of course, were at the federal level, so that nationwide figures are very much larger. Uniform Crime Reports do not include embezzlement as a regularly reported item but do report the number of persons arrested for embezzlement—12,000 in 1973.[11]

A study by Professor Donald R. Cressey of 130 embezzlers in institutions at Joliet, Illinois, Chino, California, and Terre Haute, Indiana, found that all became violators of trusts after they thought of themselves as having a financial problem which they could not share with others, knew that this problem could be secretly handled by violation of the trust, and were able to rationalize their conception of themselves as trusted persons into conceptions of themselves as users of the trusters' property.[12] Would more effective ethical training have prevented this rationalizing process?

Organized Crime

Organized crime—the so-called Mafia or Mob operation—relies heavily on political corruption; so it is discussed in Chapter Four which deals with political corruption. It is mentioned here only because it is not *poverty*-inspired crime. Many members of organized crime own legitimate businesses; they are well financed; their sons and daughters are sent to good colleges. It is middle class crime in every sense. It is true that organized crime preys on poverty areas, but it is not itself a result of poverty.

Undoubtedly there are men drawn into organized crime from poverty areas. This is especially true of the "soldiers" or "trigger men" who do the actual threatening and murdering. It is also true, however, that poverty is not the reason for maintaining organized crime. The fact that a substantial amount of legitimate industry is owned by organized crime is itself an indicator of the middle class status of the persons who motivate organized crime.

Business and Union Crimes

Also discussed in the next chapter because of its close relationship to political corruption is the problem of business and union dishonesty. It is fairly well established that American unions rank below those of other modern democracies in honesty; some portions of American business also run a high fraction of fraudulent activity. These activities are mentioned here only because the participants are practically all "middle class." They are another segment of America's criminal world which cannot be explained by poverty origins.

Professional Groups

Ethics is still a major problem with important and well-educated professional groups in the United States. The number of lawyers involved in "Watergate" has reminded us of the frail ethical standards of some lawyers. A survey of the Missouri Bar in 1963 came up with the remarkable conclusion that 29 percent of the laymen who had never used a lawyer's services thought that about half the lawyers were not ethical. Worse, 27 percent of the lawyers thought that half their fellows might be unethical at times.[13]

A sociological-legal study of the New York City bar found that ethical levels were higher among the successful lawyers. They were correspondingly lower among those lawyers whose poorer clients put them under pressure to practice less ethically. Bar association disciplinary measures are reported to be only mildly effective.[14]

Even the medical profession, which includes some of the most conscientious of professional men and women, has real ethical problems. Fee splitting, the size of fees, the use of the insurance principle, and the degree of socialized control are among the problems which have not always been illumined by completely ethical handling in the profession. However, there is probably no harder working or better educated professional group in the world, and they have a very elaborate professional code.[15] Courses in medical ethics are now standard in medical schools.

Other professions, like the architects, engineers, teachers and ministers, also have elaborate professional codes. Yet the public is at times surprised at the ability of engineers employed by different interests to arrive at varying conclusions on important problems. Nor have architects kept themselves out of political corruption.

Civil Disobedience and Disorder

The campus revolts of the 1960s were a worldwide phenomenon. Violence was a major facet in many of these acts of civil disobedience. There were substantial student demonstrations in most modern democracies and even in Soviet Russia in 1969–70. In France, students were hurling paving stones at police in Nanterre and near the Sorbonne for several days. In West Germany and Britain a few of the riots came to a degree of violence.[16] But in the United States violence was much more frequent. Bombings killed and injured several people. The President's Commission on Campus Unrest noted:

> Assistant Secretary of the Treasury Eugene T. Rossides reported that, between January 1, 1969, and April 15, 1970, almost 41,000 bombings, attempted bombings, and bomb threats were recorded in the nation as a whole. Most could not be attributed to a specific cause. Of those that could be attributed to some cause, more than half—over 8,200—were attributable to 'campus disturbances and student unrest.'[17]

Mr. J. Edgar Hoover (Director of the FBI) reported to the same Commission that disruptive and violent protests resulted in over 4,000 arrests in the 1968–69 academic year and about 7,200 arrests during 1969–70. The Commission also noted very substantial destruction of property, papers, and records.[18]

This relative proclivity to violence among American students, as opposed to European, may be partially accounted for by the larger number of American youth in college and the closer proximity of the supposed causes for the disturbance—conscription for the war in Indochina and discrimination against minority groups. The fact that some of our police forces are not too professional may have excited more violence from rioters.

Perhaps the most disturbing feature of the campus youth revolt was the willingness of comparatively well-educated youths—from good family backgrounds and with excellent career possibilities—to use violence against fellow human beings. The campus disturbances represent serious questions about the ethical level of the American students. It is one thing to riot or to demonstrate; it is another to kill innocent people.

Middle Class Tendencies to Delinquency

The crimes mentioned in this section have been singled out in order to counteract the notion that most crime comes from poverty, as most sociological analyses of the source of crime seem to contend. For some time, however, criminologists have also been aware of the fact that middle class delinquents are less likely to be included in law enforcement statistics because police are not likely to prefer charges against middle class boys whose parents guarantee good conduct in the future. Hence, sociologists have suspected larger amounts of potential for middle class delinquency than crime statistics show. A few studies of self reporting of crime have partly supported this position. Nye, Short, and Olson, using samples of several thousand boys and girls from different socio-economic strata in western and mid-western communities "failed to uncover enough significant differences to reject . . . the null hypothesis that there is no significant difference in delinquent behavior of boys and girls in different socioeconomic status."[19]

Studies with somewhat similar conclusions are reported by Rodman and Grams in a special study for the President's Commission on Law Enforcement and Administration of Justice.[20] Another study by Reiss and Rhodes of several thousand white school boys in Davidson County, Tennessee, found that the class structure of the area in which the boy lived is a very important factor in determining actual delinquency, often without regard to social class.[21]

These materials are not conclusive. The reported delinquencies are subject to the possible errors that delinquencies were invented out of bravado or that middle class delinquencies were less violent. But they also avoid the pitfall of official statistics of middle class crime, which is that parental influence secured the waiving of charges against middle class youth.

Comments on Crime

Chapter Three will review the reasons advanced by professional criminologists and by others for the existence of crime and corruption in America. There is no effort to duplicate consideration of the area, of the association, of the family, of poverty, and of other theories about the cause of crime in this chapter.

Attention is called to three factors which are usually omitted in most considerations of the reasons for crime. First, as noted above, America's crime rates are surprisingly high. In view of the many assets which we could use for crime control—leadership in education, high per capita income, highly developed electronic communication system, and well attended and supported churches—we have reason to be deeply ashamed of our high crime record.

Second, this high crime rate, if continued, bodes ill for America's economic and social future and for its influence in the world community. We are very much in need of new, fundamental reanalysis of the reasons for crime.

Third, this chapter has reviewed evidence which indicates that crime in the United States goes considerably beyond the poorer classes. Shoplifting, which is perpetrated by people in all economic classes, is a major crime. Employee theft is estimated to be even larger. Auto theft, which is usually not committed by poorer people, is a large and growing crime. Embezzlement results in few arrests, but is estimated to be an important crime. Even the well-educated professions show considerable concern about levels of ethics. Civil disobedience in America has often taken the form of criminal middle class activities. Some general studies indicate that middle class youth is as much or almost as much inclined to delinquency as are the poorer classes.

In another sense, however, the spread of middle class crime is also disappointing. The United States has been the middle class country of the world—valuing equality and other middle class attributes, educating its youth for a great middle class, setting its laws for a great middle class. If we cannot keep that class relatively honest, our entire society will be deeply affected. We must rethink our entire ethical education program.

Reasons for America's High Crime Rate

Explaining the high crime problem in the United States is not easy. As is the case with many social problems, intelligent people often favor apparent but erroneous explanations. It is the privilege of each citizen of a democracy to make up his own mind—and many people do so without benefit of sociological, historical, or comparative judgment. The first section, Speculative Explanations, analyzes some of these suggestions.

Unfortunately, experts on this problem do not agree. Most of their explanations are discussed in a second section on sociological reasons for crime, and show that they tend to concentrate on poverty and poverty areas—correctly, since higher rates of crime are found in poorer urban districts. But the sociologists do not agree with each other. While we attach great weight to their recommendations, we cannot help believing that they have not told the whole story.

A third section of this chapter discusses explanations for the crime which arises out of important deficiencies in our law enforcement mechanism. This brings in another group of "experts" who often disagree among themselves. Again we respect these informed judgments, but believe that more is involved.

Finally, we draw our own conclusions. The element of ethical education is introduced, something which the other three groups have almost completely ignored. But we believe that lack of ethical education is only one of several explanations of crime, and we try to select those recommendations of the two groups of experts which are most likely to be effective.

Speculative Explanations

One of the least satisfactory aspects of social science is the effort to isolate and to emphasize a single reason for an observed phenomenon. Each potential reason tends to acquire supporters, but the scientific assessment of their relative importance is seldom possible. Thus it is that we present here "reasons" which have been proposed by thoughtful analysts but which—after comparative and historical checks—do not seem to be of dominant importance.

A Nation of Violence

As noted above, a National Commission on the Causes and Prevention of Violence, chaired by Dr. Milton S. Eisenhower, correctly reported in 1969 that the United States is the clear leader among modern, stable, democratic nations in its rates of homicide, assault, rape, and robbery, and that it is among the highest in incidence of group violence and assassination.[1] The first chapter of the report lists various evidence of the history of violence in the United States.

Violence occurred, says the Commission, because of the struggle of newer immigrant groups against a "so-called Anglo Saxon elite"; *nativist* movements directed violence against *ethnic* scapegoats. There was violence between competing social and ethnic groups in 1863, like the New York draft riots of the Irish against New York's Negroes. Other violence came from frontier lawlessness, and from *vigilante* movements against frontier conditions.

Organized labor's battles for recognition and for power often met violent resistance. The family feuds of the border states after the Civil War were another kind of violence. The Indian Wars resulted in a bloody reduction of the Indian population. The Ku Klux Klan engaged in terrorism; lynching was widespread, particularly in the South. From 1882 to 1903 antagonism was especially racial.

The Commission does not maintain that America's traditions of violence make continued violence inevitable. In fact, the recommendations for improvement of the situation bear little reference to such a history. Two of the research studies published by the Commission indicate somewhat similar records of violence in Britain, France, Germany, Italy, and Spain.[2] The real question for the Commission, as for us, thus becomes one of elimination—or at least control—of the present violence.

The writers do not believe that this tradition is an important reason why America cannot solve her ethical problems. Australia and Canada both had frontier conditions without generating permanent violence.[3] Western European countries have had much violence in the past, but today they are all well ahead of the United States in control of crime. We *are* a nation of violence but we do not need to remain one.

Urbanism

A great deal of evidence shows that crime increases with urbanized and industrialized life. With few exceptions, Uniform Crime Reports show higher rates of crime—in proportion to population—in larger cities. Research results from Iowa and Sweden indicate a relationship between the degree of urbanism and the rate of property offenses.[4] Urbanized Sweden has crime rates double those of less urbanized Norway. There is, however, some evidence to indicate that criminalistic traditions continue in some rural areas.[5] But in general it is still true that the larger cities have the higher crime rates.[6]

Several possible reasons for this phenomenon have been advanced. Criminal cultures are more likely to exist in urban areas. The rural young man may be identified more easily as a working member of his community than is a young man in the city. One can "belong" more readily to smaller communities.

It may be that—at least in part—America's high crime rate is a result of this being one of the first nations of the world to urbanize and to industrialize. Countries like Germany, Japan, Britain, and Sweden, however, have become urbanized and have been able to maintain much lower crime rates than ours. England was industrialized before we were. Urbanism is thus a cause of crime, but it is not the major reason for our high incidence. The impact of urbanism on crime in the United States should be controlled as has been done in other countries.

Business Civilization

It is often argued that the excessive devotion to business civilization in this country results in lower ethical standards, and hence in crime. According to this reasoning, when the purpose of our society is to grab for money, people will grab it by whatever means they can use, legal or illegal.

In the next chapter, the effect of business on political corruption—which deeply affects crime—will be discussed, so consideration here will be confined to the direct effect of business on crime. There are cases where individual businesses have financed or otherwise encouraged criminal action. But most businesses do not want crime and will work to discourage it.

Before generalizing on the effect of business on ethical values, it is wise to remind ourselves that pre-capitalist societies had a great deal of crime. Communist countries have significant problems of crime and violence.[7] Other capitalist countries have much less crime than the United States. The comparative record does not justify the assumption that capitalism necessarily brings crime.

Population Mobility

Another frequent explanation given for our crime rate is the mobility of our population. The migration of millions to California after World War II has been described as one of the greatest peacetime movements of people in world history. The average American is said to move every fifth year.[8] The impact of such movement on social institutions has often been observed. It is apparently true that industrialization beings increased mobility and higher crime rates to most nations.

Vance Packard, in discussing the mobility of America, cites one estimate that the average American moves fourteen times in a lifetime, whereas the Britisher moves eight, and the Japanese only five.[9] The rate of movement is especially large in the Western states. It tends to include persons of higher social and economic brackets, and those between twenty-five and thirty-four years of age are the most mobile. Renters are three times as mobile as homeowners.

Packard also finds evidence of "malaise," if not mental upset, among people who move frequently. At aerospace centers where people are frequently transferred, he reports little community involvement, few close friends, more alcoholics, and more infidelity.[10] Cirrhosis of the liver is an unusually frequent killer in

"rootless" California.[11] Packard also mentions an area in the
Borough of Queens (Maspeth), inhabited by stable lower middle
class *ethnics*, which presumably has a lower crime rate.[12]

None of the above evidence is convincing proof that mobility
leads to crime. Such evidence is rather sparse. The mobile Western
states do not have higher crime rates, and crimes related to political
corruption are fewer in those states.

It is possible that the countries with educational and economic
levels similar to ours—northwestern Europe, Canada, Australia—
have lower crime rates because of lower mobility. All of them are
much smaller than the United States and, if the figures cited by
Packard are correct, have less mobility. Perhaps the smaller, more
stable population knows its delinquents better and supervises their
activities more effectively.

There are, however, several other possible explanations for the
lower crime rates in these countries. Many of them have monarchs
and established churches which give important psychological
support to ethical standards. All have programs for teaching religion
and ethics in the schools, and most have more rigid class structures
which may support ethical values.

Both difficult and elaborate opinion studies along with intellectual
analysis of ideas regarding crime are necessary before full appraisal
can be made of the effect of mobility on American crime and
corruption rates. Our current guess is that it is a significant but not a
major factor. Even if mobility were a major cause of crime—which
we doubt—it is constitutionally impossible to issue laws against
mobility, although financial or social legislation could be used to
discourage it.

War and Crime

The Vietnam War is used as an "explanation" of the U.S. crime
rate. It is argued that if our government is shooting people overseas,
people will assume the right to shoot other people at home. Hence,
our soldiers have been learning to be murderers.

The evidence of a relationship between war and crime cannot be
called strong. Crime rates rose during the Vietnam War, and there is
evidence of rising crime rates following the Civil War and World

War I. The increase at the end of the earlier wars may have resulted from major demobilization problems, which did not occur with the Vietnam War. There was no increase of crime after World War II, possibly because of the GI Bill of Rights and other veteran benefits which also functioned during the Vietnam War. The period since the Vietnam War ended has been marked by increasing crime rates.

Another difficulty with this hypothesis is that countries which have been much more involved in war than has ours have kept crime under much better control. Great Britain and West Germany are two examples.

Sociological Explanations of Crime and Corruption

The "sociological" analysis of crime is presented with great respect by the writers. American criminologists have made careful efforts to determine the causes of delinquency and of crime. Their theoretical explanations are often correlated with detailed statistical studies. This section will note that the sociologists do not explain all crime, but that the validity of their explanations of much of it is fully accepted.

Poverty and Delinquency

In a country which until recently has had the world's highest per capita income, few Americans dare to use poverty as the sole reason for American ethical troubles. Many, however, use "pockets of poverty" and "relative expectations" as explaining crime and corruption. This closely relates to explanations given by criminologists.

Most criminals were once delinquents, although many delinquents do not become permanent criminals. There are several important sociological theories to account for delinquency. Most of them indicate a greater attraction to criminal action than to more laborious means of securing funds.

A major theory of the origin of crime has been its prevalence in certain "delinquency areas." Various large cities have districts in which as many as one-fifth of the boys are arrested each year. In other areas there are almost no arrests. Clifford Shaw and his collaborators studied certain Chicago districts which regularly had high delinquency rates. As newer, poorer ethnic groups lived in these areas their crime rates went up, but when the groups moved to better districts the rate declined. The neighborhoods highest in crime seem to be in the low rent central city districts and near large commercial or manufacturing sub-centers.

The social order of a given district may explain its concentration of delinquency. Gangs exist in certain neighborhoods. Younger delinquents are taught how to steal and to rob, and how to avoid penalties for a crime. Usually there is little community organization working against crime. Parent-teacher associations are often non-existent. Churches are supported from elsewhere, if they exist at all.[13]

A second interpretation of area concentration is that the people most prone to crime are likely to be drawn to certain districts. Persons with lower income, who are less educated, and who have recently immigrated—including Southern blacks—concentrate where there is high incidence of crime. Exceptions to this theory include a Japanese group who lived in a high delinquency area in Seattle for a number of years without any of its children becoming delinquent. Many other families live in similar neighborhoods without their children being affected, eventually moving to areas where delinquency is less frequent.

Other theories of delinquency center around the affluence of our society. Professor Jackson Toby has summarized them for the President's Commission on Law Enforcement and the Administration of Justice. Citing Japan and Sweden, Toby gives examples of the increase of crime—especially among the young—as the society becomes more affluent. He suggests that in all industrialized societies the extended family has become less influential. Parents become more important to the child, but divorce and working parents become more frequent. Parents then may reject children, causing mental disorder, or neglect them, causing the child to orient with peer groups rather than the family. Toby suggests that the weakness of adult control has its source in "the increasing social fluidity resulting from the allocation of education, recreation, work, and family life to separate institutional contacts."[14]

Affluence does, of course, increase the opportunity for education.

It is fairly sure that children who do well in school are less likely to become delinquent. But affluence may increase the temptation for less able scholars to become delinquent, and to get more easily what they want of the cars, television sets, radios, or other examples of affluence around them.

The late Professor Edwin H. Sutherland developed a theory of "differential association" which has been expanded by Professor Donald K. Cressey. This suggests that high crime rates occur in areas which encourage "criminalistic subcultures." Youths learn how to commit crime and are encouraged to do it by groups or individuals who are already committed to crime. Sutherland hoped that this theory would help to account for the distribution of high and low crime rates. However, Cressey points out that the theory is not a precise explanation of how one becomes a criminal.[15]

Professor Albert K. Cohen argues that lower class boys wish to attain middle class goals and values. When they find the chances of reaching these goals to be slim, the boys turn to patterns of gang behavior which help them achieve self-respect within the gang.[16]

Professors Richard A. Cloward and Lloyd E. Ohlin argued that youths tend to choose delinquency when the legitimate path to material success is blocked by failure in school or by lower class origin—much as Cohen suggests—and when they find simulta-neously that circumstances favor the delinquent path to success. They noted that there are three types of delinquent groups. First is the criminal pattern in which the young man learns to use criminal techniques and to work with criminals. The second involves conflict, in which the youth learns to fight against other gangs, to be courageous, and to follow gang rules. And the third is the retreatist pattern in which the individual or the group goes into drug subcultures.[17]

Professor Walter Miller suggested that lower class life tends to develop a set of lower class values—toughness, emphasis on excitement, autonomy—which run counter to middle class values.

A substantial number of studies found correlation between broken homes and delinquency, but there are important statistical problems as to what constitutes a broken home.[18]

In reviewing these theories of delinquency, it should be noted that many sociologists have made field studies to determine the cause of delinquency, but no one theory has been fully supported by indisputable evidence. This is unfortunate, because confirmation of theory would enable us to offer clear-cut programs for eliminating delinquency.

The theories are not mutually exclusive. Delinquency may be found in an area where it has been produced by family neglect or by family rejection or by the attraction of delinquency offered by a gang. It may also be produced by a combination of these factors.

Rodman and Grams made a valuable effort to summarize various sociological theories of delinquency and the family in a "paradigm of delinquency" (presented more fully in Chapter Seven on the family). In this paradigm there are three main reasons why living in a lower class family or community tends to increase the possibility of delinquency:

1. The community's limited ability to provide opportunities to achieve in accordance with middle class values lessens legitimate opportunities for youth, increases the opportunity for illegitimate or gang behavior, and results in pressure against middle class values.
2. The family's limited ability to maintain external controls: the poorer family has a less attractive life; the father's role is handicapped by his occupational position; parents are less able to maintain control.
3. The family's limited use of child rearing techniques that lead to effective internal controls with the result that lower class families have more instability; are more likely to have lax or inconsistent discipline, show less affection as a result of economic privation, and children identify themselves less with parents or parental norms.[19]

Most of the explanations of delinquency and crime are related to poverty or to poverty areas. If life in these areas can be improved through better housing, better education, better policing, better employment services, and better health conditions, most sociologists believe that crime would be greatly reduced. The writers are inclined to agree that improved district services would probably help reduce their crime rate. Even if the case is unproven, it would seem to be sound public policy to keep trying.

All of these explanations of delinquency omit the factor with which this book is concerned: the teaching of ethical standards. Criminologists *assume* that youth is taught these standards. The writers suspect that many fourteen-year-old delinquents have not received from school, from church, or from their parents any reasoned analysis of what is wrong with killing, assaulting, or stealing from a fellow human being. Later chapters on the church, the school, and the family will give some of the reasons for this vacuum. If the largely unstated assumption of criminologists—that children have received adequate ethical instruction—is incorrect, then their theories need to be modified to that extent. In addition to feelings of deprivation, and to the appeal of lower class codes or of delinquent associates, there is another factor: that the young person has not been adequately educated in doing right.

Poverty explanations of delinquency do not apply to middle class crime. This criminal was usually raised in a middle class area, and was not forced into his crime by lack of money. If customary sociological analyses do not explain the substantial amount of middle class crime, there is even more reason to stress ethical education, which is needed for *all* social and economic classes.

Race and Ethnic Problems

A frequent explanation of crime is that it is a result of American racial and ethnic problems. The Western European powers, which do much better than we in crime control, are all cited as racially homogenous. It is true that Britain has almost two million "colored" and several millions of Scotch and Irish citizens. Sweden has Laplanders. West Germany has absorbed many Volks-Deutsch (German-speaking refugees from Eastern Europe). Canada and Switzerland have very real mixtures. But these are minor compared to America's twenty million blacks, ten to twelve million Italians, twelve million Latin Americans, and many other ethnic groups—so runs the argument.

There is validity to this argument. Many Americans have overlooked the ethical shortcomings of members of their own ethnic group. Undoubtedly the London bobby has an easier time dealing with people who know and respect his methods of operation than does the Irish-American policeman in New York who must deal with a number of other ethnic groups of vastly different social backgrounds. Part of the solution to the American problem is to get some of the ethnics in the police force, but civil service regulations and other factors keep that mixture from happening as fast as it might.

However, if the United States has been able to bring this vast mixture of peoples together in a reasonably respectable governmental process, it should also be able to bring these diverse groups into reasonably effective relationships with the law enforcement process. Immigrants to this country have traditionally been law abiding and a large majority of them come from countries which have a law enforcement record as good as or better than that of the United States. A recent trend toward securing citizen participation in various aspects of municipal government will undoubtedly help our law enforcement agencies work with the ethnics.

How important is the ethnic problem in crime control? Canada and Switzerland, also with heterogeneous populations, keep better order. Our answer is that the ethnic problem is significant but not overwhelming. Well-run police departments and an ethically educated population could cope with its difficulties.

The Blacks

Overwhelming evidence indicates that American blacks commit a much larger proportion of violent crimes than do non-blacks. In 1972 Negroes made up 60 percent of those arrested for murder and 53 percent of the victims were black, although Negroes constitute only 12 percent of the population. In the same year, 49 percent of those arrested for forcible rape were black. Sixty-seven percent of those arrested for robbery were black. But only about a third of those arrested for burglary, larceny, and auto theft were black. Black participation in other middle class crime and in political corruption has been small.[20]

Since blacks are proportionately less affluent than whites, a higher crime rate should be anticipated. But the present rate of black crime goes beyond what poverty would produce. There is also evidence of increase of black crime in recent years at a time when black incomes were rising rapidly.[21]

Two other comments should be made. If black crimes of violence were scaled down to the white rate, America would still have a higher rate of such crimes than do northwestern European nations. Cutting our murder rate by 40 percent would still leave it ten times higher than the British rate. Second, the higher proportion of victims of these black crimes are other blacks. Efforts to help blacks develop their own leadership will some day result in effective black leadership against black crime.

There are also observers who believe that civil rights militancy and riots have produced a temporary "ideological justification for crime."[22] Evidence is not yet available to indicate whether the recent rise in black economic status will reduce the proportion of black crime. Perhaps the rise in status is, at least temporarily, offset by the "ideological justification" of black crime.

The remedies for this situation seem fairly obvious. Efforts to improve the quality of schools for blacks, to ameliorate their living conditions, and to help them find employment will do much to bring their crime rate down. Continuation of such efforts will in time reduce the ideological thrust toward crime mentioned above. If we are right in believing that ethical education is needed, it should help blacks as well as whites.

Youth in the Population

Professor Edward Banfield has pointed out that one of the major reasons for current crime rates is the high proportion of youth in the delinquency-prone areas of the city.[23] The point is undoubtedly valid. It helps to explain cycles of increasing crime. However, it does not explain America's long-range tendency to higher crime rates. Other modern democracies also have larger numbers of youth in urban areas, but their overall crime rates seem to remain below those of the United States. Banfield's explanation, like the sociological explanations, does not cover middle class crime and delinquency.

Law Enforcement

Administration of Justice

America's high crime rate is often blamed on the existence of a decentralized and spotty system of administering justice. There is real validity to this criticism. In recent years the scholarly Advisory

Commission on Intergovernmental Relations (of the National
Government) and the private Committee on Economic Development both have issued reports on our system of law enforcement
which recognize substantial problems, and which recommend
desirable centralization within states on patterns already worked out
in Western European countries.

Major recommendations of the Committee for Economic
Development include:

—A Federal Authority to Ensure Justice.

—Creation of additional judges to ensure speedy court trials.
  Merit selection of judges and consolidation of courts on a
  statewide basis; federal aid to be conditioned on acceptance of
  these recommendations.

—Placing all state and local prosecuting staffs on a non-partisan
  merit basis, with adequate financing. Control of administrative
  operations through a State Director of Prosecutions.

—Expansion and strengthening of state police forces. Improvement of police management and recruitment. Improvement of
  police communication with the public. Federal and state aid to
  be conditioned upon acceptance of standards.

—Maximization of rehabilitative efforts in correctional apparatus. Greater consistency in sentencing. Strong reenforcement of probation and parole forces. Better equipped, more
  suitable prisons.

—Repeal of limitations on unorganized gambling. Experimentation with government control of organized gambling.

—More appropriate and more strictly enforced penalties for
  drunk driving.

—Elimination of private control of handguns. Reform of criminal
  codes.

—Strengthening of state Departments of Justice.[24]

The Advisory Commission on Intergovernmental Relations has
more detailed and legalistic recommendations than the CED
proposals. However, their general tendency is largely the same—
toward more state control and more effective performance of law
enforcing agencies.[25]

Should the recommendations of these two groups be carried out,
what would be the impact on crime? The writers would guess that
such changes would bring about only a partial reduction of crime.

Those areas where the administration of justice is most decentralized happen to be in rural areas where crime rates are already low. So the merging of a part-time district attorney, or a part-time justice of the peace, or an untrained five-man police force into larger, better-trained, better-administered units will give the rural area some gains of security. But such merging will not have much impact on crime rates in the larger cities where a major portion of the crime is located.

The great usefulness which centralization of law enforcement machinery could have for the larger cities would be in securing substantial aid from federal and state grants for law enforcement, coupled with central pressure for reduction of corruption. The continuous endemic corruption of some metropolitan police forces, especially in the eastern United States, is undoubtedly a factor in the continued high crime rates in those cities. Corruption, its causes and cures, will be discussed in the next chapter.

Attention should be given to a unique feature of American law enforcement: its interminable delays. Fred Graham, in a scholarly defense of the "Warren Court" decisions safeguarding the rights of accused persons, grants that the delays these decisions have brought into the judicial process are their greatest defect. According to Graham, Chief Justice Warren realized that these delays might result in a "dangerous paralysis of justice," although he never admitted that the Supreme Court "was partially responsible."[26] The Supreme Court makes each decision as it arises and does not calculate its effect on the time of the judicial process. Graham gives examples of long delays in court action due to the Warren Court decisions. His point is that the decisions have not "handcuffed the police" but that the long process of appeals has greatly delayed final decisions. Graham cites one bank robber whose final conviction, after appeals on all Constitutional points, required ten years.[27]

A frequently cited comparison to show the slowness of American justice is the case of two citizens who broadcast over enemy radios in World War II. The Englishman, "Lord Haw Haw," was arrested, tried, given final appeals, and executed in less than eight months. The American, "Tokyo Rose," was in and out of court for eight years before she received a moderate prison sentence.

Much more could be said about the uncertainty of the judicial process in the United States. Studies indicate that certainty of punishment is a more important deterrent than its severity.[28] It is not the purpose of this book to review the whole process in detail, but to indicate that the weakness of the process is one reason for our problems of law enforcement.

There have been several studies of the lawlessness of government and particularly of the police.[29] Government lawlessness varies from police "third degree" (forcing confessions from suspects), to failure to prosecute corrupt officials, to maltreatment of prisoners (especially minorities), and to selective enforcement of laws. "Third degree" methods have largely disappeared. As police forces become professionalized, rough treatment of suspects is being reduced. But other forms of lawlessness probably continue.

This kind of odd-handed administration of the law has a bad effect on volume of crime. If poorly-trained policemen treat minority groups illegally, they are cutting off needed cooperation of that part of the public. Resentment against illegal actions by other groups may encourage some unlawful measures. The English police secure great cooperation from the populace, in part because the police have been ordered to be "civil and obliging to every rank and class."[30]

Handguns

The right of the individual to possess handguns is a frequent reason given for America's crime problem. Most Western European countries limit the legal possession of such guns to police officers. The United States has refused to ban handguns completely and has only inadequate laws regarding registration.

Evidence seems to indicate that handguns are a major contributor to violent crime. Over 60 percent of murders are currently committed with handguns. Since a high proportion of murdered persons are acquainted with the murderer, it is probable that some other means of killing could be found, but the possession of such weapons is undoubtedly an important adjunct to hasty killing. Handguns are used in a substantial number of robberies—reported by the FBI as 385,910 in 1971. Sixty-five percent of these were cases of armed robbery (in contrast to mugging), and 63 percent of the armed robberies were committed with the aid of firearms. Knives are the principal alternative.

The effect of more complete handgun restrictions on murder and armed robbery is not known; even if it cut murders by a third and armed robbery and assault by a fifth, the incidence of these crimes in the United States would still be very high. There would be little effect on corruption, white collar crime, or on the FBI's estimate of 2,540,900 burglaries or 4,304,000 larcenies as in the year 1973. It would take a number of years before handgun legislation could reduce the estimated 30 million such weapons in the hands of American citizens. During that period of time, criminals with handguns would have greater strength against honest citizens lacking such weapons. As they became known as contraband and were confiscated or surrendered, however, the number in private possession would diminish.

Probation and Parole Policies

The policy of probation rather than immediate jail for a convicted prisoner is generally accepted in many American states. This policy is suspected of being responsible for the high volume of crime. It is argued that by keeping the person out of jail, probation makes the consequences of his act seem less serious; he is less likely to hesitate before taking criminal action and is free to repeat the crime for which he was convicted.

While the argument may have some validity, Britain, Scandinavia, and the Netherlands have somewhat similar policies with crime rates well below those of the United States.[31] It may be that some American jurisdictions do use probation more freely than most northwestern European countries. A careful study of the effect of probation policy on criminal thinking in all countries would be welcome. But it is probably fair to say that probation is not a major cause of our excessive crime rates.[32]

Parole, the release of a prisoner prior to completion of maximum sentence but under supervision by a parole officer, has also been charged with leading to disregard for the law. Now in very general use in the United States, it was originally borrowed from the northwestern European countries which still use it extensively. Since their crime rates are below ours, it seems improbable that parole is a reason for our excess of crime. As in the case of probation, a comparative study would be helpful.

"Victimless Crime"

A reason often advanced to explain America's crime problem is the fact that our statutes unnecessarily forbid certain victimless crimes. If such acts were not illegal—runs the argument—police, prosecutors, and judges would have more time for other crimes and would be able to keep them under control. "Victimless crimes" usually cited include abortion, intoxication, homosexuality, drug addiction, and gambling.

There is some validity to this argument. However, abortions have been legalized in some very important states in recent years, so they are no longer a victimless crime in some jurisdictions.

There is little public purpose served in arresting and bringing chronic alcoholics before a judge. At first sight the establishment of an overnight "drying out" place would seem to be adequate. Drunks can be a public nuisance, so most communities are bound to demand a minimum degree of control. Perhaps some time of prosecutors and courts could be saved by an informal treatment of intoxicated persons, but it is hard to see how the police could avoid the responsibility for supervising persons who disturb public order. Some countries have moved further towards control of the drunk in certain circumstances. Sweden has reported good results with a program of short, mandatory sentences for even mildly drunken drivers.

Laws against homosexuality are not very vigorously enforced in most American jurisdictions and the tendency is towards greater leniency, so it is improbable that any substantial fraction of police or prosecutor time is lost in this field. The question of whether or not all laws against homosexuality should be repealed is a fascinating one. Theoretical pros and cons were well discussed in recent British debates,[33] but there are also important practical considerations. However, an extended discussion of the problem does not seem to have major importance for the questions of crime and corruption discussed in this book.

Much more serious problems are raised by the suggestion that laws against drug traffic and off-track gambling be abolished. These two fields of currently illegal endeavor are the major activities—and almost monopolies—of organized crime which, as will be pointed out in Chapter Four, is one of the most important and dangerous sources of crime and corruption in America. Since the two fields are quite different, each will be discussed separately.

Drug addiction is a very knotty problem. Unquestionably, the outlawing of drugs raises their price and thus makes the selling of such drugs at the wholesale level into a substantial source of income for organized crime and a major cause of corruption in local governments (and occasionally at higher levels). The high price also sends the addict to criminal activities in order to pay for his daily ration of drugs. Since many were criminals before becoming addicted, we cannot tell how much such addiction contributes to crime.[34] But it is surely the source of a substantial percentage of burglaries and robberies.

The remedy proposed by many in discussing the crime problem is the British practice of allowing clinics to prescribe drugs legally to addicts. The British have been doing this for some years and still have a proportion of addicts well below the estimated American figures. If we should follow the British practice, we might reduce street crime substantially and cut down both criminal income and governmental corruption.[35]

However, there are major difficulties with this theory. The British did have an increase of addiction by a factor of forty under their drug issuance policy, as well as a good deal of illegal selling of prescribed narcotics by addicts.[36] They were forced to tighten their programs in 1968, and are not yet sure that addiction is decreasing. Such a program of cheap, prescribed narcotics might greatly magnify the already high degree of addiction in this country. These prospects are especially frightening because use of drugs has been an "in thing" among portions of our younger generation, which probably would resist the smaller, less euphoria-producing rations of the clinics under the British scheme. Wilson and his collaborators agree that American addicts will not accept a voluntary reform program unless it includes free heroin.[37]

A modified form of the drug suggestion is that American law be modified to permit legal sale of marijuana, which is viewed by many people as harmless, or relatively harmless. It is very widely used, easily grown, and very difficult to control. Would it not be simpler to make it legal, or at the very least modify the rather strong penalties imposed on its sale? Should it not be treated, like tobacco and alcohol, as a drug which the human race can learn to use in moderation?

There is a good deal to be said for this view of marijuana. If current research does indicate its relative harmlessness, a matter which is still far from certain, its legalization is likely to follow. One important caution is necessary, however. The plant, cannabis, from which marijuana is derived can also be used to make the more powerful and dangerous hashish. Legalization of the one would probably have to be accompanied by restrictions on the sale of the other. The burden of marijuana control on police and prosecutors would thus be only partially reduced.

Legalization of gambling would have advantages similar to the legalization of drugs, although of lesser importance. It might deprive organized crime of one of its main sources of income, and could free the police, the prosecutor, and court time for other more important offenses. It would remove an inconsistency in our law, since many states already permit race track gambling.

Again, however, there are difficulties with this proposal. Organized crime would remain important in legalized gambling because it has the capital and the skills. Professor Cressey comments: "Since World War II, we have witnessed four major experiences with legalized bet taking—in Nevada, in Cuba, in the Bahamas, and in England. In all four cases, Cosa Nostra members and their associates moved in."[38]

There are still many opportunities to cheat the customer and the government in legalized gambling. Legalization would increase the amount of gambling opportunities and cause still greater financial loss to those with low incomes who can afford it least but who are the principle customers of the policy game and the lottery. Should it still be decided to legalize all gambling, such action would probably not do much damage to organized crime. It should be done only after serious consideration of the major public policy difficulties involved.

Many of the victimless crimes are in fields which lead to police corruption. Protection of brothels, gambling houses, and the drug traffic are common reasons for bribing law enforcement agencies. Elimination of those laws might reduce some of these corruption problems, but could increase other difficulties.

In summary, it is our conclusion that some of the "victimless crimes" should be decriminalized if careful study indicates that the crimes do not, in fact, lead to general social disadvantage. But there is little evidence to indicate that legalization of victimless crimes would benefit law and order in the United States.

Conclusion

Reviewing the various reasons offered for crime in America, a few conclusions become obvious. If any of the speculative explanations offered in this chapter are valid, little can be done about them. We cannot change our history of violence. We cannot eliminate urbanism. We are likely to stay with our business civilization, which has produced a high living standard and a great deal of freedom. We could not constitutionally reduce our mobility. Fortunately, no one of these speculative explanations is so important that it will keep the United States from establishing reasonable controls over crime and corruption. Other countries have overcome similar difficulties.

The group of sociological difficulties must be taken much more seriously. If we could eliminate the basic problems of the core city poverty area, we could substantially reduce crime—especially crimes of violence. What is needed is a combination of health, education, housing, welfare, vocational training, and employment services which will assist residents of those areas in becoming a productive part of American life. Unfortunately, no major city seems as yet to have found the appropriate combination of public policy, financial assistance, and citizen support to accomplish this. Federal grants do not encourage coordinated effort. Much local effort is needed to find the right pattern.

The problems of law enforcement have an important relationship to crime. If the recommendations made by able agencies, like the U.S. Advisory Commission on Intergovernmental Relations and the Committee for Economic Development, are carried out, crime should be substantially reduced in the United States. Police must be better trained in detection and patrolling methods, and should develop better relations with the community. Handguns should be outlawed. Courts must function more expeditiously. Some centralization of police supervision is necessary if we are to defeat the corruption discussed in the next chapter. No reforms can be accomplished without honest government.

Complete acceptance of the sociological and law enforcement recommendations, however, would leave American with still substantial crime problems. Middle class crime and corruption would be only partly affected; other kinds of crime would probably continue at a high level.

It is on account of the inadequacy of the measures approved

above that this book explores another possibility: that officials and citizens alike need better ethical instruction. Later chapters will indicate how ethics may be taught, but it is first necessary to analyze that important aspect of crime called corruption.

— 4 —

The Payoff in Business, Unions, and Government

Closely related to the criminal activity which we have just discussed is another group of crimes that is commonly spoken of as "corruption." This chapter will explore the extent of that corruption, say something about its relationship to the crimes discussed in the last two chapters, and discuss its relationship to America's ethical situation. There will be a special section on "organized crime," which is almost completely dependent on political corruption but also draws heavily from business and union corruption.

Corruption is defined in Webster's *Collegiate Dictionary* as "a corrupting or state of being corrupt as: (a) decay, (b) depravity, impurity, (c) bribery." In this chapter the term is used to cover not only bribery but also cases, either within or between interest groups and bureaucracies, in which official position is used to secure illegal or unethical ends. The acceptance of a bribe for an official favor is a simple example, but there are much more complex "conflicts of interest" which are generally recognized to be bad. Uncertainty occurs in certain cases. If a senator accepts corporate or union support in his campaign and, after election, votes for legislation supporting the interests of that corporation or union, the action is not necessarily corrupt. But if the support is conditioned on an express promise of the senator's vote, the action probably is corrupt.

Since men are not angels, some corruption occurs in every society. In certain cases it becomes a dominant feature of a society. The later Roman Empire, the Chiang Kai-shek regime on the mainland at the end of World War II, the "Kingdom of the Two Sicilies" prior to unification of Italy, and Britain in the first quarter of the last century are unhappy examples. On the happier side of the ledger, Great Britain in this century, the Scandinavian countries today, and Switzerland are examples of relatively honest administrations. One thermometer for judging the health of the body politic and economic is the extent of the corruption within it.

Corruption has always existed but there is obviously more opportunity for it in a complex organization of large bureaucracies, like today's United States, than there is in simpler societies. The Mosaic law has detailed regulations about people and oxen and their inter-relationships, but few of its regulations help solve the ethical problems of economics and politics faced by a Jewish American in contemporary New York City.

Opportunities for corruption are present in business, in unions, in politics, and between those agencies. There will be sections in this chapter devoted to each of these institutions of American life. But other institutions are not exempt. The university professor who requires a large class to buy his textbook, thus securing more royalties for himself, is creating a "conflict of interest" which is not dissimilar from that of the politician whose helpful constituent wants a favorable vote on legislation.

How great is the extent of corruption in the United States, and how does it compare with that of other countries? This chapter will attempt to answer the above question in sections on the three different fields of business, unions and government, with a special section on organized crime. The existence of these separate sections does not imply, however, that corruption in each of these fields is separate; on the contrary, they are closely related to each other. They also have much to do with the high rates of crime described in the last two chapters.

Corruption in Business

Much of American business is conducted on reasonably high standards of moral excellence. Reputable firms of certified public accountants audit the transactions of most of the nation's large corporations. While accounting firms have often been criticized for failure to check inventories or other specific records, there have been relatively few cases in which these "outside auditors" have been convicted of collusion with fraudulent operators in business.

In addition to outside auditors, almost all larger firms have effective internal auditing mechanisms. Dishonest employees are usually discovered and discharged quite rapidly. A problem for American firms working in many foreign countries is the difficulty of adapting their own high standards of honesty to the prevailing business mores of the host country.

Throughout several decades the American Institute of Certified Public Accountants has been working to raise standards of company reporting. There have been difficulties with false representations of inventories, and with shifting of items to make profit and loss statements or balance sheets look better (or worse) to shareholders or prospective investors. In recent years substantial lawsuits have been brought against accounting firms, as well as against companies, for presumably misleading statements. As a result of the whole process, however, it appears that American business is moving towards much more honest standards of presenting its financial results.[1]

This general honesty of American business is not as complete as one might wish. One lapse is the free giving and accepting of favors. With few exceptions, executives of large concerns accept gifts or free entertainment from companies which wish to sell to their companies. A later section on governmental corruption will indicate that the too-easy customs of businessmen in accepting favors have done great damage to the reputations of some of those who hold temporary positions in government, where higher standards must be observed. It is probably true that the executives of corporations which do not discourage gifts justify their position on the ground that the real decision of buying or selling is made by market factors. Competitive market conditions are a basic safeguard against the influence of gift-giving. No matter how many presents he may receive from Company X, a purchasing agent will hesitate before paying 15 percent more for the products of Company X. But he may not realize how much the act of gift-taking leads to a weaker view of business ethics.

A few other discouraging aspects of business ethics should be candidly presented. The reader is reminded, however, that none of these are typical of American business.

In spite of the fine progress of accountants there are cases of business men who succeed in committing major frauds in spite of, or in collusion with, accountants. The most recent is that of Equity

Funding, the first great example of computer fraud. A few executives invented millions of dollars worth of life insurance policies and sold them to other companies for reinsurance. Computers were rigged so that auditors could not identify the fraudulent policies. Losses may run as high as $350 million. Local inquiries tell us that executives seem to have been reasonably well-educated men who were brought up with good religious background.[2]

Certain general findings on corporate practices are discouraging. While some of the following activities may not rest strictly within "corporations," they represent more than the "shady" small-scale operator. A President's Commission Task Force in 1967 estimated $500 million to $1 billion losses to customers per year through questionable home repair and improvement policies; $500 million to $1 billion in security frauds; and $500 million annual expenditures on drugs and therapeutic devices which were either totally worthless or at least vastly misrepresented in advertising.[3] In most cases these are the work of individual or small defrauders, but responsible business should have moved against them.

A 1948 study indicated that every one of our seventy largest corporations had committed some crime and had received adverse decisions in the preceding forty-five years. The average number of adverse decisions was 14.8. About 60 percent of the corporations had been convicted by criminal courts.[4] Some of these convictions may have been on undefined technical points of law (especially anti-trust law), but the general implication for corporate morality of the first half of the century is not as high as one could wish.

Other indications of questionable ethical standards in large business are outlined in the report of the President's Commission on Law Enforcement and the Administration of Justice. Three large electrical manufacturing concerns, Westinghouse, General Electric and Allis-Chalmers, admitted in 1961 to deliberate violation of the anti-trust laws. They were fined almost $2 million and jail sentences were imposed on thirty individuals. There was no evidence that top management of these companies was involved, but high ranking and very well-paid executives were. These executives knew the illegality of their actions and were even careful not to tell their own company's lawyers. Only a year later similar charges were made against two great steel companies. In 1960, Chrysler discharged a newly-made president when it discovered that he and his wife were major owners of two large suppliers to Chrysler—a complete conflict of interest of which he had not informed the board.

There may have been technical problems in the anti-trust cases. But clearly the executives involved knew they were doing wrong. The Chrysler president must have known what he was doing.

There is a very substantial amount of illegal tax evasion. The President's Commission Task Force estimated $25 to $40 billion unreported taxable income per year. When dividend and interest reporting by banks to the Internal Revenue Service was instituted in 1964, 29 percent more income was received from these sources.[5] It is generally known that where assessment of personal property by the owners has been required for local property taxes, a high percentage goes unreported. Some Americans have the impression that our tax-paying morale is higher than that of other countries. It is certainly true that less developed countries have great difficulty in collecting income taxes. But we have not been able to find studies which indicate that American tax-paying morale is higher than, or as high as, that of other modern industrial democracies.

Small-Scale Swindles

An older study indicates another level of crime by the service section of industry which is familiar to all of us. The *Reader's Digest* staff in 1941 disconnected a coil wire in an automobile and took it to 347 garages in the then forty-eight states. Almost two-thirds of the garages either overcharged, inserted parts that were not needed, charged for work which was not done, or took other such action. Similar results from almost half the jewelers consulted were received when a small screw was loosened on a watch and shops were asked to repair it.[6] There is reason to believe that the ethical level of this type of activity has not risen much in the last three decades.

OPA Violations

A study of events of 30 years ago is summarized here because the writers have no reason to believe that it could not be repeated. Professor Clinard published in 1952 an interesting analysis of "The Black Market" in contravention of Office of Price Administration regulations on price and rationing during World War II. His statistics indicate a surprising amount of violation by businessmen, most of whom were definitely not criminal types. Courts were notoriously easy in their sentences. A large majority were married white men in their thirties or forties. A great many other sanctions such as consumer's treble damages, administrators, settlements, suspension orders, injunction suits, and "miscellaneous sanctions" were available—in all, 259,966 such sanctions were instituted between 1942 and 1974. In many more cases informal adjustments were made.

Clinard is understandably pessimistic about such frequent disobedience to rules which were clearly necessary for the operation of the war effort. He notes that the government made mistakes, had inadequate enforcement efforts, and failed to enlist business and public support as much as it should have. Nevertheless, he wonders if the amount of violation of OPA regulations does not indicate a "disorganization in our society," and quotes Herman Mannheim, a distinguished British criminologist of socialist leanings, that our "acquisitive society" perhaps forces this amount of crime. Clinard concludes that we need a greater consensus on "accepted social values".[7] This conclusion is obviously in line with the thought of this book that America needs reenforcement of its ethical values.

Evaluation of Business Crime

The importance of business crime in America is difficult to appraise. Obviously crime costs American business as a whole far more than has been gained by the wrong-doers described in this section. The number of such criminals arrested is small, but the amount of their swindles exceeds many thousand ordinary crimes.

Business also contributes to the American ethical delinquencies described in the next section. Much political corruption comes from business sources. Legitimate business supports legitimate lobbies, but too often goes further into bribery. Business would do well to set strict standards limiting this type of activity.

However, as we commented above, some portions of business have been working hard to raise ethical standards. It is also true that business has done a great deal to help reform corrupt politics. The committees supporting civil service reform in nineteenth century America were half businessmen.[8] Today it would be impossible to secure support from the associations of American business in Washington for any measures which reacted against more honest government.

The writers have not been able to secure good comparative data on business honesty. Some American businessmen tell us that their firms operate much more honestly than is the practice in most of the foreign countries where they do business. Others say that British and Canadian businesses operate on a higher plane. We venture no judgment. American business does not operate on as high a plane as we and as many business leaders would wish, but we have no hard evidence that it is below that of other nations.

Corruption in Labor Unions

There is little doubt that American labor unions have been more corrupt than those in other modern democracies. Lipset, the leading sociological analyst of unions, and Hutchinson, author of a leading book on union corruption, agree on this conclusion. Hutchinson writes: "Alone, among its peers, the American labor movement has been accused of corruption in intolerable degree."[9] Lipset comments: "There seems to be much less corruption among union officials in Australia and Canada, as compared with the United States. However, English visitors to Australia are struck with the extent to which they 'will put up with boss rule in corruption in trade unions.' "[10]

A summary of some of Hutchinson's findings well illustrates the problem. New York City's building trade unions in the first half of the century were cheating the city, violating building regulations, and accepting bribes from larger companies. Officials used union funds for their own purposes. Unions conspired with employers to reduce competition.[11] Similarly, union leaders in Chicago exacted a great deal of graft and unions began to be controlled by "convicts and professional criminals."[12]

In the 1920s gangs of criminals gained control of some major unions in New York City and extorted money from both unions and business.[13] The needle trade unions found themselves subject to gangsters demanding constant protection money. Even the International Ladies Garment Workers Union was the victim of racketeers and received little help from local government.[14] The New York waterfront unions were invaded and often run by criminals for more than a half century—a control which is slowly being broken by a Waterfront Commission.[15] Labor-management combinations using professional coercion were active in a score of trades in Chicago in the 1920s and 1930s.[16] During the latter decade, the Building Service Employees International Union had a "professional criminal" as its president who kept gunmen on the union payroll and extorted funds from building owners.

Union employees themselves were frequent victims of dishonest practices. In the 1940s there was graft in the administration of the rapidly spreading welfare plans.[17] Officials of the meat cutters' union in the 1950s used their position to develop their own business, and there was exploitation of members of the bakers' union.[18]

An unhappy example of a union which was defrauded by some of its own leaders was that of the teamsters, where a strange alliance was made with management in the disposal of garbage and rubbish in California, favoring particular employers and unfavorable to the public.[19] Hoffa worked out several methods of defrauding the union to his own benefit. He borrowed widely from union officials, and he used ex-criminals on his staff.[20]

While these and other examples of union dishonesty were going on, the American Federation of Labor slowly moved to control union corruption. Later the AFL–CIO took stronger action. Congress hesitantly legislated against union corruption. The Taft–Hartley Act in 1947 did forbid bribery of a union official by an employer. The New York–New Jersey Waterfront Commission, authorized in 1953, has tried to improve labor conditions on the docks, eliminating many undesirables from union office. Legislation providing supervision of welfare plans was passed in 1959 and strengthened in 1962. The Landrum–Griffin Act of 1959 was "an ambitious attempt to regulate the government of unions and the relation between labor and management as to greatly reduce the opportunities and increase the dangers of corruption."[21]

Why did American labor unions bog down with so much

corruption and dishonesty? Hutchinson suggests that there was more corruption in the AFL "business unions" than in the CIO "social unions." But he grants that it is not a precise differentiation. He cannot find that autocracy of union management always produces dishonesty, but he believes that "the indifference of satisfied union members is a stronger inducement to corruption than the heavy-handedness of union leaders."[22] In a compendious sentence he notes about the United States:

> Far into the twentieth century the heritage of frontier justice, the contempt of the pioneer for the law, a restless population, an individualistic culture, an entrenched philosophy of acquisition, an admiration for the sharp transaction, a tolerance of the fix, and a legacy of politics viewed as a business have brought to American criminal behavior a boldness, and to law enforcement a capriciousness, foreign to most civilized societies.[23]

The writers agree with Hutchinson's implication that union corruption came largely from poor law enforcement, but do not accept his list of reasons for this failure, which will be further discussed at the end of this chapter and in Chapter Five.

Lipset has a sociological reason for union corruption in America. America lacks the traditions of aristocratic societies. Workers in America are less likely to think of themselves as members of a deprived class, and are inclined to drive ahead economically. This pressure to succeed may lead individuals to serve social needs which are illegal, through rackets. Union members do not necessarily complain about union leaders who use such devices to put themselves ahead.[24]

The writers cannot judge the validity of Lipset's suggestion. We suspect that the general low level of ethics instruction in America may be as important as the lack of aristocratic tradition or more so. At the end of the chapter will be found some suggestions as to common causes of business, union, and government corruption.

Corruption in Politics

Political corruption has existed for at least a century and a half in the United States. This section will first review the facts for the federal government and then for state and local government, including a section on organized crime. It will then appraise the comparative amount of political corruption in this country with that in other modern democracies, and try to assess the reasons for America's continuing difficulties with corruption.

Political Corruption in the Federal Government

There was corruption in the original colonies and during the early days of the Republic. Samuel Chase is said to have been denied reappointment to the Continental Congress because he tried to corner the supply of flour. Robert Morris was investigated on charges of personal gain.[25]

In his administrative history of the Federalist period (1789–1801), Professor Leonard White notes very little corruption. Washington's policy of appointing well-connected people—a policy followed by Adams and, in large part, by Jefferson—gave the federal government a level of administrative rectitude which was well above that of the contemporary British regime. There was some nepotism,[26] a few political removals took place,[27] and some gratuities were accepted.[28] In the first four decades of the Republic the level of ethics was much higher than that of England during the same period of time.

White gives a continuous record of relatively honest administration in *The Jeffersonians* (1801–1829) but there were important exceptions. He does not mention Jefferson's over-reliance on General James Wilkinson, an American officer who had drawn pay from Spain. But he does write of the trial of President John Adams's son-in-law, Colonel William S. Smith, for flagrantly disobeying the law. (Smith was not appointed to any office in the Adams administration.) According to Secretary of the Treasury Albert Gallatin, Smith also "presented fallacious statements of his emoluments."[29] The War of 1812 was handled in part by some contractors for military supplies, who did a poor job.[30] Numbers of officials and clerks took commissions for doing part of their jobs,[31] and there were a few cases of embezzlement by public officials.[32] But there was little corrupting of public officials by outside interests.

White's volume on *The Jacksonians* (1829–1861) shows a marked change in American political ethics. President Andrew Jackson did not intend to lower the standards of governmental conduct, but his theory of rotation in office had the almost inevitable result of placing persons of limited character and intellectual capacity in positions which tempted them too much or in which they could not control the rapacity of others. There was an accompanying deterioration of the moral standards of politics. The level of ability of Congressmen declined sharply. In 1853 it became necessary to forbid members of Congress to take compensation for prosecuting claims against the government,[33] and by 1860 importers were regularly blackmailed at the Port of New York for payment of fictitious charges to avoid excessive delay.[34] The Army rank and file suffered from a low general level of morality,[35] and politics in the Navy Yards resulted in "glowing abuses," according to a Congressional committee.[36] Jackson's Postmaster General, William T. Barry, was "misled by corrupt men about him."[37] The Chief Clerk of the Post Office, a clergyman, accepted a personal fee for settling a controversy between contractors.[38] The Public Printer's Office functioned very expensively, and helped the party in power.[39]

In the 1840s and 1850s the Collector of the Port of New York subjected his staff to regular political assessments for Tammany Hall.[40] Large numbers of pension claims were fraudulent,[41] and Land Office officials embezzled substantial sums.[42] Samuel Swartwout, Collector of Customs in New York, defaulted for over $1 million in 1838.[43]

During what White called The Republican Era (1869–1901), morality in the federal government reached a new low during the Grant administration (1869–1877) before it moved slowly upward.[44]

The actual incidents are unpleasant. Senator George F. Hoar, when a Representative in 1876, commented that he had seen five federal judges driven from office by threat of impeachment, four judges of the "foremost state" impeached for corruption, the political administration of that state's principal city (New York) "become a disgrace and a by-word throughout the world," the Chairman of the House Military Affairs Committee ask for expulsion of four of his associates for selling Military Academy selections, and a transcontinental railroad built through fraud in House and Senate.[45] Grant's Secretary of War, William W. Belknap, resigned, was impeached, and barely escaped conviction. Congressman James A. Garfield in 1869 said that the Indian Bureau was "spotted with fraud, . . . tainted with corruption."[46] The disposal of public lands was often marred by fraud,[47] and the Pension Office was frequently taken in by dishonest applications.[48] The Post Office official in charge of the Cuban postal service after the Spanish American War embezzled about $130,000[49] and money was stolen in a variety of ways from Post Office activities.[50]

In this century a low point was reached in the Harding administration (1921–1923), when Cabinet members were bribed to grant oil rights, the Veteran's Administration was looted by its Commissioner, and the Attorney General sold favors by the Department of Justice. The next bad point was in the Truman Administration when a number of officers of the Internal Revenue Service were found to be selling favors, and various other charges of corruption were made.

In addition to these unsavory episodes, our national administration continued to be marred by a number of episodes which range from poor administrative practice to downright criminality. Professor David A. Frier has written an interesting volume which attempts to demonstrate that the Eisenhower Administration had as much corruption as the Truman Administration or more. Whether or not he proved his point, he does outline a number of somewhat similar events in four successive presidential administrations: those of Truman, Eisenhower, Kennedy, and Johnson.

In many of the cases cited by Frier, a "gift" was the questionable item. A White House stenographer, married to a Reconstruction Finance Corporation loan examiner, received a $10,000 mink coat from a lawyer whose clients wanted RFC loans. Presidential assistants accepted gifts of deep freezers or Oriental rugs. Other cases involved misuse of official position to help personal business interests of the official, such as using a Navy yacht for a party to which business customers were invited or soliciting for a private business with letters written on departmental stationery.

In these and similar episodes the official was usually asked to resign—which he always did—and was not prosecuted. In most cases the men were using in government standards of conduct which were acceptable in at least some parts of business.[51]

In addition to executive corruption, there have been continuing corruption problems in Congress, probably not as bad as in the 1870s but enough to be a cause of concern. Professor H. H. Wilson of

Princeton in 1951 reviewed several cases of Congressional corruption. Representative James T. McDermott, a Chicago Democrat, resigned in 1914 after sharp criticism of his connections with the District of Columbia retail liquor lobby, the pawnbrokers' lobby, the National Brewers' Association, and the National Association of Manufacturers. Representative John Main Coffee, Democrat from Tacoma, Washington, was sharply criticized but not punished in 1946 because his administrative assistant accepted a $2,500 check from a contractor-constituent for having arranged a meeting with the Commanding General of Army Service Forces in World War II. Representative Eugene Cox, Democrat of Georgia, was forced by public opinion pressure in Congress to resign from the chairmanship of a special committee investigating the Federal Communications Commission, which was checking on a Georgia radio station for which the Congressman had been counsel. Representative James Michael Curley, Democrat of Massachusetts, was indicted and convicted of using the mails to defraud. He left Congress with no effort to punish him and with major support from the Majority Leader. Representative Andrew Jackson May, Kentucky Democrat, in 1946 was subpoenaed by a House Committee, but never actually testified, for constant support of a shady war contractor. The House of Representatives in each of these cases, says Wilson, was much too easy on corrupt Congressmen, in sharp contrast to the high standards set by the House of Commons for its members. These cases happened to involve Democrats; Republicans are not exempt from such findings. In the case of three errant Senators, Wilson found a better record than the House, but still it was poor.

Wilson notes substantial differences between American and British legislative situations. An individual Member of Parliament does not have the high degree of authority which committee chairmen in Congress possess over some parts of administration. National party discipline is much tighter in England. The kind of local support which Curley received from the Boston Irish, or Cox and May received from fellow Southerners—in spite of their indefensible positions—is less likely to be found in England. Because of these differences, one cannot avoid the view that Congressional ethical standards are much lower than Parliamentary ones.[52]

A more recent book by Professor Robert Getz on Congressional ethics tends to confirm Wilson's judgment that British ethical standards for legislators are higher than ours. Getz does note some improvement. In 1967 Bobby Baker, Secretary of the Senate, was convicted of diverting campaign funds to his own use. The Senate Rules Committee performed badly but the Senate later established a Select Committee on Standards and Conduct whose actions were a partial cause of the censure of Senator Thomas J. Dodd of Connecticut, resulting in his later defeat. The House also set up an ethics committee, but one without policing power.[53]

A fundamental problem which the Congress is not likely to solve in the near future is that of "conflict of interest." Americans, with their great emphasis on constitutionalism and legalism, tend to believe that a major cure for corruption is the avoidance of conflict of interest. The English, on the other hand, assume that some conflict of interest must exist in legislative work and that the cure for corruption is more honest legislators.[54]

The obvious difficulty with eliminating conflict of interest is that legislators are likely to be connected with the economic interests of the areas which they represent. Some persons hope that public disclosure of candidates' property will help prevent corrupt conflict of interest. Others fear that such disclosure will drive many good candidates out of competition for legislative seats. Common Cause of California in 1974 secured state legislation for disclosure. Experience will indicate whether it helps or damages.

Since the Watergate scandals, discussed in the next section, there has been a tendency to be more careful in legislative circles. Some Congressmen have ordered their staffs not to accept gifts of candy or cheese; greater care is being taken about accepting free airplane rides.[55] But Congress is still very far from having resolved the problem of conflict of interest.

Watergate

At a time when political corruption seemed to be disappearing from the federal government, Watergate and related scandals received tremendous public attention. The chief transgressions in these scandals have been:

1. The establishment by the Committee to Re-elect the President of a staff which broke into the Democratic National Committee headquarters with the intention of bugging the telephones there. One of the men who broke in was on the White House payroll.
2. Two members of the White House staff broke into the office of the psychiatrist of Daniel Ellsberg (the man who published the "Pentagon Papers").
3. Efforts were made under the supervision of some White House staff members to "cover up" both these crimes. The President was aware of—and to a certain extent approved—some of these efforts.
4. Persons who prepared President Nixon's income tax put in a very large deduction for the gift of his Vice Presidential papers to the National Archives, under questionable circumstances.
5. The President countenanced efforts to use federal agencies to investigate and perhaps harass political opponents.
6. Associates of the President accepted large corporate gifts for campaign funds under circumstances which clearly indicated an effort to direct federal government policies for the unions. Particularly questionable were gifts of ITT and the milk cooperatives, both of which also gave freely to Democrats.

The Watergate scandals are quite different from most of our political corruption. These crimes were of no great numerical significance when compared to the vast amount of on-going political chicanery in American local government. In sharp contrast to most public graft, none of the higher officials involved seemed to have benefitted financially other than what they gained by staying in office. But the fact that an ex-Attorney General and two principal assistants to the President of the United States had apparently known about and tried to legally hide major crimes shocked the nation.

Related to the Watergate scandals was a more frequent type of political corruption. The Committee to Re-elect the President (Nixon) staff apparently asked for substantial contributions from corporations and individuals who were interested in securing favorable decisions from federal agencies. Some illegal corporate contributions were returned. Several corporations and corporate executives have been successfully prosecuted for breaking the law against corporate contributions—a law which had previously gone unenforced.

As the pursuit of the Watergate episode resulted in the resignation of President Nixon, other comments are necessary. Reading of the transcripts of the tapes kept on conferences in the White House clearly indicates a lack of concern by the President for his responsibility "that the law be faithfully executed." He apparently did not set a policy of rectitude firmly before his staff. He did not report to the Department of Justice when he learned of illegal actions by staff members. He was not the kind of moral leader that Americans expect their President to be.

Unfortunately, it is not possible to predict change of American thinking against political corruption because of the Watergate affair. A heavily Democratic Congress was investigating a minority party President in the Watergate case. A similar Congress avoided investigation which might have involved a Democratic President in the Bobby Baker case.[56] A Congress will probably never again be able to subpoena tapes, because future Presidents will not keep them. Most corruption is at a local level where it attracts much less attention from the media and the chances for a basic ethical reform because of Watergate are small.

If television and major newspapers would use the amount of energy against local and state corruption—including organized crime—which they used against Watergate, the prospects for reduction of political corruption in the United States would improve. But it is difficult to imagine the media concentrating on such problems outside the federal government.

The relationship of Watergate to America's problem of ethical instruction is still puzzling. The major conspirators were not criminal types and secured no financial gain from their transgressions (unless one counts the President's temporary gains in real estate which really were not related to Watergate). Former President Nixon is a well-educated man, with good church as well as school connections. So were most of the principal conspirators. Ivy League, Catholic, and prestigious state universities, as well as strong liberal arts colleges, contributed to the education of almost all of those convicted for Watergate and related crimes. Nevertheless, it would be our guess that very little thoughtful ethical education was included in the background of these men. One of the Watergate participants, Magruder, blamed his plight on the "situation ethics" which he had been taught at Williams College. Whether or not he was correct, it is certain that most of the Watergate conspirators would have been better public servants if someone had taught them the virtue of truth.

State and Local Government

The story of state and local corruption in America is too long to detail here, but must receive some review. Since national politics is based on state and local politics, and since business and unions must operate in states and localities, dishonesty at this level affects all business and political operations. There will also be a sub-section on organized crime, which is intimately tied to poltical corruption.

The citizens of the new America probably ran their states and towns fairly well in the first few decades of the Republic. From 1830 on, however, American state and local government had major encounters for graft. Most discussed by historians was the Tweed ring of New York City. Tweed, leader of Tammany Hall in the 1860s, was not the first Tammany politician to mulct the taxpayers of New York City but was the most publicized. His ring put all sorts of relatives and friends on the city's payroll for services which were often minimal or non-existent.[57] City printing contracts were let at exorbitant prices to companies owned by Tweed or his associates. Their bank became a city depository.[58] A plasterer aide-de-camp of the ring was paid $133,187.20 by the city for two days' work.[59] All contracts for supplies and work were increased by 55 percent to 65 percent with the increase paid to members of the Tweed ring.[60] In less than three years (1869–1871), the city's debt increased from $36 to $97 million as a result of the Tweed ring's operations.

It is interesting to note that when Tweed was prosecuted, his attorneys included David Dudley Field, a leader of the bar and member of a very distinguished family, and Elihu Root, later a most distinguished lawyer and statesman.

Tammany Hall operations included the state government of New York. Tweed, who was a state senator, was also the agent for the Erie Railroad and was involved in representation of other corporate

interests. Bribes were used frequently, and underpaid "respectable" legislators from rural areas accepted them as well as did big
city representatives.[61]

In the last half of the last century, other major cities suffered the
same kind, if not the same dollar values, of corruption as New York
City. James Bryce, in *The American Commonwealth* (first
published in 1888), describes the Philadelphia Gas Ring. Griffith
mentions Philadelphia (1880), Cincinnati (1880s), Indianapolis (1886),
and Detroit as examples of major electoral frauds. Boston and
Philadelphia are given as examples of corruption by banks and real
estate owners; Memphis, Tacoma, Cairo, and Des Moines were
smaller cities where an underworld influenced politicians to tolerate
lax enforcement of laws against vice, gambling, and use of liquor.
Franchising of public utilities caused corruption in Detroit,
Milwaukee, Jersey City, Providence, Pittsburgh, Chicago, and
Minneapolis in the 1870s and 1880s.[62]

Municipal corruption in the United States (1840–1900) was a
result of several factors. The absorption of many millions of
immigrant voters was probably the largest single factor. To
foreigners who know little of American politics, political machines
like Tammany Hall could offer services ranging from social
recognition by attending funerals or weddings through minor
material help, or release from law enforcement to the ultimate help
of a job. All the machine asked in return was votes. It was an
obvious bargain until members of the ethnic group became educated
and sufficiently prosperous to be able to take care of themselves in
American life.

Jacksonian theories of rotation in office had resulted in chaotic
forms of municipal government which encouraged corruption. As
Griffith puts it: "in the hodge podge of elected officials in America,
in the indefinite relationship between the council and the executive,
and between both and the state, and in the lack of any sort of
statutory budgetary procedure, some coordinating force was
needed. In fact some such force was inevitable, if the government
was to function at all. The boss was almost a necessary evil."[63]

There is no ready summary of the amount of corruption in state
governments in the last half of the nineteenth century, but one can
guess that it was almost as widespread as city corruption. Just as the
Tweed ring extended its operations to Albany whenever necessary,

such organizations in other cities could easily move to the state capitol for special legislation to serve their purposes.[64]

Griffith speaks optimistically of the reform movements sweeping through city government about 1903–1904.[65] However, state and local corruption has shown a surprising amount of vitality since that time. In the first quarter of this century the Vare machine in Pennsylvania, the Southern Pacific control of California, and—as late as 1930—Anaconda Copper–Montana Power control of Montana were well known. Tammany Hall continued to control New York City government off and on until the 1960s. Chicago is still run by the Daley political machine.

The reader should remember that during this century and a half of corruption in state and local government, there have been fairly constant efforts at reform. Even New York City has elected many reform mayors: Seth Low, John Purroy Mitchell, Fiorello La Guardia are well-known names. Few machines have kept an unbroken control since the 1920s like that of the Chicago Democratic group. But we must also add that few reform mayors have been able to effect a complete or on-going reform of their cities. In many major cities the machine, or other corrupt forces, has returned to power shortly after a reform victory.

In recent years there has been a revival of state corruption. Reichley in *Fortune* magazine writes:

> The last two years alone have seen: the conviction of Federal Judge Otto Kerner for taking a bribe in the form of race track stock while he was Governor of Illinois; the conviction of Attorney General of Louisiana Jack Gremillion for perjury; the conviction of Gus Mutscher, former Speaker of the Texas House of Representatives, for participation in a stock swindle; the conviction of former U.S. Senator Daniel Brewster for taking a bribe; the indictment of close associates of Governor William Cahill of New Jersey for promoting a scheme to evade income tax laws covering campaign contributions. None of these deeds approached Watergate in seriousness, but all are evidences of the low level to which ethical standards have fallen in many areas of government.[66]

Since 1950 the large city and state machines have lost their power. The reason most frequently advanced by political scientists is that the development of more universal welfare programs, with federal support since the 1930s, has removed the value of the small economic privileges which the machine could give its supporters. The other reason often cited is that the education of many ethnic groups improved their job opportunities and their chance to make independent judgments. Radio and television have also altered the general nature of politics.

The machine, however, has been survived by much local political corruption. In early 1973 the Knapp Commission reported that very many of New York's 30,000-man police force were violating laws repeatedly.[67] Other cities have similar sorry stories. A relatively recent study of Reading, Pennsylvania, indicates continuous corruption.[68] Widespread law-breaking by police officials is reported by Professor Reiss in a study of Boston, Chicago, and Washington.[69] Since reform mayors rarely had time to clean up an entire police force, it is probable that those of New York, Chicago, and other cities have been substantially corrupt for over a century.

Oragnized Crime and Government

A new machinery for political corruption has been introduced by organized crime—more familiarly called the "Mafia" after the name of a series of Sicilian criminal organizations. Actually the American "Mafia," "Mob" or "Syndicate" is not organically related to the Sicilian organizations, though many of its executives are of Italian origin. Michael Dorman, in an undocumented but carefully-written book, lists organized crime operations which had attained some control of state or local government (as well as control of several Congressmen and a few federal officials) in Chicago; in the state of Illinois; in New York; in Massachusetts; in St. Louis; in Louisiana; in Reading, Pennsylvania, and in the state of Pennsylvania; in Tucson, Arizona, and in Gary, Indiana; in Seattle; in Honolulu; in Detroit; in Hot Springs, Arkansas; in Newark and in Jersey City; in Long Branch and other small cities in New Jersey; in Youngstown, Ohio; in New Orleans and in the state of Mississippi; in West Virginia; in Nevada; in Houston; and in the office of the Speaker of the House of Representatives.[70]

The "Mafia" or "Mob" group secures its control by contributing to campaign funds, by offering other political assistance, by helping business friends of the candidate official, by control of a union which is essential to a business supporter of the candidate, or in other ways. Opportunity for some form of political corruption is apparently necessary for organized crime to operate. The actual enforcement machinery of the gangster is the "soldier," or gunman. The latter's services can be purchased much more readily if there is some means of reducing legal penalties—a friendly police officer, a prosecutor, a judge, or a legislator with influence.

Organized crime is even more widespread than the above instances of known political corruption would indicate. The President's Commission on Law Enforcement and the Administration of Justice reported in 1967: "In response to a Commission survey of 71 cities, the police departments in eighty percent of the cities with over one million residents, in twenty percent of the cities with a population between one half million and a million, in twenty percent of the cities with between 250,000 and 500,000 population, and in over fifty percent of the cities with between 100,000 and 250,000, indicated that organized criminal groups exist in their cities. In some instances federal agency intelligence indicated the presence of organized crime where local reports denied it."[71]

Organized crime members are harder to prosecute than ordinary criminals. A New York legislative study indicated that although 536 organized crime figures had been arrested for felonies in the New York area in a decade, only 37 were sent to prison. Syndicate lawyers have connections or friendly judges can be found.[72]

In addition to control of gambling, brothels, and drug traffic, organized crime has taken many businesses away from their legitimate owners or subjected businesses to "protection" payments which are sometimes very severe. Businessmen who fail to comply with the racketeers' demands find themselves or their businesses damaged or destroyed.

Professor Cressey in his thoughtful analysis of *La Cosa Nostra* tells us that the members of the nationwide organization

> control all but a tiny part of the illegal gambling in the United States. They are the principal loan sharks. They are the principal importers and wholesalers of narcotics. They have infiltrated certain labor unions, where they extort money from employers and, at the same time, cheat the members of the union. The members have a virtual monopoly on some legitimate enterprises, such as cigarette vending machines and juke boxes, and they own a wide variety of retail firms,

restaurants and bars, hotels, trucking companies, food companies, linen supply houses, garbage collection routes, and factories. Until recently, they owned a large proportion of Las Vegas. They own several state legislators and federal congressmen and other officials in the legislative, executive, and judicial branches of government at the local, state, and federal levels. Some government officials (including judges) are considered, and consider themselves, members.[73]

Organized crime has been able to eliminate legitimate competition in certain industries and to undermine the integrity and efficiency of many of our governments. How has it advanced so far in American life?

It is no coincidence that most leaders of organized crime are of Italian or Sicilian origin. The portion of southern Italy and Sicily from which they come had had low levels of governmental honesty under a corrupt Bourbon monarchy prior to unification of Italy. One must recognize that a very large majority of our many millions of Italian-American citizens are honest individuals. An Italian-American, Frank Serpico, was the policeman who forced Mayor Lindsay to begin reform of the New York police.

In this case the ethical explanation of crime is not very cogent. There is little or no poverty problem in *La Cosa Nostra*. "Mob" sons are sent to good colleges to acquire business administration education for further misdeeds. Italian immigrants have not introduced organized crime into Britain, Canada, or Australia, where there are large numbers of such immigrants. The reasons for development of organized crime in the United States must include some flaws in the American system of law enforcement which have permitted organized crime to develop.

How Corrupt is America?

The unpleasant fact we must first face in analysis of our corruption is that America may be most corrupt of advanced modern democracies. Our high educational and economic levels have not brought us to a high level of governmental honesty. There are no international statistics on graft, but analysis of a number of studies satisfies the writers that there is probably more political corruption in the United States than in other advanced modern democracies including, specifically, Britain, West Germany, Switzerland, the

Low Countries, Scandinavia, Canada, and Australia. Some of the evidence follows.

Corruption occurs very seldom in the British national government and infrequently in British local government. Britain did have a great deal of corruption in the first quarter of the last century—probably more than occurred in the United States—but what Professor Friedrich describes as a "little short of miraculous" reform overcame this corruption and incompetence.[74] Later in the century the British central government succeeded in helping local government to eliminate most of its corruption. The late Hiram Stout, in his *British Government*, says, "On the score of integrity, no major scandal has touched the Civil Service in recent years."[75] A 1972 *New York Times* article indicates that corruption is negligible in the British judiciary, as well as being low in France and West Germany.[76]

Roland Huntford is sharply critical of Swedish governmental policies, but comments, "It is vital for an understanding of Swedish society to realize that public corruption, in the form of personal bribery, does not exist."[77] Professor Heidenheimer tells us that the German Civil Service had a minor wave of corruption in the 1850s, but the German public official is still widely admired.[78] Hans Rosenberg gives us some background of the more than century-old Prussian bureaucratic efforts to maintain honesty.[79] Holland, after a good deal of effort, has succeeded in setting high standards against corruption of government officials.[80] Switzerland seems to maintain high standards of honesty in its government.[81] The only modern democracy which may have had amounts of corruption parallel to ours was France under the Third Republic.[82] It is our impression that France now has less corruption than the United States.

It should be noted that all of these modern democracies secured their relative freedom from corruption only after substantial effort. In the first quarter of the nineteenth century, several of what are now European constitutional democracies probably harbored more corruption than did the United States. By 1900 the tables were completely reversed. In most of these countries the monarchy, the smaller size of country, the established church, and the class system, may have been of value in helping to overcome corruption. In all of them there is a greater tradition of centralization, especially that of law enforcement, than in the United States.

After moving generally backward into corruption in the

nineteenth century, America has made some progress in this century. Most of the federal Civil Service is now free of corruption. Many states and cities have improved their standards of administration considerably. But it is still puzzling that this country has more persistent corruption, especially at the local level, than is the case with other modern democracies. The practical demise of the political machine (except in Chicago) has not been succeeded by honest government.

A few words should be added about costs of corruption, particularly since some of the theorists noted in the next section tend to minimize its expense. Costs in this case include not only the amounts of extra money secured by contractors, bribe receivers, and other malefactors. Far greater costs lie in other directions: the undermining of public confidence in government or portions of the government. A few examples will be given.

Studies of poverty areas which were hard hit in the black riots indicate that in various cities a substantial part of the local political workers queried were aware of widespread corruption in the police.[83] One can guess that similar reactions in the numerous major cities where the police accept bribes may be one cause of the almost catastrophic rift between the police and the less affluent citizens of these cities. Certainly the fact that the police are known to accept bribes cannot improve their status in public opinion.

The subsection on organized crime indicated that this factor is largely dependent upon securing some degree of corruption in government. It could be said that much of the real cost of organized crime is thus attributable to political dishonesty. We have no figures on the national cost of organized crime, but without estimating the psychological tragedy for those victims who are driven out of business by such criminals, the figure must be in the hundreds of millions of dollars.

Political corruption can seriously interrupt the flow of important government business, as was exemplified in the effect of Watergate on the work of the Nixon administration. More typical examples occur in state and city government when significant decisions are ignored because political leaders are concerned with graft.

The danger that corruption may undermine the moral fiber of the nation should not be overlooked. Friedrich has outlined some of these difficulties, indicating that it may produce inefficiency,

mistrust of the government, waste of public reserves, discourage-
ment of enterprise, and political instability. "Corruption may affect
a society in its ideatic core."[84]

Why Does America Have
Continued Political Corruption?

An effort to control political corruption in America must be based
on correct analysis of its causes. Our particular concern is why so
much corruption has continued after the demise of the political
machine. Unfortunately, there is no thorough study of corruption
known to the writers. A variety of reasons suggested by various
political scientists, historians, and others will be rapidly reviewed.
At the end of the section, the three reasons which seem to the writers
to be most important will be stated.

The Modernization-Functional Theory

Political scientists have written in recent years about a
"functional" theory of corruption. One of the principal statements
of this is in Professor Samuel Huntington's book, *Political Order in
Changing Societies*, which argues that corruption comes with
"rapid social and economic organization."[85] New sources of wealth
and power make new demands on government, and they resort to
bribery or other forms of corruption if their demands are not met
legitimately. Modernization has changed the values of society
toward "universalistic and achievement-based norms." It also
creates new power and wealth, and increases the laws and
regulations operating on society, sometimes establishing "unreasonable puritanical standards." Reducing corruption may
involve scaling down of norms for officials as well as leading the
behavior of those officials toward the norms.

Corruption, says Huntington, also appears to be less likely to
function in a highly stratified society, which already has a well-
developed system of norms. Since corruption involves exchange of
political action for economic wealth, the form of corruption depends
on whether wealth or political power is easier to gain. "In the United

States, wealth has more commonly been a road to political influence than political office has been a road to wealth.''[86] In societies which have fairly strong national political institutions, the incidence of corruption is likely to be greater in the lower levels of government.

Huntington's "functional" theory of corruption is best given by a quotation:

> Just as the corruption produced by the expansion of political participation helps to integrate new groups into the political system, so also the corruption produced by the expansion of governmental regulation may help stimulate economic development. Corruption may be one way of surmounting traditional laws or bureaucratic regulations which hamper economic expansion. In the United States during the 1870s and 1880s corruption of state legislatures and city councils by railroad, utility, and industrial corporations undoubtedly speeded the growth of the American economy.[87]

Huntington grants that corruption weakens a governmental bureaucracy. However, he believes that corruption may help party organization which eventually helps to overcome corruption.

This book has not concerned itself with ethics in developing countries, and will not challenge Professor Huntington's generalizations in that field. However, if his theories are correct as an interpretation of a part of American history, it is obviously important for the purposes of this volume.

The thesis that corruption comes with rapid social and economic organization is valid for the nineteenth-century United States where an economy was expanding, cities were developing, and new immigrant groups were entering communities. During most of that century, many American cities, some states, and at times the national government itself became corrupt. "Modernization" was not creating new norms as Huntington suggests (perhaps he was discussing only developing countries), but there were new forms of wealth and power. The third effect of modernization, creating new laws and regulations, was not noticeable in the United States; in fact, we were probably as busy shedding old regulations as we were adopting new ones. However, the whole problem of the application of the Huntington theory of corruption in nineteenth century America deserves close historical analysis.

If two of Huntington's three reasons for modernization creating corruption did not apply in nineteenth-century America, this development is probably not an adequate explanation of the extent of our corruption. Huntington's theory of modernization certainly does not explain the surprising amount of continuing corruption in twentieth-century America.

However, his observation that class stratification can help to save a country from corruption may be borne out by our experience. It is generally granted that America has not had a class structure comparable to that of the northwestern European countries, and it is probable that class structure did help those countries establish traditions of governmental honesty. Class structure is more fully discussed in the next section.

The theory of the functional uses of corruption seems to be one of Huntington's positions which is least applicable to the United States. It does not explain a large fraction of American nineteenth-century corruption or the preponderant amount of our continued twentieth-century corruption.

The histories of Tammany Hall show a looting of the New York City treasury, which had no significant connection with advancement of economic life. Exorbitant prices paid for city purchases, "kickbacks" on city contracts, and large paychecks to non-working people are simply methods of stealing. The Tweed ring's activities were largely of this simple type of plundering. The granting of franchises for operating street cars and for selling gas services may be interpreted as "functional," though it is also possible that the bribes used to secure these franchises were extorted from the utility and its customers rather than spent for a functional activity. Certainly the exploitation of brothels, saloons, and gambling houses through the police departments served no substantial economic function. If these are to be regarded as normal economic activities, corruption may have hindered rather than helped them.

Examination of municipal corruption in twentieth-century America leaves little place for the "functional" theory. Most utilities are now regulated at the state or federal level. The continued corruption evidenced by fraudulent contracts, police exactions, and protection payments for organized crime is not "functional."

Some elements of "functional" corruption continue at the federal and state level where regulations regarding prices, rates, types of service, amount of imports, and other controls affect economic groups which in turn try to influence government action. It is quite possible, as suggested later, that there should be careful consideration of such regulations to see if the amount of regulation could not be reduced or the process of regulation made more impersonal and automatic to lessen the possibility of corruption. But elimination of all such "functional" corruption would leave intact the great mass of persistent local government corruption, which is more personal exploitation than economic functionalism.

Class Against Corruption

Another reason has been offered for our continuing corruption. In northwestern Euope office-holders are said to be better respected than in the United States, so there is more reason for them to feel a sense of *noblesse oblige*.[88] Some have put the same point differently: that other modern democracies have a ruling class or an upper class which has more responsibility for governing honestly than does the group which happens to be in charge of government in a less class-minded America. Huntington asserted that societies with rigid class structures were less likely to become corrupt. Lipset's comparison of Canada with the United States supports the same conclusion.[89]

There is merit in the class theory but there are also problems. There are honest business and political systems maintained in America without the aid of social classes. Czarist Russia, Britain in 1800, caste-ridden India had or have corruption along with class stratification. America may not have social classes in the European sense, but it has many families which have been well-established educationally and economically for generations. It is difficult for the writers to avoid the belief that the United States could find honest political leaders, if Americans believed that honesty is sufficiently important. However, Americans will not introduce a class sytem in order to lessen corruption. If lack of such a structure has caused our corruption, we must find other means of getting rid of it.

The Business Dominance Theory

A third reason which is frequently cited for the continuing corruption in American political life is our "business system." (The similar argument that "business civilization" is a cause of general crime was discussed in Chapter Three.) The theory is that most of the bribes come from business: since business is more important in the United States than it is in other modern democracies, its low standards are forced on the body politic. An elaboration is that business emphasizes success, regardless of ethical standards. Lincoln Steffens held to this view at times. It was the theory on which the prosecutions of the corrupters of the Ruef-Schmitz machine in San Francisco were held.[90]

Although there are elements of truth in this theory, there are obvious objections. The other modern democracies which have much lower political corruption records have free or semi-free systems of business operations. In one important respect, the opportunity for cartellization, these modern democracies control their industries less than does America. There are also many recorded instances in which the business leadership of American communities has worked hard to eliminate political corruption. The very fact of competitiveness in American business makes unpopular the payment of funds to corrupt political groups.

An element of truth in the "business system" explanation of America's continuing political corruption seems to lie in the bad example set by some of the businessmen discussed earlier in this chapter. When businesses make a habit of giving expensive presents to purchasing agents, the practice may not wreak great havoc in a competitive market but it may easily be carried over into the non-competitive field of government where such gifts are either illegal or highly inappropriate. If business could raise its own standards through industry agreement or statute, the elevation would help reduce political corruption.

A reverse twist to the "business" explanation of political corruption is to be found in a book by a distinguished academician-senator, Paul H. Douglas. Douglas was usually classified as a "liberal" Democratic senator, which in contemporary American usage means one who advocates more governmental control. Surprisingly, Douglas pointed out that elimination of a number of control statutes and restoration of a free market would reduce the occasion for political corruption.[91]

The Party Dominance Theory

A fourth reason advanced for corruption, especially in the last quarter of the nineteenth and the first quarter of the twentieth century, was the dominance of party machines. Direct primary elections, the right of voting referenda on legislation, and recall of public officials were mechanisms intended to reduce the influence of party leaders. White cites Charles Francis Adams in putting the blame for corruption on a party organization "bred in the gutter of New York politics."[92]

The obvious difficulty with this theory is that other nations have learned to operate non-corrupt politics through party machinery. Huntington assumes, perhaps correctly, that party organization will end corruption. Adams' theory was a example of a frequent American mistake: the premise that mechanical changes would eliminate our political difficulties. A current example of a similar effort to reform by mechanics is the Common Cause effort to limit the size of campaign funds. This reform may or may not make for more moral campaigns; it is unlikely to result in any serious reduction of the amount of government corruption in this country. It may simply insure the perpetuation of one-party control of legislative bodies.

Theories of Change in Form of Government

From the Civil War to World War I, several "mechanical" causes for corruption were cited. The Civil Service reformers believed that enactment of their legislation would end the graft. In our judgment it has been only partly successful in doing so. Another group believed that clear delineation of political responsibility in city charters, through the strong mayor or the manager plan, would eliminate much of the strength of the corrupt machine. A variant of these proposals was Henry Jones Ford's suggestion that separation of powers causes our troubles and that concentration of responsibility in a political executive would end them.[93] It is true that the simplification of governmental machinery by the city manager plan was accompanied by reform in many cities.

The chief difficulty with these mechanical causes is that their elimination has not stopped political corruption. Civil Service has probably lowered the amount of it in the federal government, in some of the states, and in many cities; but Civil Service is no panacea, as the amount of continuing corruption indicates. Some of our "strong mayor" and even some "manager" cities have continued to be regrettably corrupt. The change has been helpful but not conclusive.

Professor James Q. Wilson, an unusually perceptive writer, gives three theories of political corruption.[94] The first is that immigrant groups want immediate help and are not concerned about the loss of long-range justice. The second is that corruption is a result of extraordinary temptations facing ordinary public officials. The third is Ford's theory, already discussed, that separation of powers forces corruption. Accomplishments can only be effected through the exchange of favors between branches. All of these reasons have merit but none of them fully explains the large amount of persistent corruption in the United States. However, it is true that the first reason is subsumed in one of the reasons which we will now present.

Conclusions

The writers would welcome further research, but are inclined to regard the main causes of continuing political corruption in this country as the following:

1) Although the political machine is dying, the traditions of ethnic voting (including overlooking a fellow ethnic's departures from political morality), of semi-corrupt police forces, of bribe-offering contractors continues strongly in many American cities. As an example, New York City's mayoral election in 1969 was one of the most ethnic in its history.[95] Police Commissioner Murphy, serving under a reform mayor, commented that he had vastly underestimated the difficulty of developing an honest police force. The writers' guess is that New York, Philadelphia, Chicago, and Boston have rarely had honest police forces—reform mayors and police chiefs or commissioners not having had time to root out all the dishonest men on the force.

If corruption continues in large cities, some of it is almost certain to spread to state governments and to some portions of the federal government. For example, organized crime is most strongly rooted in a few cities, like New York and Chicago, which are still influenced by political machine traditions, but it spreads itself to control state legislators, judges, prosecutors, or congressmen, as needed for its tasks. New York State has held this extension to a minimum; Illinois has been less successful. There is no specific cure for the tradition of corruption left by the political machine. The remedies suggested for the next two problems could be helpful here.

2) A second fundamental difficulty with ensuring rectitude in American political life is the high degree of decentralization of law enforcement machinery. All other modern democracies retain some degree of supervision of law enforcement machinery by central government agencies. If a British city police force becomes corrupt, the inspector of the national government makes suggestions to the appropriate local authorities. In France the Ministry of Interior would order corrections. But in the United States the badly run city or county is usually left to wallow in its own corruption, with federal assistance limited to a few income tax prosecutions.

The writers are firm believers in local self-government, but do not believe that state or federal governments are free from responsibility to help maintain the quality of local self-government. Without honesty, local self-government loses its advantages of securing respect and citizen participation. Accordingly, the writers favor state supervision to secure better law enforcement machinery.

3) The third underlying reason for America's political corruption seems to the writers to be ineffective teaching of moral standards. This problem may arise from the great variety of religions in America, or from the failure of any one religion to prepare its youth for the complex ethical problems of our society, from the almost complete elimination of ethical education in the public schools, from the amorality of television, or from a mixture of these stresses.

It may be true that the churches, traditional purveyors of ethics, have tried from time to time to stem the tide of corruption. White, in discussing the worst corruption of the Grant era, says: "The churches did not waver in holding man's duty to his fellowman before him."[96] Individual clergymen have led movements against corrupt political machines.

But the instruction given by most churches to youth involves almost nothing which would lead a young man or woman to avoid corrupt political action. The nineteenth-century teaching of Biblical texts opposed corruption only indirectly; the twentieth-century teaching of social ethics does not oppose corruption at all. Professor Clebsch, after noting that denominations have concerned themselves with their own ritual and dogma, queried: "What American denomination has developed moral norms that are at once realistic and genuinely religious to guide persons who are perplexed by a welter of new problems such as abortion, divorce, euthansia, extra-marital sexual intercourse, financial manipulation?"[97] He might have added political corruption and ordinary crime as items that are ignored.

The failure of the schools to teach ethics is fully outlined in later chapters. School courses in "civics" are quite general, but have been ineffective educationally and have almost ignored problems of basic honesty.[98]

The media, newspapers, magazines, television, and radio are all ostensibly in favor of honest government. Some newspapers have at times conducted courageous campaigns against corruption. Otherwise, however, the media have not viewed the general level of ethics of the population as one of their major concerns.

The obvious recommendation, developed more fully later in this book, is that churches, schools, and media should pay more attention to the development of higher ethical standards in the community.

Common Causes of Business, Union, and Political Corruption

The reader can hardly have failed to notice our country's unhappy position below other modern democracies in union and governmental honesty, and perhaps in business honesty. Are there any common causes of these difficulties?

Government is at the center of the ethical problem. It is clear that governmental corruption has an unhappy effect on both business and union levels of honesty. If police will not arrest the malefactor, district attorneys not prosecute him, or courts not convict him, there is not much use having laws for business or union honesty. Our actual situation is not as bad as the previous sentence would imply, but the sentence does illustrate the basic importance of governmental rectitude.

There are other important relationships. Gangster-run unions work to exploit businesses and to force the latter into dishonest action. Dishonest business action may provoke unions into dishonesty, and both may exert dishonest pressures on government.

After reading many explanations by specialists on business,

union, or political corruption, one cannot help reflecting that an injection of basic honesty would help eliminate all three fields of trouble. Elaborate explanations based on century-old frontier influences or lack of class distinctions seem to be less important than the problem of rearing and educating honest prople. Thus, the third underlying reason for political corruption—the failure of America to conduct effective ethical instruction—seems to apply also to business and union corruption.

Earlier in this book three major methods of correcting crime and corruption in America were outlined. These included improvement of conditions of human life in poverty areas, improvement of law enforcement, and improvement of ethical instruction. If the analysis of reasons for corruption given above is correct, then the improvement of law enforcement and better ethical instruction are necessary to cure corruption.

Succeeding chapters will indicate the possibilities of teaching ethics so that the level of politics, business, and union life may be raised. After demonstrating that ethics can be taught we will appraise the possibility of ethical instruction on the part of a number of institutions of our society. As was the case with crime discussed in the two preceding chapters, there are several reasons for the prevalence of corruption in America and a number of things must be done if it is to be eliminated.

— 5 —

You Can Teach Ethics

An oft expressed dictum about moral education is that people learn their behavior from the example of others: "Ethics are caught and not taught," or "you can't teach ethics." The man from Missouri declared, "Show me!" This pragmatic approach to ethical instruction is typically American.

Such a view of morality reflects two notable facets of the American character. As "the first new nation," to use Seymour Lipset's apt title, Americans distrusted moral formalism because it was believed that it impeded progress. Second, American egalitarianism tends to regard moralizing as a hypocritical attempt to prove one's greater class or self-worth. Beyond these persistent reasons for skepticism toward ethical instruction there are three difficulties generally cited in teaching ethics: ideological, administrative, and methodological.

Ideological Difficulties

The ideological arguments are perhaps the strongest. We are all familiar with the different reasons why it would be wrong to teach ethics. They include:

1) The psychological belief that ethical instruction hurts the child's development and capacity for self-determination. This was the position of many Freudians. An even more general belief of psychologists, both Freudian and behaviorist, is that ethical instruction will have no effect because behavior is determined by non-rational experience.

2) The sociological argument, which is specifically relativistic.

97

According to this view, each group has its own values, so that ethical education will inevitably be an imposition of one group's values on another.

3) There are several philosophical arguments against ethics. The major one is positivism, which extends the relativistic viewpoint of the sociologists into individual life. Positivists assert that it is impossible to determine what values are universally true; therefore, there is no such thing as moral truth. I may believe that it is wrong to steal or murder, but if this belief is only a result of my experience, and has no objective validity, who am I to say that it is wrong for someone (particularly someone who is underprivileged) to do so? His experience may be very different from mine.

Another major line of argument used against ethical instruction is that if ethics are learned from social experience, in an unjust society the teaching of ethics perpetuates injustice. This approach often has a Marxist root: morality and justice are defenses of the economically-privileged against the just claims of the underprivileged. In American society the social justice argument frequently has racial or pacifist overtones. How can one teach ethics, it is asked, in a society where so many minorities are discriminated against and when thousands are being killed in an unjust war or billions of dollars are being spent for weapons of death while other pressing social needs are ignored?

Administrative Problems

The administrative or institutional reasons are also distressingly familiar. The schools probably should not teach ethics because this might be a violation of the separation of church and state. As William Ball has pointed out, the Supreme Court's recent cases, including *Schempp* and *Torcaso*, could possibly include "ethical culture" and "secular humanism" as expressions of religion forbidden by the First Amendment.[1] Ethics also represents the danger of governmental interference in private life. Is it not likely that the government will seek to set ethical standards, as it has set those for health, environment, safety, and racial discrimination in the past decade?

Almost everyone recognizes the increased influence of mass media, particularly that of television, in our daily lives. And yet when it is suggested that television should assume a greater role in acting as a democratic ethical instructor, television executives argue that their role is only that of entertainment and information—defending their right to make huge profits, with a minimum of social control, on the basis of freedom of speech.

Over 40 percent of America's population regularly attends church and even more consider themselves associated with religious denominations. Yet in religious schools surprisingly little attention is given to ethical matters except in some of the more "fundamentalist" groups.

It is generally agreed that the family is the first place where moral instruction should be given. Realistically, however, the family is incapable of assuming the entire job of moral instruction. Nearly 50 percent of the marriages in some areas end in divorce, and there is a 25 percent illegitimacy rate in several minority groups. In addition, the time spent with television and with peer groups has greatly increased. Such are only a few of the administrative difficulties in teaching ethics in a mass, pluralistic society.[2]

Methodological Problems

The third major objection to teaching ethics is methodological. How can it be done? In Plato's dialogue *Meno*, the question is asked: "Can you tell me, Socrates—is virtue something that can be taught? Or does it come by practice? Or is it neither teaching nor practice that gives it to a man but natural aptitude or something else?"[3]

As Plato was aware, you cannot tell a hardened criminal to be good nor explain to him that all men are brothers and expect an immediate—or, indeed, any—change in his behavior. It might only make him a greater hypocrite. Ethics represents a complex of differing ingredients, including natural temperament or passions (psychologists have noticed a great difference in disposition of the newborn), childhood experience and habits, perception of social possibilities for individual goal achievement, concepts of social justice and reform, and possibilities of punishment for social infractions, to name a few. Sociologists tell us that a member of a minority community who comes from a broken home, has a poor education and low income, and believes that society discriminates against him is a much more likely candidate for crime than someone who is better situated and better disposed toward society. Nevertheless, it frequently happens that the one least provided for may succeed and the one most privileged drop out.

It is improbable that anyone will ever prove how a person becomes ethical. Perhaps it is a question of innate character, or social class, or church membership, or the proper degree of discipline and love in the family, or the example of a successful parent, or a desire to conform, or a fear of social authority, or some mysterious thing (the presence of a divinity or absolute experience in one's life), or the cognitive power which enables one to choose the right ethical alternative, or racial or social history—or more likely a combination of many of these variables. We do not know what is the best method for ethical education because we do not know what—outside of coercion—makes people behave responsibly toward others.

Many analysts believe that there are no common values in our society, or that our political system is too corrupt or too libertarian to permit ethical instruction. Others believe that our social institutions are so fragmented that they cannot cooperate in the area of ethics. Such analyses pose hard questions. But given sufficient time and space, most if not all of their objections could be adequately answered. As political scientists, however, we are more impressed with the fact that people act as if there were values such as justice, equality, and honesty, and that their willingness to act on these principles is the basis for political life. Far from being moral skeptics, the majority of citizens seek to perpetuate the social and individual virtues: opportunity for all, elimination of poverty, increased political liberty, world peace, and the reduction of crime. The existence of this informed political consensus is something which should be prized and perpetuated. Public policy must reflect these ethical attitudes.

Ethical education is thus a complex subject. However, it stands to reason (to use a somewhat old-fashioned phrase) that if a person's ethical habits and attitudes can be improved, it will be more likely, other things being equal, that ethical behavior will also be improved.

What do we mean by ethical education in this sense? There are two major areas of moral education: (1) affective—those things involving personal habits, passions, and so on, and (2) cognitive— those things which are aspects of one's understanding of what is right and wrong and reflect knowledge of the consequences of ethical activity. If ethical education is to be successful, it must be so in both affective and cognitive areas and must be carried on in a wide variety of life situations whose cumulative impact contributes to the ethical conscience of the individual. For a discussion of the totality of ethical experience in life, the reader should consult John Dewey's *Human Nature and Conduct*.

The real test of whether ethical education works can probably never be carried out. However, in spite of all the arguments advanced to assure the inadequacies of moral education, there is considerable evidence to suppose that other societies have been able to transform the lives of their members through explicitly ethical means. In this chapter we will concentrate on the practical effects of ethical instruction observable in other societies and present some of the pedagogical techniques which have been and still can be used to promote ethical standards.

Comparative Ethical Reforms

Perhaps the best proof that we can teach ethics is the experience of other societies. In the latter half of the eighteenth century and on into the nineteenth, British life was marked by a high incidence of public corruption and considerable general criminality. The mistreatment of the poor, a political system based on rotten boroughs, the corruptibility and inefficiency of British officials in America and in other parts of the British Empire, are a few of the familiar manifestations of British decadence during this period. From this low ebb, British life underwent what Carl Friedrich has called a recovery which is "little short of miraculous":

> The process by which the British pulled themselves out of the morass of corruption which had made a Burke defend the "rotten borough" as a sound political institution and developed what is, in the opinion of many, the most thoroughly honest public service ever organized is little short of miraculous. It also shows that pathological phenomena are not necessarily destined to go from bad to worse, and the corrective for them is often quite readily at hand.
>
> By the second half of the nineteenth century what had been considered "normal behavior" had become corruption sharply condemned by the majority of Britons.[4]

What caused this marked improvement in the ethical standards of British public and private life? Historians differ in their interpretation. Some cite the increased wealth generated by the industrial revolution and the democratization of the society. Others, and perhaps the most influential group, make a persuasive argument for the view that the reforms were brought about by the increased moral conviction of large numbers of British citizens. The ethical teachings of the Wesley brothers, reflected in Methodism, in Thomas Arnold's program at Rugby, and in the English public schools in general in addition to the writings and speeches of many lesser known individuals were major contributors to the change. According to one authority, the root of the reforms was "latitudinarian evangelism."

> Utilitarianism, Darwinism, Positivism, Rationality, Biblical Criticism, and Atheistic Humanism—none of these succeeded in undermining morality, as some had feared, or in providing a 'new motive' for morality, as Macauley and others had hoped. *In the end what sustained the Victorian ethic was essentially what had first inspired it—an unsectarian, latitudinarian evangelism.*[5]

To support her thesis, Himmelfarb quotes George Eliot:

> Evangelism had brought into palpable existence and operation . . . that idea of duty, that recognition of something to be lived for beyond the mere satisfaction of self, which is to the moral life what the addition of a great central ganglion is to animal life.[6]

In the course of the nineteenth century, Prussia, Bavaria, and France underwent "similar although less dramatic reforms." A properly trained bureaucracy and a responsible public service was developed in this period.[7]

There are countless other examples of the influence religious instruction has had in different societies. George LaPiana states: "There is no doubt that the moral principles taught by the Christian church contributed much to the moral and social progress in European civilization."[8] Max Weber, writing of the early Protestants, comments:

> But still, through its numerous related features, Old Testament morality was able to give a powerful impetus to that spirit of self-righteous and sober legality which was so characteristic of the worldly asceticism of this form of Protestantism.[9]

Ernst Troeltsch, in his monumental work *The Social Teaching of the Christian Churches*, argues that Catholicism based society upon "the Christian conception of the family—that combination of the elements of authority with those of personality and individualism." He also believes that under the aegis of the church, "the whole of social thought and feeling in general has been deeply influenced by the idea of an objective fellowship with absolute values and truth."[10] Many other historical authorities, including W.E.H. Lecky, G.C. Coulton, and A.C. Adcock, have shown that the fundamental moral reforms of pagan Rome and among the Jews were brought about by Christian teachings.[11]

In other cultures, even more distant from our Judeo-Christian experience, there appears evidence that religious faith and practice have had a profound effect on individual behavior. The historian James Breasted is confident that the Pharoah Ikhnaton was able to maintain high standards of morality through moral instruction.[12]

In most cases one might argue that ethical behavior was compelled through political police power.[13] But in the cases we have cited the moral instruction frequently was founded on faith alone, often in opposition to social authority. Early Christians seemed to thrive without the help of any coercion other than the expection of future rewards and punishments promised by their faith. Perhaps the early Christian communities were influenced by the habits and examples of their committed leadership.

Ethical Education is a Joint Responsibility

Study of the societies in which ethical standards have been raised suggests that in order for an ethical conscience to become a significant part of the national character, many of the important educational institutions must support one another. English ethical reform started in the churches, spread to the schools and colleges, and then reached the economic and political institutions. It seems a reasonable conjecture that the major reason why England and the United States reversed positions during the nineteenth century—the English rising from a period of public corruption to one of world-renown for honesty, and America tracing almost the opposite course—may have been due to the fact that the ethical teaching of the American churches and schools was not sufficient in itself to counteract the profound strains on the social fabric. American business was perhaps too free during this period in its expansion of capital and production irrespective of social ends. United States politics became dominated by recent ethnic immigrants who were confused by the new social system, who practiced widely different religions, and who—in later decades of the century—came from political societies which did not put as high a value on civic honesty as did the puritanical, Protestant North Europeans.

If we accept the evidence that societies have successfully taught moral principles, how have they done so? What are the techniques which have been employed, some of which will be discussed more fully in Chapter Ten?

Teaching the Law

The first approach in terms of history and of importance was the teaching of divinely-inspired law. Both the ancient Greeks and the Jews understood their moral duties through a divine law given to them at the beginning of their history. Many Christian groups continued to use the decalogue as the basis of their moral instruction. Christianity, however, tends to be more oriented toward a creed than toward a law. There is evidence to support the view that the longevity of the Jewish people has resulted from the continuity provided by the Mosaic statutes, successively interpreted by the rabbis.

In contemporary American society the teaching of the law could be effectively employed not only in the religious denominations, which possess an historical body of laws, but also in secondary and higher education to familiarize students with accepted standards of behavior, reminding them of the need for social regulation and for democratic processes to enact laws.

Individual Virtues

A second major approach to teaching morality is by the "individual virtues" common to Aristotle, Castiglione, and Lord Chesterfield. Although there are significant differences in the desirable character traits which each describes, the general attempt to inculcate standards of human excellence through moral instruction or discussion is clear. Aristotle, for example, lists liberality, magnanimity, courage, in addition to the most impor-tant—justice.

Aristotle understands the virtues to be the result of the proper ordering of character. To take courage, which is the first virtue Aristotle discusses and the most illustrative of the virtues, as an example: "With regard to feelings of fear and confidence, courage is the mean." According to Aristotle, the greatest fear is that of death, particularly violent death in battle. There follows a detailed discussion of the proper end of courage, why it is necessary for human existence, and how it should be limited. The most interesting part of Aristotle's analysis is how courage, or any of the virtues, is promoted. According to him, virtues are acquired mainly through activity or experience.

> Moral virtue comes about as a result of habit. . . . It is plain that none of the moral virtues are in us by nature; for nothing that exists by nature can form a habit contrary to its nature. Neither, by nature, then, nor contrary to nature do the virtues arise in us; rather, we are adapted by nature to receive them, and are made perfect by habit.
>
> The virtues we get by first exercizing them, as also happens in the base of the arts as well. For the things we have to learn before we can do them, we learn by doing them, e.g., men become builders by building and lyre players by playing the lyre, so too we become just by doing just acts.[14]

In this democratic age, many of these virtues must be reinterpreted to fulfill greater standards of equality. As discussed in Chapter Ten, this has been successfully done in at least one character education program.

The individual virtues approach appears to be most applicable at younger age levels. It provides a very effective introduction to good habits using simplified concepts of ethical decision-making. If a child is used to telling the truth and to being forthright, he can later learn in what situations one should temper the truth by kindness or by the knowledge of a greater good. Similarly with the other virtues, good habits need to be developed first. Therefore, what Lawrence Kohlberg has called the "bag of virtues" approach seems

appropriate for primary school and younger religious schoolgoers.[15]
The "bag of virtues" seems a particularly effective way of teaching
the Christian virtues, for example.

Case Study

A more sophisticated and democratic technique which has been
used by different societies and their leaders is known as the case
study approach to individual moral decision-making. The case study
discussion is a technique which can be applied in almost any
context, and is perhaps the least dogmatic of approaches. When
Christ proposed a parable to His disciples, or when He forced the
crowd stoning the adulteress to reconsider their own moral
positions, He was in effect framing a moral case study. The major
advantage of the case study discussion is the greater emphasis on
individual ratiocination about the consequences of ethical or
unethical acts, in addition to the opportunity it gives each individual
to think through his own moral apparatus.

The case study method seems to have some measure of
applicability in almost every ethical training situation. It probably
has the greatest benefit for older and more sophisticated participants, such as secondary and college students. But if an individual
has no previous moral training and his peers are not supportive of
ethical decisions, the case study method may be fruitless.

Learning Ethics Through Experience

Dewey and Tufts, in their renowned textbook on ethics,
comment:

> Moral theory . . . emerges when men are confronted with situations
> in which different desires promise opposed goods and in which
> incompatible courses of action seem to be morally justified. Only
> such a conflict of good ends and of standards and rules of right and
> wrong calls forth personal inquiry into the bases of morals.[16]

It was from this general position that Dewey derived his theory of
teaching morality through experience in the school, which is
discussed more fully in Chapter Ten.

Just because the studies of the curriculum represent standard factors in social life, they are organs of initiation into social values. As mere school studies, their acquisition has only a technical worth. Acquired under conditions where their social significance is realized, they feed moral interest and develop moral insight.[17]

This belief that morals can be learned through the development of habits while learning in the school is at least partly borne out by pedagogical studies also described in Chapter Ten.

Comparative Approach

The comparative approach to ethical knowledge is another possible source for general moral rules. Scholars of religion, anthropology, law, and sociology have explored the similarities between the ethical principles of different societies. C. S. Lewis's *The Abolition of Man* is a comparative analysis of major religions and outlines the remarkable ethical similarities among them.[18] Clyde Kluckhohn also maintains that sociological studies of values show common ethical standards in at least five cultures.[19] Professor Ralph Linton has argued the comparative thesis from an anthropological point of view.[20]

However, these social scientific attempts to bridge the is/ought controversy in order to provide universal social values have been challenged by Paul Taylor, who argues that even if one could demonstrate that every society had similar ethical standards one would still not have shown why societies or individuals ought to behave in the socially approved fashion.[21]

The comparative approach may be used most profitably in schools. The knowledge of differing societies and religions can serve as an effective introduction to the remarkably similar ethical basis underlying most of these apparently different religions and societies. The fact that the differing approaches and techniques exist is illustrative of the persistent attempts which have been made to teach ethics.

Comments

In reviewing several of these techniques, it becomes clear that they have a greater suitability for some institutions than for others. An important consideration is that different institutions must work together, along the lines of the Parent-Teachers Association, to have any lasting consequence. Thus, if there is to be a renewal of interest in individual ethical responsibility and education, it will be most effective if there is a similar emphasis—if not a similar message—from several or all concerned institutions: the churches, the schools and colleges, mass media, business and government, and most important, the intellectuals.

One might think that in a mass society such as ours popular enthusiasm would tend to exert influence on every social segment. Occasionally this may happen. Our research indicates, however, that there continues to be such a pluralism of values and a division of functions that the suggested reform measures can only be carried out by effective leadership in separate institutions acting cooperatively with each other. The United States lacks the centralization found in other nations, so the problem of reform is more difficult.

Another proof of the "teachability" of ethics is the wealth of research in the area. In Chapter Ten we analyze theories of moral development given by Bandura and Walters, Piaget, Kohlberg, Freud, and Erickson.

— 6 —

Ethical Reform:
An Opportunity for the Intellectuals

Importance of the Intellectuals

In a mass society such as our own, intellectual leaders wield great power through their influence on popular opinion. This power is enhanced by the importance of education in our society. Americans have always been devoted to free universal education, and since the second World War increasing emphasis has been given to higher education. Over 50 percent of all young people (not just 50 percent of high school graduates) now pursue some form of post-secondary academic study—more than double the average of Western European countries. Moreover, academic degrees have increasingly become employment credentials: lawyers, doctors, scientists, and college professors are required to have an approved diploma. This may now seem natural to us, but not too long ago the majority of lawyers had never seen the inside of a law school. Sigmund Freud once thought that psychoanalysts should be amateurs, without an M.D. degree.

Another factor contributing to the increased importance of the intellectuals is their ability to utilize the electronic media, particularly television. Talk shows, documentaries, news reports and analyses, while not strictly "intellectual," present a forum for intellectual ideas at first or at least at second, hand. Newsmen, while rarely intellectuals themselves, are usually university graduates attuned to intellectual/academic currents.

In addition to these factors is the general receptivity of our society as a whole to intellectual ideas. Ours is the first society explicitly founded upon intellectual principles or truths, spelled out in the Declaration of Independence. Our emphasis on individual educa-

109

tion and enlightenment makes us more receptive to intellectual theories, if not necessarily to intellectuals. The absence of any long standing religious, class, or intellectual traditions may also make us more open to new intellectual currents. Certainly within this century the principles of psychology were accepted more quickly and more widely in the United States than they were anywhere else in the world (exclusive, perhaps, of the Soviet Union).

There are many occupations which intellectuals may pursue; however, one seems to be more central than the others. Among intellectuals the written word is still more influential than the spoken, as Marshall McLuhan affirms by continually writing books. Those who write books and articles in magazines of opinion have an enormous influence on the attitudes of other intellectuals and the intellectually-influenced professions, e.g., college and secondary school teachers, members of the mass media, theologians, and even judges and politicians.[1]

The intellectuals are crucial to the fate of ethical instruction in the United States because of their power over public opinion. They help to determine the importance or lack of importance of ethical training in the schools, on TV, even in the home. They train the teachers, broadcasters, public officials, administrators, and even give instruction to parents on how to rear their children. If, for some reason, ethics were to come into intellectual favor, the intellectuals would play a central role in formulating and disseminating the new approach.[2]

The intellectuals, in other words, have the power to define the consciousness of the nation regarding fundamental human and social problems. For example, the psychologists tell us how to rear children and treat criminals; the political scientists tell us a great deal about the efficacy and justice of our institutions; the economists play a similar role regarding economic policies.

Intellectuals and Ethics

Before beginning a critique of the intellectuals' approach to ethical education, it is important to note their moral strength.

The intellectuals, particularly the academicians, are highly ethical as a group. In their own fields their standards of truthfulness and painstaking search for evidence are usually high, as is their concern for their students' welfare and education. In comparison with the other institutions of our society, the institutions with which intellectuals have been associated (for example, colleges, newspapers, magazines) have had a good ethical record. Even though these institutions are on the periphery of political and economic power, the areas in which there are potentials for abuse (e.g., accepting bribes for grades or for the acceptance of scholarly articles) have been almost entirely free from corruption. Moreover, intellectuals involved in political activities and community work evidence a highly ethical social concern. Most demands for social reform in recent years have been based on their writings.

The intellectuals are highly ethical in a social sense. They have consistently explored the condition of the disadvantaged and the ravages of modern life. Gunnar Myrdal's analysis of the Negro's plight, Rachel Carson's treatment of the ecology danger, and Harrison Brown's warning about the population explosion are all fine examples of intellectual concern. Further, they have been the active leaders of many political and moral causes.

However, many of them seem to be indifferent to the maintenance or even the need for individual ethical standards in business and governmental bureaucracies. Several studies by political scientists of corruption in developing countries have concluded that injustice and bribery sometimes pay off by making the system more adaptable to change.[3] Robert Merton, the famous sociologist, has offered a rationale and defense for the political machine: Machines come about when "the functional deficiencies of the official structure generate an alternative (unofficial) structure to fulfill existing needs somewhat more effectively."[4] Carl Friedrich, a noted political scientist, criticizes the defenders of corruption and points out that "corruption is closely linked with other (political) pathologies, especially violence and betrayal." He goes on, "Corruption may, therefore, afflict a society in its ideatic core," e.g., destroy the general belief in the ideological or political principles of a regime.[5] In their rejection of ethical considerations, the intellectuals carry over the libertarian, laissez-faire position of the eighteenth and nineteenth centuries. About the only way one can rationalize this lack of concern about individual habits and attitudes with the desire for a good society is through Mandeville's famous quote that "private vice equals public virtue."

Intellectuals are skeptical of individual ethical instruction. An example of this attitude can be found in Richard Hofstadter's description of himself and his friends in the 1930s:

> We were intensely vague about what it was we were positively committed to in terms of human values, though we thought we knew what certain particular programs of social reconstruction ought to be. . . .
> Our elusiveness about values was not merely an oversight. It was a philosophical myth that arose out of the assumption that the important changes were only structural and institutional changes, and that, once these were properly taken care of, human values would somehow take care of themselves.[6]

The "philosophical myth" which Hofstadter mentions is what we have been referring to as the substitution of social ethics for individual ethics. The new understanding of man brought about by scientific materialism places a heavy emphasis on social and environmental influences, reducing the role of the individual.[7] Many intellectuals tend to be relativistic when standards of individual ethics are discussed, yet when speaking about social issues—such as world peace, social or economic injustice, or pollution they become highly moralistic. Their approach stems from a one-sided, or social ethics, view of morality.

To understand the greater emphasis on social ethics over individual ethics one needs to study the ideological/historical origins of modern intellectuals. Although there are analogies between modern intellectuals and ancient sophists or medieval philosophers, intellectuals have their roots in the Enlightenment of the seventeenth and eighteenth centuries. They are the spokesmen-promoters of modern science. By and large, they seek to make society more rational, better organized, and independent of religious authority. Their second desire, faithful to the goals of the Enlightenment, is to increase the social advantages of all and to eliminate suffering. To secure these ends they have frequently opposed the privileged classes—often while they lived off their beneficence—and some of them have contested the influence of religious authority. These characteristics have continued from the seventeenth century to the present.

In recent decades, for example, the majority of intellectuals have desired a more regulated economy, equal representation, therapeutic treatment of criminals, and so on—all in the interest of greater rationality and fairness. At the same time they have opposed religious influence in public schools. We realize, of course, that these generalizations do not fit them all. There are, for example, Christian intellectuals, conservative intellectuals, and radical intellectuals. But available studies indicate that the general characteristics we have discussed are the most common.[8] We believe that Christian and conservative intellectuals would be the first to admit that they are a decided minority in intellectual circles.

The intellectuals are spokesmen for modern science, and they are also influenced by philosophic trends. We mentioned in Chapter One that most of the major philosophic movements of the twentieth century have been generally opposed to the concept of the individual found in religious tradition and in the earlier philosophical movements (such as Kantianism and utilitarianism) which encouraged ethical instruction. Included are both the scientifically oriented theories, such as logical positivism, Freudian psychology, and Deweyan pragmatism, and the post-scientifically oriented ones, such as existentialism, all of which tend to work against ethical instruction.

The intellectuals may also oppose individual ethical instruction because many of them believe that it is being adequately done at the present time, or even overdone. Their general attitude is remarkably similar to that which we found in Dewey and Freud. This position has been well expressed by Lionel Trilling, probably the leading American literary critic of this century:

> [The] particular course of literature over the past two centuries has been with the self in its long-standing quarrel with culture. . . . This intense conviction of the existence of the self apart from culture is, as culture well knows, its noblest and most generous achievement. At the present moment it must be thought of as a liberating idea without which our developing ideal community is bound to defeat itself.[9]

Much intellectual thought about ethics is rooted in the idea of liberating human nature from the repressions of religious education and the competitive selfishness of capitalism. This understanding seeks a new morality, as represented by "situation ethics," "Consciousness III," or the "Summer Hill Experience." The far-sighted vision of many intellectuals is perhaps the major reason why

they are occasionally short-sighted about contemporary ethical
needs.

There are other minor reasons why intellectuals are not leaders in
individual ethics. Too often they are unclear about the attitudes and
lifestyles of non-intellectuals. It is well-known that personal
experience has a great deal to do with social expectations. Life on a
college campus and in upper-middle class offices and neighborhoods, where one associates with generally well-behaved students
and highly educated persons, tends to make intellectuals forgetful of
the problems of life in lower-middle class and poverty-level
communities.

Intellectual Support for Ethics

One can easily be too critical of the intellectuals for subjecting
society to logical theories which short-change individual ethics.
Therefore, this section is devoted to an appraisal of the
contributions made by sundry intellectuals to ethical instruction.

Some of the "elite intellectuals" mentioned earlier have focused
their attention on the problem of ethical education. Irving Kristol,
professor of Urban Values at New York Univeristy, editor of *The
Public Interest*, and regular contributor to the *Wall Street Journal*,
has attempted to sketch the roots of American morality. Kristol
writes: "It is said that the institutions of our society have become
appallingly 'impersonal.' I take this to mean that they have lost any
shape congruent with the private moral codes which presumably
govern individual life."[10] On another occasion, Kristol attempted to
analyze the means or forces conducive to ethical revival. He thinks a
revival of the religious spirit would be helpful. Any possibility of
such a revival taking place faces obvious difficulties, as Kristol
knows. Our world is still moving toward ever-greater secularity.
This fact can nowhere be better seen than in the increasing reliance
of ministers and theologians on essentially secular-academic
theories. Also, and perhaps more important, the absolute separation
of church from state in our political system restricts the institutional
avenues down which religious influence may flow.

Kristol's second suggestion appears more plausible. The political
consciousness of the American people respecting the institutions

and principles which form our free representative government are also, in large measure, ethical principles or at least the basis for ethical principles. If this political consciousness could be raised, it seems likely that the American people's ethical consciousness might also be increased.

This proposal would involve instruction in the implementation and preservation of the principles of free government. D. W. Oliver and J. P. Shaver, arguing in the same vein as Kristol, have shown that a liberal democratic political system requires clarification of and commitment to democratic ethical principles:

> Democratic constitutionalism, as we are using the term, is more than a principle of government; it implies a set of procedures for designing questions in a rational, intelligent, humane way. It depends, too, upon certain assumptions about the nature of man himself. The most important are (1) that he can be trained to restrain his own impulses in the interests of others, and (2) that he will inevitably strive toward some degree of personal freedom and self-expression.[11]

Irving Kristol has also criticized the American university for its total inattention to questions of ethical or character education:

> I recall Leo Rosten observing that, so far as he could see, what dissatisfied students were looking for were adults—adults to confront, to oppose, to emulate . . . I agree with Rosten that this is what is wanted, and I am certain it will not be achieved until our institutions of higher education reach some kind of common understanding on what kind of adult a young man is ideally supposed to become.[12]

Occasionally, college presidents or other well-intentioned speakers at commencement time will emphasize the connection between education and ethical standards. Praiseworthy in itself, one suspects that the speakers are trying to remedy the deficiencies of the previous years of education. While definitely a minority position in the academy, this is represented by an excerpt from the address by Edmund E. Day, former President of Cornell University:

> In our formal education at all levels we must abandon, once and for all, the idea that it is not the task of our schools and colleges to deal with moral and spiritual values. We cannot go on tolerating the failure of the schools to deal constructively with the inculcation of habits and

ideals of simple honesty. In both curricular and extra-curricular activities, the enduring values of honorable living must be cultivated by all available means. Performance without character and ambition without integrity threaten to be our undoing.[13]

If attitudes such as those expressed by Irving Kristol and Edmund E. Day were to become prevalent in the major journals of opinion and in American colleges, it is safe to say that institutional reform would be very rapid, because the popular support for ethical education is strong. What is missing is a broadly-based intellectual leadership.

In the summer of 1973, the authors tried to test the reactions of their colleagues in the social science faculties of the six small colleges which comprise the Claremont Colleges. Of our fifty-plus respondents, a clear majority favored ethical instruction. Although many thought that it would do little good, because larger social and intellectual forces are at work, the majority said that if it could be done in a non-dogmatic manner they would favor it. While we do not put too much stock in the generalized applicability of the survey—for our sample was small, and perhaps the greatest opponents of ethical instruction did not bother to reply—one tentative hypothesis seems appropriate. In spite of their general commitment to mechanical-structural solutions, when the question of individual ethics is brought to their attention intellectuals will accept its logic.

In England there is much greater support for individual ethics among intellectuals than there is in America. *The Journal of Moral Education*, established in 1971, serves as a focal point for intellectual efforts in ethical education.[14] In addition, research units located at both Oxford and Cambridge Universities have done basic and applied research in ethical education. On the Continent, several countries are developing moral education programs for their public schools. Therefore, it is obviously not impossible for contemporary intellectuals to support ethical reform.

Can America Have Intellectual Support for Ethical Reform?

There have been intellectually inspired reforms. Within the last two decades we have seen two major changes in the popular consensus which have produced dramatic reforms in our society. Both of these have had leadership from the intellectuals. The greater of these two movements brought the black American out of second-class citizenship and set him on the road to full equality. The second committed the nation to a limitation on the harmful effects of technology for the sake of a healthier and more beautiful environment.

In both cases reforms were anticipated by zealous, educated reformers who saw the need for change. In the case of the blacks, a vociferous group of intellectuals has called for an improvement in their status since the early 1930s. A notable example of this effort was Gunnar Myrdal's *An American Dilemma*. For a long time their calls were ignored because there was no broad, popular consensus to support them. Professor Alexander Bickel traces the turning point in the struggle for black civil rights to the televised portrayal of racial hatred which alerted the majority of Americans to the grave problems faced by the blacks in our society.[15] Once a consensus was formed, all the legislation and litigation which went into the "civil rights movement" was made possible and meaningful. This reform would not have been possible, at least at the time at which it took place, without intellectual leadership.

A second example of reform has been in the attitude toward the environment. The ecology movement has followed essentially the pattern of the civil rights movement. Even with a few early intellectual studies, which were rhetorical successes, such as Harrison Brown's *The Challenge of Man's Future*, the environmental reformers' warnings went unheeded. However, as the air grew worse, the water fouler, and the countryside more blighted, the ecology issue steadily grew in popularity. Finally, with the creation of the Environmental Protection Agency and the passage of the Clean Air Act of 1970, the ecology movement arrived. Barring an error of judgment by the policy leaders, it seems reasonable to assume that the national consensus they have persuasively helped to create will stand behind more legislation which will solidify and broaden their gains.

Ethics is a field where the popular consensus for change already exists. It does not have to be created as it did for the civil rights and ecology movements. The Gallup Poll is frequently a reliable source for estimating popular attitudes. From 1968 to the present, crime—because of its consistent position as one of the top two public concerns—has been one of the major domestic issues in the United States, according to the Gallup Poll. A further indication of the national mood can be found in a Gallup Poll completed in November 1968. To the question, ''Do you believe that life today is getting better or worse in terms of morals?'' a staggering 78 percent said worse. This is a sufficiently high figure that even if the use of the word ''morals'' is partially reflecting a concern with sexuality and obscenity (which are not the principal interests of this study), a concern with ethical matters, even prior to Watergate, is obvious.

Conclusion

The intellectuals are to a significant extent the moral guides and spokesmen of American society. They have become the ''sermonizing clerics'' of the twentieth century, due to the continuing secularization of the modern world.

The intellectuals approach ethics from a social point of view which, to a certain degree, precludes any great interest in individual ethics. At the same time, it should be noted that intellectuals are not doctrinaire on this subject. They recognize that if social attitudes can be changed about the ecology and minority rights, they can also be changed concerning an individual's ethical responsibility to others and to society. Both changes involve a comprehensive and sophisticated approach to education in our pluralistic, libertarian democracy. However, before we can be confident of success in the reform of ethical education, we must re-educate the intellectuals concerning the importance of individual ethical education. In large measure that is the challenging task of this book.

— 7 —

Bringing Them Up Right

A striking phenomenon of American life is the almost complete responsibility for ethical education placed upon the American family. For various reasons schools have largely withdrawn from this task—a problem discussed in Chapters Nine and Ten. "Main line" Protestant, Roman Catholic, and some Jewish churches are giving little attention to ethics, as readers of Chapter Eleven will find. Government has not proven to be a leader in ethics, as noted in Chapter Four. By default, then, the family bears the major responsibility in this important field. This chapter will discuss the durability of the family, the methods of family ethical education, the weaknesses of the family in such education, and some suggestions about steps which would strengthen the ethical role of the family.

In reading this discussion, it is well to remember that the American family is functioning in a changing society. Many ethnic groups came to this country with a pattern of extended family life which could not be fitted into American urbanized living. Many families of older American stock have found their pattern of life disturbed by industrialization and the mobility of people which has been forced by industrialization. More liberal divorce laws have made the family structure at least appear to be weaker. The very frequent proximity of families from different cultural backgrounds often weakens the family influence on children. It is probably true that we have left to the American family a complete responsibility for teaching ethics at a time when it has been least able to do so.

Durability of the Family

In spite of some statements to the contrary, the family appears to be a permanent social unit. In the United States the youth

119

movement of the later 1960s brought some experiments in
communal living. But, like earlier experiments of this type, these
seem to be small and short-lived. One can search the literature on
families in vain for any serious suggestion of large-scale communal
rearing of children. Americans seem to recognize that the family,
truncated though it may be by divorce, is here to stay. In some ways
the prevalence of divorce is an improvement on the European
practice of taking on mistresses.

The writers are concerned about the potential effect of the present
high rates of divorce on the American family structure. A later
section will indicate that divorce probably reduces the ethical
education given by the family. Numerous marital changes may
weaken the ties of individuals to their community. But we still
believe that the family will remain a basic unit in our society.[1]

Another indication that the family is here to stay is found in Soviet
experience. Soviet Russia began its communist experience with a
deliberate effort to reduce the importance of the family through a
series of laws, including "divorce by post card," which were
intended to support "a dissoluble marriage and not a lifelong
union." But by the 1930s, the Soviet regime had decided to support
the family, and new legislation did that. A 1954 law was clearly
intended to make divorce more difficult. Evidently the family was to
be a unit of communist as well as of capitalist society.[2]

Methods of Ethical Education

How much strength does the family display in ethical instruction?
The writers have found few specific studies on this score. However,
there are a number of studies in a parallel field—that of political
socialization—which reflect a great deal of strength in the family
impression on youth.

A few examples will suffice. One American study found that
three-quarters of party preferences of students came from parents.[3]
Hyman lists a number of studies which indicate positive correla-
tions, a few without correlation, but none with negative correlation
between parental and children's opinions.[4] Jennings and Niemi, in a
study of almost seventeen hundred twelfth graders, found agreement with parents on party identification but smaller agreement on
issues.[5]

It is difficult to appraise the implications of these and other studies of political socialization for ethical instruction. The fact that parents have had great influence on political opinions would seem to argue that they will have great influence on the related field of moral opinions. However, some of the studies indicated a closer parent-child correlation on party identification than on attitudes toward issues. This may mean that ethical attitudes, which are somewhat similar to viewpoints on issues, are not too easily transmitted from parent to child. On the other hand, the opportunity for parents to instill ethical *habits* in their children may be far more important than either party or issue orientation.

The study which seems to us to be most effective in describing sound family programs of moral education is by an English writer, Norman Bull. Our readers must remember that Bull is describing a society which has been more successful in ethical education than has our own. Bull comes to the conclusion that the home is the most important part of a child's moral development.[6]

How does the family achieve moral training? Bull notes an important class difference (perhaps greater in Britain than in the United States): "The broad distinction is between the working class tendency to punitiveness and typical middle class moderation, with the use of reasoning and the effort to inculcate guilt feelings."[7] Bull, following Piaget's studies, finds four stages of a child's moral development: (1) anomy (or state of no rules), mostly up to age seven but sometimes continuing later; (2) heteronomy (or moral codes determined by others, e.g., parents, teachers, or police) from age seven until a sharp decline at age eleven but with some continuation to age seventeen; (3) socionomy (judgment shaped by relationships with others in society, beginning at age seven, sharply developing at age thirteen, but becoming a minority factor by age seventeen); (4) autonomy (self-determined moral codes) which takes over heavily, but not completely, by age seventeen.

Professor Bull does not have an exact testing device to know how much of each of these stages is a result of family influence. But his tests of 360 children in towns of the southwest region of England, a largely rural area, give an opportunity for children to state why they have adopted certain moral positions. In the heteronomous period of the child's life, the opinions of parents are frequently cited as decisive. Since Bull believes that his figures also demonstrate that the formation of moral opinions in the heteronomous period is essential to the opinion of the socionomous and autonomous periods, it is evident that he believes that parental opinions are a very significant factor in moral development.

In discussing his English test children, Bull finds in his "lying test" that children are less likely to lie to their parents if the parents have had a friendly relationship with them.[8] Heteronomous responses are often a result of physical discipline which "stands as a barrier between parent and child." Some parents use psychological discipline, e.g., "Since mother cares for you and does not lie to you, you shouldn't lie to her," or "Since father pays for everything, you should repay him by telling the truth."[9] This moves on to loving trust by age thirteen.

Bull points out that parents serve as models for children: they give explicit moral teaching, establish unconscious moral assumptions in the home, and determine the psychological atmosphere of the home. The home itself reflects the moral ethics of its own socio-economic background, which permits higher moral judgments by children of higher socio-economic status.[10] In discussion of particular years of growth, Bull notes that during childhood, nursery rhymes, fairy stories, folk tales, and fables all have some moral significance. Parents, especially mothers, have much to do with their children's learning or reading of these ancestral moral conditioners.

Much of the family's success in moral training is said by sociologists to come from the process of "identification." This means more than simple imitation of the parent; it means adopting the parent's "vantage point as the perspective from which he sees and understands situations."[11] However, there is some evidence that sons of criminal fathers do not identify with their fathers' criminal careers. "Rather, it would appear that rejection by the father creates aggressive tendencies in the child."[12]

There is also the pressure of the family on the individual to follow family standards.[13] Obviously the fact that love, food, clothing, shelter, travel, and all the good things of life come from the family gives the latter a degree of authority for ethical instruction. The family is known by the community to be the principal agent of character formation, so many things are referred to it. If a child creates a problem, in most communities the first step is to report to his parents. Most policemen will refer first offenders to their parents rather than arresting them.

To those persons who sometimes wonder about the bustling American household, with members rushing off to a wide variety of activities, there may be comfort in a 1950 judgment by the psychiatrist Erik Erikson:

> The American family . . . tends to guard the right of the individual member—parents included—not to be dominated. In fact, each member, as he grows and changes, reflects a variety of outside groups and their changing interests and needs: the father's occupational group, the mother's club, the adolescent's clique, and the children's first friends. These interest groups determine the individual's privileges in his family; it is they who judge his family. The family becomes a training ground in the tolerance of different interests—not of different beings; liking and loving has little to do with it.
>
> The meaning of it all is, of course, an automatic prevention of autocracy and inequality. It breeds, on the whole, undogmatic people, people ready to drive a bargain and then to compromise. It makes complete irresponsibility impossible and it makes open hate and warfare in families rare. It also makes it quite impossible for the American adolescent to become what his brothers and sisters in other large countries become so easily, uncompromising ideologists."[14]

Erikson might have written less surely about the American family's non-production of ideologists two decades later. However, it may be that the family federation he describes is the best training ground for a competitive individualist society. One may wonder if such a family is an adequate sole source of moral education.

Weaknesses of the Family

Historically, the American family has had a reputation for indulging children, as we have noted earlier. In a pluralistic society like ours these observations are testimony only for the observed families; children in many immigrant, or special religious, groups have been reared very strictly. But the person who believes that leadership for ethical education must come from the parents is overlooking the fact that different American families make vastly different efforts to lead their children ethically.

If we turn from Bull's description of reasonably effective British processes of family ethical instruction and Erikson's happy description of American families to American poorer class efforts, we find a good many difficulties. Rodman and Grams summarized some of them for the Katzenbach Commission in 1967. There is a good deal of evidence that broken homes weaken the family's chance to teach ethics and, hence, produce more delinquents. The unhappiest effect is on younger pre-adolescents and on girls.[15] Quarrelsome and negligent homes may well be worse than broken homes, since several studies show that children are more likely to be delinquent if their parents have poor conjugal relations.[16]

Many parents also seem to be unaware of or unable to administer fair, consistent disciplines for their children—again with the consequence of higher delinquency rates. Parents of delinquents were more likely to use physical punishment; those of non-delinquents were more likely to have reasoned with their children. Affection in the household, especially of the father for the son, will result in less delinquency. After reviewing numerous studies of delinquency, Rodman and Grams constructed a "paradigm of delinquency," summarized in Chapter Four of this book. The portions of that paradigm which relate to the family indicate that a lower class family is handicapped by the following facts:

a. social, economic, and occupational deprivation (by definition);
b. lesser attraction for the family and for one's father, given the emphasis that is placed upon the man's occupational position and earning power;
c. a lower concept of personal and family worth;
d. a lesser ability of parents—stemming from limited resources which make the manipulation of rewards and punishments more difficult—to maintain external controls over their children, especially in anonymous urban areas;
e. a lesser degree of attractiveness of community agencies—for example, schools—and therefore their lesser ability to maintain external controls.

Rodman and Grams' paradigm of delinquency goes on to conclude that living in a lower class family involves:

a. more family disharmony and instability, stemming from the members', and especially the father's, greater difficulty in fulfilling expected roles;
b. a greater likelihood of lax or inconsistent discipline and of discipline focused upon the child's actions rather than intentions—

stemming in part from the constraining situation represented by lower class occupations;

c. a lesser degree of affection within the family, stemming from the pressures imposed upon the family by the need to adapt to deprived circumstances;

d. a lesser degree of identification with parents or of internalization of parental norms.[17]

Another way of viewing the effect of poverty on family life is an appraisal of types of delinquency. British and American studies of family life are summarized by Wright for three kinds of delinquents:

The home backgrounds of these three types of delinquent vary in predictable ways. The neurotic delinquent tends to come from a small, middle class, and intact family, where attachments to parents are strong, where the mother is over-protective and over-anxious, where there is some emotional instability in either or both of the parents, and where the parents set austere and uncompromising standards for their children . . .

The unsocialized, aggressive delinquent more often comes from a lower-class family in which parent-child relationships are marked by mutual hostility, rejection and distrust, and where the parents are punitive, erratic, and unjust . . .

The main feature of the homes of pseudo-social delinquents is not so much parental rejection and punitiveness as parental neglect, distance and coldness; the boys' relationships with their parents are characterized by mutual indifference. This is particularly true of the father-son relationship.[18]

These conclusions are based upon the theories of a number of distinguished criminologists. Many Americans who have known the sting of poverty will know that not all deprived families suffer from the above difficulties. But it probably is fair to conclude that a substantial number of such families do. If so, it seems doubly important to help these handicapped families with other forms of ethical training.

The contemporary family is in some ways declining in importance. In recent decades a number of social functions have been transferred from the family to other agencies, such as the transfer of old-age security to government or private agencies. Educational functions have been assumed by schools, with the single exception of ethical education in America. Many of these transfers were made to help the family and its members, but they cannot help reducing the importance of the family in our lives.[19]

Some families are much weaker than others. It has often been suggested that the first generation of immigrants in America are at a disadvantage. If father does not speak English well and is occupying a low-level economic job, how can he command the respect of a son who has learned English in the schools and sees himself as rising in American society? If the son does not respect his father, he is less likely to pay attention to his father's admonitions; hence the higher delinquency rates of the first generation born in America.

The necessity for many immigrant groups to shift from an extended family (where everyone helps the child with his ethical development) to a nuclear family (where only parents may make suggestions) is in itself a temporary weakening of the ability for ethical instruction. Parents have to assume greater responsibilities, the rules of the game are altered, and new psychological barriers to ethical education are introduced.

Divorce, which has been increasing at a startling rate, may augur badly for the family's role as ethical educator. In some jurisdictions, like Los Angeles County where the writers live, the number of divorces is now approximating the number of marriages. In many states divorces are a third or a half of the number of marriages.

However, the above statistics do not mean an end to the family as ethical educator. Step-parents sometimes assume this role with a real sense of responsibility. Many divorces come in families which have not yet had children or from which the children have "graduated." Some families need divorce, and the children will receive better ethical upbringing because of it.

Family troubles are not confined to America. Jean Piaget, in his ground-breaking studies of character development in Swiss youth, came to the conclusion that families had a negative influence on character development. Parents load their children with too many instructions. They try to catch up with wrong-doing rather than avert catastrophes. They take pleasure in inflicting punishments and in using authority.[20]

Another difficulty which faces the family as a moral instructor is that some parents do not know what to instruct. It is well known, for example, that blacks in large city ghetto areas have high crime rates. Frequently the uneducated parents of these black families had no preparation for the difficulties to be encountered in these areas—drugs or different methods of crime—to enable them to warn their children. The shift from life in Southern rural areas to life in Northern societies has had a tremendous impact on family values.

Similarly, Oscar Lewis, in his study of Puerto Rican families living in the poverty areas found serious gaps in their ethical equipment. "People with a culture of poverty are aware of middle-class values, talk about them, and even claim some of them as their own; but on the whole they do not live by them."[21] These Puerto Ricans were not bad people, Lewis observes. But it is easy to understand that they were unequipped to train children for life in a city like New York.

Even middle class families may have another kind of inability: in our complicated society, do the parents know what ethics to teach? Many of the Watergate conspirators came from families who did their best to bring up their children well, but who were totally unprepared to pass on the kind of instruction needed to help avoid the arrogance of great power. Probably none of these parents foresaw the kind of authority which their sons one day would have.

In some ways the basic authority of the parents is a handicap to their role in ethical education. They are, as noted above, the source of many of the good things of life for the child, but they are also a constant source of frustration. Parents who have had to say "don't do this" and "don't do that" are not the most appreciated source of moral inspiration.

The large-scale employment of married women in this country clearly reduces the amount of time parents can spend with children and, thus, the opportunities for ethical instruction. Nye's study indicates a slight association between employment of the mother and delinquency of the child.[22]

Patrick Moynihan, in a much publicized 1965 report, "The Negro Family: A Case for National Action," pointed out that "the family structure of lower class Negroes is highly unstable, and in many urban centers is approaching complete breakdown."[23] The report goes on to note that "nearly a quarter of urban Negro marriages are dissolved, nearly one-quarter of Negro births are now illegitimate, almost one-fourth of Negro families are headed by females, and the breakdown of the Negro family has led to a startling increase in welfare dependence." The report urges that special steps be taken to help the Negro family structure.

Although Moynihan was undoubtedly trying to help the Negro family, the report generated great controversy by those who viewed the report as an attack on blacks. One of the responses, by Dean

Andrew Billingsley, points out that the difficulties of black families are largely confined to poor blacks, and grow out of the poverty and discrimination which these families must face. If economic and social obstacles are removed, the black family will perform its function well.[24]

The current difficulty of poorer black families simply adds to the belief of these writers that families alone should not be expected to carry the entire burden of ethical instruction. If, as Billingsley points out, the poor black family faces tremendous obstacles, we should not burden it with a tremendous solitary load of ethical instruction.

The belief that the family should do all the moral teaching is opposed by some of the difficulties enumerated above. In addition, there are sociological evidences that the family cannot do it alone. Peck and Havighurst concluded in their study of Morris, Illinois:

> The crux of the problem is this: each generation tends to perpetuate its strengths of and weaknesses of character, largely unchanged. A sizeable minority of adults are heavily amoral or expedient in character. They treat their children this way and their children strongly tend to turn out just like their parents.[25]

Helps to the Family

What can be done to help the modern family overcome its limitations and function more effectively in ethical development? The most effective help would probably be the revival of interest of schools, Sunday Schools, and the media in ethical development of children. Nothing helps a parental suggestion as much as reinforcement from another source which the child views as important.

Since, however, it is unlikely that any of these institutions will suddenly change their policies, it is important that methods be worked out to help parents in their all-important ethical responsibilities. The most significant one is the suggestion of education programs to help parents with their tasks. The British Ministry of Health and Welfare is planning a program to help parents rear their children mentally as well as physically. Much may soon be learned from it.

If Wright is correct in the summary of studies noted earlier, all three of these family failures could be corrected, at least in part, if parents were informed about what they are doing wrong. The neurotic delinquent's parents could be shown how to reduce the pressure.

The aggressive delinquent's parents could learn some of the disadvantages of being punitive and erratic. The pseudo-delinquent's parents are harder to reach, for the father is often absent, but such parents as are available could learn something about being friendly with their children.

If the family is disorganized because of absence of a parent or because of a pathological parent, other methods than working with parents must be devised. Perhaps the children of such families should be placed in foster homes more frequently than is now the case. The recommendations regarding improvement of conditions in poorer areas are also likely to reduce the number of such disorganized homes.

It is easy to imagine programs which could help parents with their task of ethical instruction. Television programs which show parents how to combine love with firmness in dealing with their children could easily be developed. Various methods of setting good ethical examples can be portrayed. Readings could be used in high school texts to indicate to students (who are only a few years from parenthood) what their instructional responsibilities are.

Part of helping parents do their jobs might be a deliberate parental reenforcement. This can be done with father and son banquets of various organizations, and by bringing parents into some positions of importance in recreational and school programs. The Russians in their ethical teachings try to develop the child's sense of responsibility to his parents. Our parent-teacher associations work in this direction, but one suspects that they build up the teacher more than the parent; perhaps the direction could be somewhat changed.

Bearing in mind that the greatest burden of delinquency comes in the lower economic brackets, special efforts should be made to help poor parents rear their children. Welfare requirements which place a premium on a father's deserting his family should be changed. A job program which would underwrite income and give self-respect to fathers of poor families might be very helpful.

Summary

In summary, this chapter has noted real strengths of the family as a social institution, its apparent continuity, its influence over children's opinions, its importance in the early stages of moral development according to Bull, and in its easy relationship with outside forces as noted by Erikson. There are also substantial weaknesses: the problem of the immigrant parents, the weakness of the home of low-socio-economic status, the danger of frustrating moralization described by Piaget, the ethical ignorance of many parents, the failure of all classes of families to see the ethical problems of today, the special problem of the black family, the effect of outside employment on the time of mothers, and the changes from extended to nuclear family forces by immigration into our urbanized, industrialized society.

There seem to be important steps which can be taken to help the family in its task of moral education. These include education of parents in methods of rearing children and support of parents by social institutions. The most important help would be greater ethical education in other parts of society.

— 8 —

Gang Leader or Eagle Scout?

This chapter reviews the potential of peer groups for ethical instruction: the relationships of peer groups to other institutions of possible ethical instruction such as the school and the family; the destructive possibilities of peer groups; and the constructive possibilities, including a program for better peer-group action.

Potential of Peer Groups

Peer groups—of pre-adolescent, adolescent, and immediate post-adolescent youth—possess an important potential for ethical or anti-ethical education. The easy movement of people in an urbanized, industrialized society, which handicaps the family, is little problem to youthful peer groups, which can speedily adjust themselves to new faces and new surroundings. The constitutional and political brakes set by society upon ethical instruction in the public schools do not operate directly on peer groups, nor are these groups limited by the intellectual problems of the church. If leaders of such groups have a message to transmit to their members, the group is an effective and flexible means of communication.

Writers on the subject of peer groups generally support this broad view of the group's potential. It is probably more important in the overall socialization process of lower class than of middle class children, and of boys more than of girls.[1]

While the evidence is not conclusive, it has been postulated that American peer groups are more influential than those in some other countries. In part, Hsu, Watrous, and Lord attributed behavioral differences of Chinese-American youths in Hawaii and American youths in Chicago to the likelihood that American youths were far

131

more under the tyranny of their peers than were their Chinese-American counterparts. Differences between Mexican and American children have been interpreted in a similar fashion by Maslow and Diaz-Guerrero, who see the Mexican child as learning to accept adult values more readily because he lives far more in the family and less in a peer society than does the American child.[2] This may be because society in the United States is more urbanized and hence more subject to peer group influences.

Adolescent peer groups constitute a society with a strongly institutionalized normative culture. The norms are related to the general value structure of a larger society, yet are differentiated. Peer influence is experienced in many realms: occupation, status aspirations, educational achievements and goals, morality, friendship, and courtship, to name just a few. Such groups can represent extremes, from those destined for "high" occupational status to those that reinforce analogous "low" expectations of their members—this extreme being the delinquent gang.

If the forces of the peer group could be used for instruction in ethics, the United States would make rapid strides toward better standards. Unfortunately, peer groups are probably more of a liability than an asset under present conditions.

Relationship of Peer Groups to Other Ethical Forces

In our rapidly changing society, the relative strength of peer groups in contrast to other means of ethical instruction seems to be strengthening. Ausubel states, "it is mostly in heterogeneous urban cultures that values during preadolescence (and especially adolescence) tend to acquire a wider base and peers tend to replace parents as interpreters and enforcers of the moral code."[3]

Parsons and White distinguish two main types of peer group: one which stresses youth culture values of popularity and friendliness, playing down studentship and achievement, and a second which gives almost equal value to both sets at once. They consider this second type of orientation as a direct point of articulation between the youth culture values on the one hand and those of adult society on the other. Hence, the values of the peer group are definitely differentiated from those predominant in the larger society, particularly in the occupational system, but are sufficiently in contact with those values so that the degree of divergence is consistent with the conception of a differentiated subsystem.[4] The thesis of these authors is that the peer group assumes a place complementary to the school and the family in the transmission of values to adolescents. Complementary evidently implies relative equality rather than similitude—the family may transmit one type of values, the peers another.

While Parsons and White deal primarily with pre-college youth, campus uprisings from 1968 to 1971 might indicate a superordinate role for peer groups of college age. Nevertheless, there is room for considerable divergence among college-age populations, particularly when the contrast is made between college and non-college boys. The environment of the rural or far-from-home residential college has been shown to produce peer groups different in form from those of the urban commuter college where the student is likely to remain under the influence of parental and secondary school norms.

Several studies have compared peer/parental/school influences on adolescent decision-making. Larson found that adolescents favored parent-compliant options in current-oriented situations.[5] However, Brittain's finding—that situations invoking future aspirations or school achievement produced parent-favored decisions, whereas those dealing with status-norms and identity issues produced peer-oriented choices—disagrees with Larson's conclusions.[6] Analyzing a sample of girls in a small southern city high school, Brittain found that moral items—like whether to tell the truth about which of two boys damaged school property and which of the two damaged public property—were parent-compliant items. "Choices tended to be parent-compliant when they were perceived to be important in the eyes of both peers and parents, and, conversely, to be peer-compliant when perceived as relatively unimportant in the eyes of both peers and parents."[7]

Peer groups evidently have some role in political socialization for civic values, although the evidence seems to indicate that the family and the school are more important in this field. Hyman notes that peer groups become more important in socialization as the child grows older and that "peer-oriented" youth are less interested in political socialization than are parent-oriented youth.[8] Using comparable data on Jamaican and Detroit school youth, Kenneth Langton relates peer group to social class influence: peer group influence does perpetuate the viewpoint of the child's social class background, but there is some evidence that if a child of lower socioeconomic status attends school with those from diverse social classes he is more likely to be "politicized"—more democratic, more supportive of civil liberties, more likely to vote, and more economically conservative.[9]

Bronfenbrenner, in 1970, reports a trend among American youth to spend slightly more time with peers and within schools than with their parents. Peer-oriented youngsters were found to be more influenced by a *lack* of attention and concern at home than by the attractiveness of the peer group. In general, these children held negative views of themselves and of the peer group as well as expressing a dim view of their own future. Their parents were rated as lower than those of adult-oriented children, both in expression of affection and support, and in the exercise of discipline and control. Also, such peer-oriented children were found to engage in more anti-social behavior, such as doing something illegal—lying, teasing, or playing hooky. Hence, the peer-oriented child is more a product of parental disregard than of attraction of the peer group—he turns to age mates less by choice than by default.[10]

This viewpoint is confirmed and strengthened by Bowerman and Kinch, who consider orientation as related to adjustment within the family; e.g., "A lowered orientation toward the family during adolescence is not inevitable but takes place only when a poor adjustment is made to members of the family."[11] These authors investigated students' "norm orientation" by asking them whose ideas were most like their own when it came to decisions of right and wrong, what things were fun to do, the importance of school, and what they would do if one group wanted them to do something of which the other did not approve. In the sample of fourth to tenth graders, the eighth grade represents a turning point—before that parents were the norm (moral) advisors.[12] One conclusion we may reach from these studies as well as from that of Devereux is that peer influence, contrasted with parental influence, is inversely related to parental warmth and support. Hence, it was found that British and American children who joined gangs came from homes which were either highly punitive or highly permissive.[13]

In general, a child's susceptibility to delinquency is highly dependent on the self-image and self-esteem anchored in the home, and
subsequently in the school environment. A child from an unstable
home, or one at odds with his parents, is likely to be assimilated into
a group of peers who become his *primary* reference point. Since his
disposition is less than friendly, socially-acceptable peer groups will
not court his membership. If the neighborhood is one where opportunities for deviant behavior are widespread, he is more likely to join
a delinquent peer group and to engage in anti-social activities such as
destruction of property, gambling, theft, and the like.

Even within a multi-class neighborhood, social level plays a key
role in the differential impact of the peer group. Lower class parents
exercise less control and supervision over their children's outside
activities; middle class parents are said to emphasize internal moral
codes in contrast to the lower class—a fact which implies the availability of lower class youth to external influences.[14]

Judging from this wide variety of evidence, peer groups are equal
in importance to the school or to the home as a source of ethical
instruction, and could become more influential. The rise of the youth
culture in the late 1960s and early 1970s increased the relative
potential of the peer group in the views of many observers.

Destructive Peer Groups

Unfortunately, the role of the peer group is far more important in
delinquency than it is in political socialization. Most of the major
theories of juvenile delinquency reviewed in Chapter Three involve
some degree of peer group participation. The group's increased
influence may be attributed to the breakdown of family and of
religious ties, with the resultant moral and emotional vacuum being
filled by television and by the peer group.

According to Coleman, adolescents are cut off from adult society
today probably more than ever before. While still oriented to fulfilling parental desires, they look very much to peers for approval.
Hence, "society has within its midst a set of small teen-age
societies, which focus teen-age interests and attitudes on things far
removed from adult responsibilities, and which may develop stan-

dards that lead away from those goals established by the larger society."[15]

Theories of delinquency in general refer to family, to social class, to peer group, to school, and to personality variables, with the first three receiving greatest attention. As noted in Chapter Three, the works of Albert Cohen, Richard Cloward, and Lloyd Ohlin argue that although nearly all youth internalize the goals of educational attainment and of subsequent financial-occupational success, not all have equal opportunities or are equally equipped to reach these goals. Lower class youth are at a particular disadvantage because of lack of access to educational opportunities and because adverse home experiences make it difficult to measure up to "middle class" standards of conduct and performance.[16]

While the theories of Walter Miller, Larry Karacki, and Jackson Toby assume a divergent position and refer to different youth populations, they agree on the point that some youth become delinquent because of a basic lack of commitment to conventional middle class norms and values.[17] Miller's view of a distinctive lower class cultural pattern which negates such middle class values as scholastic and occupational success is at odds with the more widely-held notions of Cloward, Ohlin, and Cohen that lower class youth, at least initially, have such a commitment, and that deviant behavior is produced when access to such attainment is blocked. However, since the two positions refer to different populations, perhaps one should not be declared correct, the other incorrect. Miller's thesis may be applicable to certain ethnic and low-status urban groups, while the Cloward/Ohlin/Cohen view may fit the more numerous working class in urban and other environments.

Lerman's study tends to further support the Cloward/Ohlin thesis. His survey of slum youth, aged from ten to nineteen years, showed that the non-deviant value of school success received greatest support. Attraction to a deviant value begins early, increases at ages twelve to thirteen, and then may persist as a counter-attraction to school and to work. There is greater attraction to deviant values on a peer level than on an individual level; an attraction which appears to be relatively constant for all ages but which does not outrank the attraction of good grades and of the job world. Youths attracted to a deviant value—either past or present—are most likely to select peers who support this orientation. Youths who shared peer values were inclined to believe that most of the people they knew were tempted to break the law. This suggests that peers lend behavioral as well as value support to one another.[18] Membership in deviant gangs demands conformity to values and to behaviors as in other peer groups, yet the values and behaviors here are anti-ethical and anti-social.

We have not been able to secure statistics on the percentage of crime and delinquency which is motivated by peer group pressure. Crime reports do not indicate whether a crime is perpetrated by a group or by an individual. But reports from police forces and from criminologist investigators indicate that gangs are a very significant factor. Such gangs do not function entirely in core city poverty pockets. They also operate in middle class urban areas and sometimes even in rural areas. In many districts gangs may be the source of a large majority of the crimes committed.[19]

While criminologist investigators vary as to the exact mechanism by which the gang takes over, they all agree that this form of peer group activity does override ethical instruction from other sources.

Constructive Peer Groups

The major question left by the host of delinquency studies is what can be done to re-direct the anti-ethical tendencies of most American adolescent peer groups? The peer group need not be a repository of anti-social tendencies. The Soviet Union and, to a lesser extent, Israel use the peer group to foster State-desired values and behaviors.

While not a dictatorship, the Israeli government promotes, to a fair extent, distinct ideological convictions within its youth population. This is especially so in the kibbutz where traditional family relationships have been replaced by a system of peer relationships. Spiro's report on one such kibbutz revealed that adolescents gave greater weight to peer-group influences in the socialization process than to other authority figures. When asked to name those things for which they would be blamed and who would do the blaming, "parents" was the least frequently mentioned response, "the group," the most. "Social irresponsibility" was the response most likely to elicit (peer) group blame.[20] Here, then, is one clear example of the positive uses of peer group pressure.

Such groups are used to foster ideological ethical values in the

Soviet Union as well, but there is neither the choice nor latitude found in Israel. Beginning with the early school years, children are organized to cooperate and compete as groups, not as individuals—hence, a sense of responsibility to a larger entity, which is rewarded by praise and renounced by blame, develops at this time. In this manner the child learns to generalize his responsibility from the classroom group to society at large. And this is a society where public confessions of wrongdoing evoke collective blame. Thus the classroom peer group, with initial guidance from the teacher, is a primary agent of socialization.

Some of the ethical values emphasized in this study (honesty, sense of obligation to society, and respect for law) received scrutiny in a comparative investigation of Soviet and American sixth graders.[21] The peer groups reacted quite differently to such unethical behavior as cheating on a test, denying responsibility for property damage, etc. When told that their friends would know of their actions the American subjects were even more willing to engage in misconduct. Soviet youngsters manifested the opposite tendency.

Bronfenbrenner explains these contrasting results by the differing role of the peer group in both societies. Soviet society creates and compels the group to foster ideologically approved goals and, therefore, the group is an extension of adult values and socialization influences; while in the United States such groups are free from adult control and, in Bronfenbrenner's opinion, outrightly opposed to socially approved values and codes. He supports his case by reference to the comparatively recent American phenomenon of middle class vandalism and juvenile delinquency. Furthermore, the Soviet Union has always regarded "character development" as an integral part of education and the principal agent of this process has not been the family but the peer group, both in and out of school.

Since the Soviet Union does not publish crime statistics, it is impossible to check on the value of their peer group instruction. The frequent newspaper reports of Soviet criminality make us suspect that this instruction is less effective than the individual ethical instruction in the constitutional democracies of northwestern Europe.

The writers are not advocating the introduction of any feature of Soviet life into the United States. Communist repressiveness and totalitarian philosophy are not needed here. We only wish to note that the Soviets have discovered some ways of using the peer group for constructive purposes.

The British Public School (and also many other British schools) has made considerable effort to teach ethics through systems of student administered justice. Prefects in the Sixth Form (senior students) are given authority to administer rules, sometimes even to administer corporal punishment.[22] As in the Russian use of the peer group, the hand of authority was heavy in the prefectoral system. The head master's, or house master's, conferences with the prefects were the place in which ethical ideas were passed on. But the peer group then supported the position very effectively for thousands of future public leaders.

Most American attempts to channel peer groups toward ethically desirable goals have come from voluntary organizations which, in contrast to Russian efforts, reach only a fraction of each age-level peer population. Examples include the Boy Scouts, Boys Clubs, Girl Scouts, Campfire Girls. YMCA, and YWCA.

For example the Boy Scouts of America have in their handbook a Scout's Oath,

> "On my honor
> I will do my best
> To do my duty to God
>   and my country and
> To Obey the Scout Law
> To help other people at all times
> To keep myself physically strong,
>   mentally awake and morally straight."

The Scout Law is that a Scout is,

Trustworthy	Obedient
Loyal	Cheerful
Helpful	Thrifty
Friendly	Brave
Courteous	Clean
Kind	Reverent

The above quotes are, of course, meaningless if they are only printed words and are ignored by scout leaders or fellow scouts. But if they are taken at all seriously, they constitute an improvement over the ethical instruction offered by most public schools and by many churches. They are subject to the charge of being a "bag of virtues" which will in some cases contradict one another. But they do offer a useful ethical arsenal for young men.

Until recently, however, most of these organizations have failed to reach youths in high-delinquency areas. Boys Clubs have always worked in poorer areas and Boy Scouts are now doing so. The government has played a small role in promoting socially-inclined, ethically-oriented peer groups. Ghetto organizations such as HARYOU-ACT and Mobilization for Youth in New York City have developed character-building programs for delinquency-prone youth with varying degrees of success. A sizeable number of groups have been sponsored by police departments, such as the Explorer units which are concerned with crime prevention and may foster positive attitudes toward law enforcement as well as stimulate interest in police work.

Not all of these voluntary units have been completely construc-tive. They face a variety of difficulties so far as ethical instruction is concerned. The Boy Scout or Campfire Girls group may be led by a well-meaning University graduate who has been told in his academic days that "ethics should be reexamined," or more bluntly, "ethics is bad." The leader finds his or her way easier if no real effort is made to inculcate ethical standards, reinforcing his university-learned skepticism on the subject.

Another difficulty is that some leaders view their voluntary group as a mechanism for inculcating their personal views of social reform. Moynihan has indicated that this may be one of the reasons for the failure of some of the War on Poverty's efforts to support local groups.[23]

Numerous writings have looked to recreational and parks department programs as the panacea for anti-ethical delinquent groups, but such programs have yielded very mixed results. In contrast to many of the adult-sponsored, organized programs listed above, the mere existence of some parks and recreational programs has provided the locus for anti-social activities such as gang meetings. Recent thinking indicates that recreation programs will be successful in areas with delinquent peer groups to the extent that they are part of an integrated community approach to the problem, one which involves frequent consultation among such groups as police officers, social workers, and neighborhood organizations, and which manifests a broadened perspective of recreation to incorporate job training and placement, health services, and the like.[24]

A Program for Peer Groups in America

In noting the interrelationship of peer groups with other means of ethical instruction, the destructiveness of American peer groups when left to themselves, and the constructiveness of the "administered" peer groups in Russia, Israel, and Britain, one is forced to the conclusion that peer groups will be ethically effective only as they receive initial leadership from persons of strong ethical conviction. The peer group may itself be self-governing and independent as seems to fit our democratic society, but if it does not have mature leadership it may well resemble the activism portrayed by Golding in the *Lord of the Flies*.[25]

It will be a long time before the public school of the poverty area can develop peer group organizations which are of great ethical value. An effort should be made, but not too much can be expected. It would be possible, however, for the voluntary peer group organizations such as Scouts and Boys Clubs to pay more attention to ethics and to make a real effort to include children from poverty areas in their work.

Other suggestions have been made to encourage adolescent peer group support of ethical, not anti-ethical, values. While recognizing the difficulty of implementation in non-dictatorial societies and the fact that such a philosophy or pattern of action has not been the focus of education departments, Coleman sees the school as the institutional base for such endeavors.[26] Such values could be fostered by increased rewards for scholarly activities in juxtaposition to the continual support of sports. Scholastic fairs could be held which would reflect competition between *schools* rather than between individuals. Coleman feels that the "impact upon student motivation would be great due to the fact that the informal social rewards from community and fellow students would reinforce, rather than conflict, with achievement."[27]

Similarly, Bronfenbrenner feels that the schools could experiment with two-pupil teams and group reinforcement, like introducing customs such as applause for correct answers and honoring classmates who otherwise show the greatest progress.[28] In general, he believes it essential to realize the contribution of the school as a whole to the development of the individual child: "If the school as a total community becomes visibly involved in activities focused on the child and his needs, if older children, school organizations, other teachers, school administrators, PTA's—if all these persons and groups in some way participate in the program and publicly support those most actively engaged in the effort, the reinforcing effect increases by geometric proportions."[29]

Going beyond the school, Bronfenbrenner suggests that if the widespread group isolation by race, age, and class is broken down, then peer groups will naturally become more involved with adults—and vice versa—in the tasks and problems of the larger society. Examples include the Head Start Program and Parent and Child Centers. The authors believe that participation in constructive activities on behalf of others will also reduce the growing tendency toward aggressive and anti-social behavior.[30]

Frequently overlooked or underestimated is the model of values and behavior provided by older peers and siblings. These youths may well be more potent socialization agents than are adults, and there is no reason to assume that they would not be interested in fostering ethical values, given the recognition and the means to do so. The desire for participation in their own and in society's future have gone largely unnoticed until recently, but there are an increasing number of examples of innovations along these lines: participation in school policy councils and in drug and ecology programs are a few.

This heightened involvement in community action programs may serve as the means by which socializers and socialized cooperate in formulating goals. It may not cure anti-ethical adolescent behavior, but providing young people with both the occasion and the responsibility for the operation of—and cooperation in—some large social projects affecting their lives might produce significant social change. Since the major institutions affecting adolescent values and behavior—family, school and peers—would all be participants in the process, it could be successful.

The writers, however, believe that peer groups will not make a real contribution to a better ethical life in the United States until members of such groups have themselves received more substantial amounts of ethical education.

9

Ethics K–12, I

Introduction

One of the major mechanisms in any society for inculcation of desired ethical standards is the schools. This is especially true of the United States, which spends more per capita on its public schools than does any other country in the world.

There must be a word of warning. No country can expect its schools to do everything. The support of ethical standards must be a responsibility of the family, the church, the media of communication, and the state as well as the schools.

Some people maintain that schools have no responsibility in the field of ethics. This position is historically wrong, oblivious of foreign experience, and pedagogically impossible. American schools have vastly reduced their emphasis on ethics in this century but have never formally renounced it. In the nineteenth century it was a major reason for existence. Ethics are clearly part of the school programs of all modern democracies into which the writers have inquired—a list which includes England, France, West Germany, Switzerland, the Scandinavian countries, the Low Countries, Canada, Australia, and two communist countries, Russia and China. Finally, it is impossible to conceive of a school in which some ethics is not taught. Telling the truth, some degree of obedience, the absence of violence, and respect for one's fellows are qualities as essential to the conduct of a school as they are to other parts of society.

This chapter will discuss the history of ethics in American public schools and the present status of ethical instruction. The following chapter will indicate that ethics is taught elsewhere and how it can be taught.

History of Education in Ethics

American schools, public and private, were deeply concerned
with ethics in most of the last century. Leading educators spoke of
moral education as their primary purpose. Readers were filled with
literary quotations of a moral nature. In liberal arts colleges, the
President gave a course in moral education to the Senior Class.
There could be little doubt that character development (with its then
almost universal bedfellow, religion) was a primary purpose of
education.

As Chapter One has indicated, several studies clearly show the
process of elimination of ethics from public school readers which
has occurred in the last quarter of the nineteenth and in the twentieth
centuries, and reasons for this change were discussed. This chapter
will develop more fully one of the most potent of them: the pedagogy
of teaching ethics as developed by John Dewey.

If the reader has any doubt about the studies of the elimination of
ethics, he can easily check for himself by buying one or two
McGuffey's Readers (reprints are now available in larger
bookstores or may be purchased from American Book Company)
and by comparing them with the required readers for the same grade
in his own state. He will find that stories involving individual moral
obligations have been replaced by stories which tell the child how to
get along with his group.

What accounts for this tremendous change in the materials of
American education? There are no exact answers to a problem of
intellectual history like this, but we will venture a few suggestions.

The hypothesis which seems most important is that moral
education went out with religion. As the United States expanded,
there was a greater diversity of religious groups. Americans (like
other peoples) grew more skeptical of sectarianism, and there was
constant criticism of any form of religion taught in the schools. It
became probable that the teaching of religion would disappear from
the public schools as the Supreme Court broadened its interpretation of the Constitutional provisions against relationships between
church and state. Finally, in the 1920s, Supreme Court decisions
effectively removed most religious teaching from the schools.

Many readers who think of ethics as separable from religion will wonder why they, too, should have been discarded. The question is a reasonable one. Perhaps the most accurate answer is that ethics, which had been tied to religion for two thousand years or more, could not be suddenly separated from it. Walter Lippmann earlier commented on the same problem, but he also threw out the moral baby with the religious bathwater:

> Now the very thing which made moral wisdom convincing to our ancestors makes it unconvincing to modern men. We do not live in a patriarchal society. We do not live in a world which disposes us to a belief in theocratic government, and therefore, insofar as moral wisdom is entangled with the premises of theocracy, it is unreal to us. The very thing which gave authority to moral insight for our forefathers obscures moral insight for us. They lived in the kind of world which predisposed them to practice virtue if it came to them as a divine commandment. A thoroughly modernized young man today distrusts moral wisdom precisely because it is commanded.[1]

As a substitute for theocratic sanctions, Lippmann advocated "the insight of high religion into the value of disinterestedness."[2]

The student of intellectual and cultural history of nineteenth-century America knows that efforts were made to divorce public school education from narrow denominational ties. Father Neil McCluskey has written a penetrating study of three major figures in public education who took positions on this controversy. Horace Mann, Secretary of the Massachusetts Board of Education from 1837 to 1849, tried to advocate a "non-denominational" Protestant Christianity for the schools, but found himself assailed by denominational leaders because his teachings were judged to be too broad. Dr. William T. Harris, Superintendent of Schools in St. Louis from 1867 to 1879 and later U.S. Commissioner of Education, advocated the teaching of morals based upon the "celestial virtues" in schools where no denominational religion was allowed. Harris was frequently criticized as an "atheist, deist, freethinker, agnostic, and skeptic."[3]

The third educational leader discussed by McCluskey, John Dewey, succeeded in setting the pattern of moral education which eventually prevailed. The pattern varied in different schools, but the general effect was that morals should be learned as a part of the pupil's experience in the school. Dewey's effect on American schools was great enough to warrant separate analysis.

Dewey's philosophy left no room for absolute moral standards on scientific grounds. "The supposed fact that morals demand immutable extra-temporal principles, standards, norms, ends, as the only assured protection against moral chaos can, however, no longer appeal to natural science for its support, nor expect to justify by science its exemption of morals (in practice and in theory) from considerations of time and place—that is, from processes of change."[4]

In addition to rejecting absolute values, Dewey rejected any authoritative pedagogy. Education, according to him, was "a continuous reconstruction of experience in which there was a development of immature experience towards experience funded with the skills and habit of intelligence."[5]

Dewey was never an enemy of morals. He wrote two books and many articles dealing primarily with the subject and discussed moral problems in many other publications. In his most famous, most influential, and most widely-published book, *Democracy and Education*, he objected strenuously to separate moral education, and thought all education led to morality.

> Moral education in school is practically hopeless when we set up the development of character as a supreme end, and at the same time treat the acquiring of knowledge and the development of understanding, which of necessity occupy the chief part of school time, as having nothing to do with character. On such a basis, moral education is inevitably reduced to some kind of catechetical instruction, or lessons about morals. . . .
>
> A narrow and moralistic view of morals is responsible for the failure to recognize that all the aims and values which are desirable in education are themselves moral. Discipline, natural development, culture, social efficiency, are moral traits—marks of a person who is a worthy member of that society which it is the business of education to further.[6]

Democracy and Education has a number of references to ethics. Dewey's chapter on "Theories of Morals" begins with a strong favorable statement: "It is a commonplace of educational theory that the establishing of character is a comprehensive aim of school instruction and discipline."[7] However, this is immediately qualified by a warning against moral education by itself: "Hence it is important that we should be on our guard against a conception of the relations of intelligence to character which hampers the realization of the aim, and on the look-out for the conditions which have to be provided in order that the aim may be successfully acted upon."[8]

In discussing the goals of education, he tries to avoid the "depreciatory estimate of the masses characteristic of an aristocratic community. . . . But if democracy has a moral and ideal meaning, it is that a social return be demanded from all and that opportunity for development of distinctive capacities be afforded all."[9] Dewey believed that a democracy must develop its own values through the experience of all students.

Writing of history, he concludes that "the great heroes who have advanced human destiny" are not the politicians, generals, and diplomats, but the scientists, inventors, artists, and poets. Through them one can understand the advance of humanity during the course of history. "Pursued in this fashion, history would most naturally become of ethical value in teaching. Intelligent insight into present forms of associated life is necessary for a character whose morality is more than colorless innocence."[10] However, historical examples are not a useful means of teaching ethics:

> The use of history for cultivating a socialized intelligence constitutes its moral significance. It is possible to employ it as a kind of reservoir of anecdotes to be drawn on to inculcate special moral lessons on this virtue or that vice. But such teaching is not so much an ethical use of history as it is an effort to create moral impressions by means of more or less authentic material. At best, it produces a temporary emotional glow; at worst, callous indifference to moralizing.[11]

In his chapter on educational values, Dewey objects to "moral goods" like honesty, amiability, perseverance, loyalty, and the Golden Rule in morals: "These principles are so important as standards of judging the worth of new experiences that parents and instructors are always tending to teach them directly to the young. They overlook the danger that standards so taught will be merely symbolic; that is, largely conventional and verbal. In reality, working as distinct from professed standards depends upon what an individual has himself specifically appreciated to be deeply significant in concrete situations."[12] The essence of his thought on teaching ethics is that it cannot be taught directly, but can be learned only in doing other things.

On the importance of work interests, Dewey writes: "Take these things out of the present social life, and see how little would remain—and this not only on the material side, but as regards intellectual, aesthetic and moral activities, for these are largely and necessarily bound up with occupations."[13]

The industrial history of mankind "is an ethical record as well; the account of the conditions which men have patiently wrought out to serve their ends."[14] This thought—that study of industrial history might have moral purposes—leads us to the one class of situation in which he advocates teaching ethics by illustrative example:

> On the more direct social side, American history (especially that of the period of colonization) is selected as furnishing a typical example of patience, courage, ingenuity, and continual judgment in adapting means to ends, even in the face of great hazard and obstacle; while the material itself is so definite, vivid and human as to come directly within the range of the child's representative and constructive imagination and thus becomes, vicariously at least, a part of his own expanding consciousness.[15]

In Chapters One and Five this book has referred to the importance of developing habits of ethical action and to Dewey's heavy stress on habits, instincts, and impulses in *Human Nature and Conduct* (1922). The pedagogical techniques developed in Dewey's *Democracy and Education* (1916) are generally consistent with the emphases later developed in *Human Nature and Conduct*. Students were not to be taught "principles," which are likely to become "merely symbolic," but were to develop through their studies "open-mindedness, single-mindedness, sincerity, breadth of outlook, thoroughness, assumption of responsibility, for developing the consequences of ideas." The difficulty Dewey most wished to avoid was that "The habit of identifying moral characteristics with external conformity to authoritative prescriptions may lead us to ignore the ethical value of these intellectual attitudes, but the same habit tends to reduce morals to a dead and machine-like routine."[16]

The great strength of Dewey's position was that he wanted to dispense with authoritarianism and help moral education to become a part of the habits of individual Americans. The ethical decision was to be determined by the individual's judgment of consequences, in a fashion appropriate to democracy. The pedagogical weakness was that his method ruled out study of the history of ethics—a history which included many concepts he would have regarded as artificial, but which also included much useful human development of ethical standards.

Dewey's influence on ethical education in the United States was profound for a half century. Almost a dozen books on character and moral education were published from 1900 to the 1960s,[17] and his ideas appeared in nearly all of those published after the appearance of *Democracy and Education*. Most were written by professors of education whose suggestions sometimes are penetrating, and sometimes are pedagogical devices. Nevertheless, the existence of this literature indicates that there has been support in schools of education for some kind of ethical training. The books, most of which are designed for teachers, also indicate a continuing interest in ethical education in the schools, and a few of the suggestions made are included herewith.

A number of them discuss "direct moral teaching" versus indirect teaching—"direct" teaching apparently meaning lectures or a teacher-led discussion of ethical responsibilities, or the use of slogans, oaths, or pledges.[18] In one poll in the 1920s, 45 percent of school superintendents were in favor of "direct" teaching. It probably would not have been approved by Dewey.

There is considerable exposition of the use of classroom or school activities to help develop character, using some ingenuity in the devising of methods. Few of the writers note frankly the sporadic and uncertain nature of this approach, and that it will not reach many non-activity students.

A book by Hartford[19] gives several examples of experimentation in teaching ethics by individual schools or school districts in Kentucky. They are characterized as "community," "supervisory," or "faculty student" approaches, and were partly social work with students who needed guidance and partly discussion of ethical materials. This variety of approach to education in moral values indicates both the ubiquity of feeling for action and the uncertainty of what action to take.

McKown's *Character Education* reviews many plans in different areas for "citizenship contests," "School Republics," "Knighthood of Youth," and similar arrangements. His summary of the trends in "character education" in Chapter Four sound as if it came directly from John Dewey:

1. A decreasing confidence in the use of formal rules . . . and similar formal material, and an increasing confidence in the utilization of opportunities that afford actual practice.
2. A decreasing emphasis upon sentiment and emotion, and an increasing emphasis upon intelligently arrived at ideals.
3. A decreasing emphasis upon ex cathedra pronouncements, and an increasing emphasis upon an understanding and appreciation of causes and effects.
4. A decreasing emphasis upon personal goodness as a sole aim, and an increasing emphasis upon social responsibility and social responsiveness.
5. In general, a decreasing emphasis upon abstract theory, and an increasing emphasis upon concrete practice.[20]

Charles and Edith Germane published a book on character education in 1929 which seems to emphasize techniques more than basic ethical objectives. Chapter headings include "Subject Matter and Character Building," "The Assignment and Character Building," "Pupil Participation in Self-Government," and "The Home Room Organization." Many of the techniques and suggestions are undoubtedly useful, but like the Hartford and McKown book, the Germane books seems to assume that the teacher knows what character values he is teaching.[21]

A more thoughtful book on *Education for Moral Growth* (1928) by Henry Neumann of the Ethical Culture School, considers the development of ethical values in various parts of education. He has a review of education in classes. some of which he does not view as necessary for ethics. A possible criticism is that Neumann did not adequately recognize the importance of basic individual ethical obligations.

Perhaps Neumann's greatest contribution is his appraisal of "the pragmatist criticism." He concludes that Instrumentalism (Pragmatism or Deweyism) "has performed excellent service in showing the folly of choosing school work without regard to student and group activities. Its service, however, has been greater in exposing the harm done by the traditional schooling than in pointing to concrete, positive ends."[22]

Analysis of the suggestions in the Hartford, McKown, and Germane books leads to a feeling that these books contain more techniques than character education. Well-intended social activities were developed instead of consideration of individual ethical obligations. Few people apparently realized that the social activities were only transitory and that the habits developed by character education were needed for a lifetime. The understandable reaction against preaching a rigid moral code had become an excuse for teaching no ethics at all, and the tendency of educators to concentrate on techniques rather than basic ideas compounded the felony. The stage was set for the amoral education of many American schools today.

Present Status of Ethical Instruction

A review of ethical instruction in United States schools is not an easy task. Some professors of education assured our staff that ethical instruction is not a responsibility of the schools; others believed that it was adequately done. Still others talked with pride about an instruction in "values" which includes few or no ethical problems.

In an effort to obtain a more objective view of the situation, the Salvatori Center staff made three surveys—two of them in California, which is the most populous state and includes about one-tenth of the population. First, a questionnaire was sent to a sample of teachers in "Elementary Reading-Literature" and "Secondary Social Studies" throughout the state (approximately equal groups). Second, the most widely-used fifth grade readers and high school social studies texts in California were examined. Third, a letter of inquiry was sent to all State Superintendents of Public Instruction.

Inquiry of the State Departments of Education produced varied results. A number of states require moral education in the public schools by state law, but often they make little or no effort to follow up on this requirement. Other states report no administrative action.

Certain states, however, are much more active. Kentucky issued a bulletin on "Moral and Spiritual Education in Kentucky" in 1958, containing rather general articles on broadly-defined values. Massachusetts has a few "values" courses. California issued a state report urging the teaching of moral and religious values.

A real desire of some school authorities to teach ethical values is indicated, but there is not much evidence that these studies have altered the trend against inclusion of ethical materials in school textbooks or the tendency of teachers to avoid this unpopular subject. The conclusion drawn from the letter survey is that the schools have not dropped moral values completely, but that they pay little attention to them.

The California school questionnaire was answered by 117 teachers from thirteen school districts, well distributed as to geographical sections of the state, racial groups, and family income.

Questioned about their own instruction in ethics, 43 percent of the teachers had taken college courses dealing with ethics, and 25 percent had followed graduate or workshop programs; 55 percent had had no ethics work. Social science courses on both undergraduate and graduate levels were counted by the teachers as courses in ethics, so it is a fair assumption that much of the ethics studied was social and not individual. When asked whether they considered their ethical training to have been adequate, 31 percent replied in the negative and a significant 45 percent did not answer the question. From these data it is probably fair to infer that only a small proportion of California teachers—perhaps 25 percent—are equipped to teach the ethics of individual responsibility.

On questions regarding the teachers' knowledge of available literature, 23 percent had used Piaget, who himself has no developed theory of ethical education. Only very small percentages had used Kohlberg, Raths, or Simon, the most important writers in the cognitive developmental approach, and the values approach to teaching ethics.

Some of the points of opposition to teaching ethics were smaller than we had anticipated. Only one percent of the teachers believed that the connection of ethics with religion was an argument against teaching ethics in schools. Teachers estimated the proportion of parents, principals, and students opposed to ethical teaching at 15 percent or less.

The large majority, 73 percent of teachers, believed that parents had the predominant responsibility for education in ethics. However, only 46 percent believed that parents actually were teaching the subject.

How was ethics taught? Sixty-one percent of the teachers stated that they cover it indirectly; 31 percent choose direct procedures. Sixty-eight percent knew of no textbook covering ethics.

When asked where the initiative for ethical instruction should lie, 72 percent of the teachers answered that it should be with them. This readiness to assume responsibility is commendable but difficult to reconcile with previously cited inadequate preparation of teachers for ethical education.

In answer to the question as to how to teach ethics, almost half (48.6 percent) of the teachers favored open class discussion. Another 13.6 percent favored study of specific cases, and 17 percent the example of the teacher's own conduct. There was thus a substantial majority for discussion of cases or problems; and less than a fifth favored what John Dewey thought was a principal method of teaching ethics—the teacher's example. An English survey reported in 1969 gave opposite results; perhaps because English teachers are more likely to be selected for their effect on the student's character.[23]

A question as to changes in student attitudes resulting from ethical education was checked by half the teachers on the item "cooperation with peers." Such ethical instruction as was available had a major effect in the field of social ethics: 12.6 percent of the teachers found that respect for authority was strengthened.

Summarizing the results of the questionnaire, it is clear that the teachers recognized that the public schools must teach ethics, even though they prefer that families assume the responsibility. A high proportion of these reading and social science teachers have tried to teach ethical awareness in spite of a clearly inadequate preparation for the task.

The school textbook inquiry was limited to fifth grade reading and eleventh and twelfth grade social studies texts. These are more representative than at first seems to be the case. Statewide circulation in California means that at least a tenth of the school children of the nation have an opportunity to use four elementary texts studied here. The two eleventh and twelfth grade texts are, as far as we could tell from various school reports, very widely used in California high schools.

The fifth grade readers were designated for "average," "culturally disadvantaged," and "culturally advantaged" readers. Only a small percentage of the stories for the "average" contained ethical values (13 percent in one reader and none in the second). The "culturally disadvantaged" text contained a few more ethical references (20 percent), unfortunately of low intellectual calibre. The "culturally advantaged" text had 24 percent of items with ethical references which were not central to the story but were not too obscure for a ten-year-old. It is not clear why the culturally advantaged students who need it least should be given more ethics; it is probably accidental.

The social studies texts showed ten out of eighty articles or readings to have some ethical reference. The twelfth grade texts, usually on American government, had a higher ethical content than did the eleventh grade ones, which were usually on American history. Particularly noticeable, however, was the failure of civics texts to discuss individual ethical responsibilities such as that of the citizen to help decrease the amount of murder or other crime.

It is interesting to observe that the fifth grade readers averaged 15 percent of stories with an ethical content; high school social studies had only 10 percent. But 59 percent of the teachers had selected social studies, and only 17 percent had chosen reading, as the best vehicle for ethical presentations.

The writers of the school textbooks are not deliberately ignoring ethics. A few stories or articles are clearly written to bring out ethical points. In some of the history readings the introduction of ethical homilies may have seemed out of place to the writer. In many literary extracts, moral issues might appear to be forced or "old fashioned." However good such rationalization, the fact remains that ethical teaching is largely absent. Perhaps it is fair to conclude that teaching of ethics does not seem to be important to the men and women who prepared these texts.

The lesson to be drawn from both the teacher questionnaire and the analysis of textbooks is that California schools have not organized themselves to do an effective job of teaching ethics, although a substantial majority of their teachers believe that they should be taught.

— 10 —

Ethics K–12, II

Teaching of Ethics in Other Countries

While America has been taking ethics out of its public schools, some of the countries which are comparable in economic and educational levels have been increasing its content in their school programs. The trends in various school systems, including those of the two great Communist countries, will be reviewed, with particular attention paid to Great Britain's new program which is likely to be worthy of study by American educators.

Before reviewing the ethics education programs of the comparable countries, it would be wise to analyze a few obvious speculations. It has been observed that other modern democracies—Britain, France, West Germany, Scandinavia, the Low Countries, Switzerland, Canada, and Australia—almost universally teach ethics in their schools, while the United States does not. That their rates of violent crime and political corruption are much lower than in America is probably true, but such a correlation does not necessarily mean that lack of ethical instruction is the main reason for America's failures. The comparison countries are smaller and more ethically homogeneous than the United States. Many of them have monarchs and established churches which may help to secure national agreement on ethical values. Their law enforcement machinery is more centralized and more honest. The media, especially television, may be less influential than ours.

While these and other factors keep us from concluding that teaching ethics in the schools would bring America up to the ethical level of the comparison countries, the correlation does at least give grounds for careful consideration of the restoration of ethics in our school system. The writers, however, recognize that ethical education in the schools is only one of the programs needed to restore ethical vitality to America.

Most ethical instruction in the northwestern European comparison countries is a part of religious education. This is puzzling, since active church attendance in many of these countries is well below that in the United States. In some nations, like Norway and Sweden, church attendance is less than a tenth of the population, whereas in the United States it is still around 40 percent. One can only guess that in some of these countries the requirement of religious education, including ethics, remains as a matter of tradition. However, it may also be that religious education has been kept in part because of its presumed ethical values. The requirement of religious education dates from 1944 in England and from 1946 in the West German Länder (states), so there obviously have been other than traditional considerations in those nations.

Before proceeding to a country-by-country review, it should be added that the writers are unable to generalize about the values of religious education for ethical training. Conversations with citizens and officials of all the northwestern European countries have yielded divided opinions. Some feel that the religious setting is a handicap to ethical education; others, that it is a help. Britain, Sweden, and Land Hamburg are in the process of adding teaching of non-religious ethics to the teaching of religion which includes ethics. Perhaps it is fair to say that higher crime rates induced by urbanization and industrialization are leading these countries to add more specific ethical values to their existing religious education.

Our nation-by-nation review may well begin with the two great Communist powers. They are not part of our comparison countries. We know little about their crime rates, although we can guess that crime is substantial in the Soviet Union—perhaps higher than in northwestern Europe, perhaps lower than in the United States.

In both countries there are programs of ethical education in the public schools. In both countries the primary effort is to teach "Communist morality" with emphasis on national economic production, national loyalty, and loyalty to communist administrators. But in both countries there is also stress on individual ethical responsibilities and on obligations to one's family.

Delinquency in Russia is in some ways similar to that in the United States. It is greater in urban areas and a large majority of delinquents are school drop-outs or near drop-outs. Excessive use of alcohol is a frequent contributor to the delinquency. In their efforts to control delinquency, the Russians are frequently concerned about schooling and its development of "Communist morality."[1]

The principal book in English on Russian teaching of ethics is Urie Bronfenbrenner's *Two Worlds of Childhood*. He paints a picture (some scholars of Russia view it as much too idealistic a picture) of Russian children learning cooperative ethics. Classes are broken down into sections and each section is responsible for the conduct of its members. The teacher punishes the section for a transgression of one of its members. American educators would probably never accept this method of discipline because of its unfairness to individuals, but they would have little trouble in agreeing with the individual ethical goals of the Russians.

The Russians in recent years have begun to give a course on ethics to all future teachers at the university and at teacher training institutes. Teachers are then responsible to teach ethics in various parts of the school curriculum.[2]

The writers have no detailed knowledge of education in Communist China. However, one book gives a careful discussion and many readings from texts (grades one through five) published in 1957, 1958, 1963, and 1964. The readings are largely "indoctrination," propagandizing for communism, for Chairman Mao, and for the People's Republic of China. There are also a substantial number of readings which are intended to inculcate senses of duty, altruism, honesty, and family loyalty, as well as the collectivist virtues. The proportion of readings instilling such virtues is probably larger than in most American school readers of today.[3]

Shifting from communism to the comparable constitutional democracies, the first country to consider is Sweden. The Church of Sweden (Lutheran) is established and supported by a state tax which is paid by 95 percent of the Swedes, although less than 10 percent attend church services. Swedish schools for many decades have required courses in religious education, which have been carried over from the days when schools were operated by the church. Currently-used courses emphasize Christianity, but include readings in the Jewish religion, in Islam, in Hinduism, in Buddhism, and in "the religions of the natural peoples." Ethical questions are constantly introduced in discussions of religious education, and can be combined with teaching about school, home, and society.

In recent years the Swedes have been concerned about a sharp increase in crime, although the rates are far below those in the United States. A joint committee of the Ministries of Justice and of Education has recommended a program in "law and right" which will be conducted as part of other public school courses. It will not replace religious education in the schools.

In Norway, as in Sweden, religion is taught throughout the school programs as well as in the university. All students who are members of the Norwegian church (over 95 percent) must take the work. The several readers seen by the Salvatori Center staff include a discussion of Christian religions, and the discussion of Christianity at home is very broad and includes social problems, missionary work, and a good deal of ethics. The writings do not seem to be designed to force religious or denominational belief.

Being less industrialized, Norway does not have a crime rate comparable to Sweden's and is not yet planning the extension of ethical instruction which is to be found in Sweden and elsewhere. Officials working on crime problems, however, were not at all sure that the ethical instruction involved in the program on religion was effective in preventing delinquency.

Largely in reaction to Nazi rule, all of the Länder in the West German Bund have programs in religious education. In two visited by Salvatori Center staff members, Hamburg and Bremen, the program is spread through the school years and includes a substantial amount of ethics. Bremen, responding to an increase in crime due to modern urban conditions, has a committee at work on direct education in the subject.

A course on ethics in Bavaria may be taken as an alternate to the required religion course. The outline is a typically thorough German review of all aspects of ethics: man in community with others; man and his personal life; conflicts and their regulation; man in difficult situations; the significance of life in world thought systems; man in society; man in responsibility for the world; authority and discovering oneself; norms and their justification; conscience; sex relations as a ripening process; world beliefs and their consequences; fundamentals of philosophic ethics; freedom and determination; norms and decisions; right and justice; happiness. Readings and discussions are encouraged; in several instances, discussion of cases is recommended.[4]

In both the Low Countries, religion—including ethics—is taught regularly in the public schools. The many Catholic or Protestant schools in Holland determine their own course, but religion and ethics are also taught in government schools. Much the same story is found in Belgium, where the public secondary schools have two hours a week for religion or ethics. The church schools, of course, teach both subjects. An active association of believers in "lay morals" urges parents to register their children in the ethics course rather than that of religion.

With almost as pluralistic a society as the United States, the Canadian provinces have usually managed a substantial amount of religious education. The systems vary according to the province, and religious education is often given by a denominationally-managed school. In Quebec there are two public systems—Catholic schools and Protestant pluralistic schools—each offering programs of religious and moral instruction. Ontario has a number of experimental projects in moral education and widespread courses in religious education. The Newfoundland school systems associate with denominations, each of which teaches religion, including values. In British Columbia religion has been excluded from the public schools by legislation, and there are no formal courses in ethics.[5]

There is variety among the Australian states. Tasmania is developing curriculum models for value education and religion studies. Western Australia has a system by which clergymen may visit schools to offer instruction, and a secondary school course called "Human Relations" which deals in part with ethics.

The British seem to have "muddled" their way through the problems of ethical education rather effectively. Most of their government schools voluntarily taught religion, including ethics, up to World War II, and independent schools frequently had denominational support. Those with Church of England affiliations frequently made church instruction of religious and moral values into one of their basic programs, following the doctrine of Thomas Arnold of Rugby that "Christian development" was the first responsibility of the preparatory school. In 1944, as a result of a long study and perhaps also in part as a reaction against Nazism, Parliament declared religious education to be a requisite, with safeguards of freedom for teachers and students in all schools.

British scholars told us that intellectual winds blow from the west (United States) to the east (Britain), and that some of the American intellectual habit of denigration of individual ethics is to be found on their campuses. Despite these winds, however, the tradition of teacher responsibility for character development in students has remained strong. There has been much discussion, pro and con, of the religious education courses, but they do not seem to be in any immediate danger of abolition. They are based on a program of objectives developed by interdenominational groups established by local school authorities. In recent years such groups have included Sikhs, Buddhists, and Liberal Humanists (a euphemism for agnostics or atheists), as well as Jews, Roman Catholics, members of the Church of England, and other Protestants.

A recent interdenominational conference sponsored by the British Department of Education and Science concluded, among other things: "It is not the business of the religious educator to impose moral concepts upon the pupil, but rather, to help him recognize the moral, social, and religious claims being made upon him by society and—if he accepts the idea—by God."[6] A study made by the Morals Education project found that religious education courses were viewed by most schools as an important method of moral education.[7]

One of the advantages of British religious education requirements may be that they have stimulated constructive discussion on the teaching of moral values among British educators. Granting that religion may bring difficulties with it, the open-mindedness of the British and their concern about the development of character in their students has resulted in thoughtful consideration of religious and ethical teaching.[8]

Not satisfied with the moral by-products of religious education, the Schools Council (an association of local school authorities) established a project on moral education in the secondary schools in 1967—a project located at Oxford for a number of years and now at Cambridge University. The staff developed a series of moral case problems for discussion by secondary school students in the hope that teachers in each school would build cases related to the social environment of that school. A well-planned and well-written handbook on *Moral Education in the Secondary School* has been written.[9] The material has been tried out on 22,000 pupils and seems to be successful in helping students to develop an attitude of concern toward others.

Pupil democracy is an important part of the British Moral Education program. Insofar as pupils can learn morals from their experiences in the conduct of school life, this is considered desirable. John Dewey's principal method of moral education thus secures recognition as a part of moral education in Britain; however, it is not the only method of ethical instruction, as Dewey would have wished.

Two sentences indicate the philosophy of the program: "Our working answer to the question 'What is moral education?' was that all education which helped a child to adopt a considerate style of life, to have respect for others' feelings and interests as well as his own, was moral education. The doctrine was confined to the assertion that a world in which people are treated with consideration for their feelings and interests is preferable to one in which this is not the case."[10]

Moral Education in the Secondary School begins with the viewpoint that boys and girls benefit themselves as well as others if they learn to live a life style which is considerate of others. A Schools Council survey shows that 70 percent of young people expect the school to help them understand what makes an action good or bad. Many psychosomatic disorders could be avoided if we were to educate children "in the considerate side of life," and to meet the challenge of variety in inter-personal behavior. Teachers are bound to form values, whether or not they try; what they do is more important than what they say.

The Schools Council found that children should be trained to help choose and construct the society in which they want to live. A program of moral education, they discovered, is a coordinating force in the academic program. Effective education is learning to care.

In place of established or personal authority, the program is based on asking questions and studying the answers. In many cases, families had failed to help the students with moral problems. "For example, orders without explanation, criticism without positive suggestions, personal remarks, exhibitions of temper and periods of sustained disapproving silence, inside or outside school, were not regarded as helpful by most secondary children."[11]

Many teachers "regarded moral and social education as a legitimate function of the school," but about half wondered if circumstances permitted them to do more. Existing programs most often mentioned by teachers included school assembly, religious education, the prefect system, team games, the discipline of work, and collaborating on a common task. However, the achievements in moral education of these activities were not clear in the minds of the teachers themselves.

Student surveys of moral education needs were enthusiastically received, and their answers indicated a desire to have persuasion rather than compulsion in determining moral standards. There was special objection to unreasonable punishment. Relations with adults were of great emotional significance to the adolescents. On the basis of these surveys, the Moral Education project concluded that the establishment of a "morality of communication" requires: (1) Reception ability, (2) Interpretative ability, (3) Response ability, and (4) Message ability.[12]

A review of Christian, Kantian, and other theoretical bases of morals concludes that moral education should describe what is meant by "moral," provide us with the means of making moral decisions, be rationally supportable, motivate us to behave morally, and understand that moral behavior sometimes requires making personal decisions which go beyond mere norms of behavior. On the basis of these considerations, the Moral Education project has worked out three types of case studies for class discussion:

> *In Other People's Shoes*—tries to develop the themes of encouraging sensitivity to others and the moral and social consequences of actions.
> *Proving the Rule?*—describes situations set in home, school, or neighborhood involving relationships between groups.
> *What Would You Have Done?*—deals with more complex situations in the modern world.[13]

The format of this new British moral education program seems to be well suited for American needs. It has no religious denominational ties; it is not a "rigid moral code," which seems to scare many people; it provokes student discussion and thought on the subject of ethics.

How Can Ethics Be Taught?

Although ethics are taught in the public schools of other modern countries, one frequently encounters in the United States the statement that ethics cannot be taught. This section will rapidly review the psychoanalytic and social learning theories of teaching ethics, and attention will be paid to cognitive developmental theories of how children acquire ethical habits. The section will then compare several practical ways of teaching ethics.

Psychoanalytic theories of the formation of "conscience" or "character" have already been discussed. Original psychoanalytic theories left almost no room for teaching ethics, but indicated that moral behavior rested on identification with parents and on guilt feelings. More recent psychiatric writing indicates that there may be a place for teaching ethics. Since these recent writings do not go into detail on the teaching methods, no further attention to them is needed here.[14]

The social learning theorists, well represented by Bandura and Walters, focus on the manner of moral learning. The child identifies with models who promote moral, amoral, or immoral instruction. To a large extent, internalization of moral behavior results from identification and the disciplinary method employed by the parents. A child with harshly punitive parents is unlikely to internalize or value moral behavior, yet he may act in accord with such values out of fear of external sanctions.[15]

The social learning theory overlaps with the cognitive developmental theory soon to be discussed, and to some extent with the psychoanalytic theory. Social learning is clearly much more useful for the majority of children who learn ethics from their parents than for those who, because of parental inadequacies, must learn from more formal instructional methods. Unlike the psychoanalytic theory, it does not exclude other ideas. Further discussion of it is not needed in this chapter, but some use of it appears in the chapters on family and on peer groups.

The third approach to learning is called "cognitive developmental." Here the ability to learn is the salient factor; moral learning depends on the level of development of the thought process which tends to be correlated with age. Two psychologist-educators have been largely responsible for growth in this field—Jean Piaget and Lawrence Kohlberg.[16]

According to Piaget, cultural factors—such as norms, child-rearing, and a minimal amount of parental nurturance—affect the choice of values by children at similar stages of development as well as the rate at which the child progresses. Despite recognition of culture, environment, and peers, Piaget nevertheless gives primacy to the cognitive process, i.e. whether the child imbibes moral values from models depends on his level of development and on his concomitant ability to understand the information. A child is not expected to demonstrate moral behavior until he is able to comprehend the moral lesson.

The dividing point between Piaget's two principal stages occurs at age seven. Prior to that time the child judges an immoral act by the amount of damage and subsequent punishment meted out by adult authority. For example, in stage one a child considered the accidental breaking of a number of cups more reprehensible than a lie that produces no visible consequences. After age seven, the morally developed judge an act not by the amount of damage but by the intent of the actor. Punishment is now meted out by the conscience through guilt feelings.

As stated above, this progression toward moral autonomy is presumed to be linear except where parents or a political system intervene to exert extreme coercion. Such coercion denies the experience of mutual interchange, and the individual is dominated by fear and dependence, which is the opposite of autonomy.

A distinguishing characteristic of moral autonomy is the individual's development of empathy—an ability to see oneself in the role of others. Prior to this stage the child assumes that his perspective is *the* perspective, i.e., that everyone's view of the event is the same as his; he also is unable to distinguish objective and subjective aspects of a situation. Piaget believes that ethics can be taught in school, but inclines towards cooperative activities as the mechanism.[17]

Kohlberg's Cognitive-Developmental Approach

Professor Lawrence Kohlberg of Harvard and a series of collaborators have been working for almost two decades on means of testing students' development of ethical awareness. Kohlberg believes that test findings indicate six stages of human ethical awareness; that movement through them is invariant; and that the direction (not the speed) of movement is the same in different countries. Kohlberg views himself as following Piaget and

ultimately John Dewey. The writers add the comment that if
Kohlberg follows Dewey, it is the Dewey of earlier writings, not of
Democracy and Education or *The School and Society.*

Kohlberg's six stages, briefly outlined, are:

Stage 1. Action is motivated by avoidance of punishment, and
"conscience" is a non-rational fear of punishment.

Stage 2. Action is motivated by desire for reward or benefit.
Possible guilt reactions are ignored and punishment viewed in a
pragmatic manner.

Stage 3. Action is motivated by anticipation of disapproval of
others, actual or imagined hypothetical.

Stage 4. Action is motivated by anticipation of dishonor, that is,
institutionalized blame for failure of duty, and by guilt over concrete
harm done to others.

Stage 5. Action is motivated by concern about maintaining
respect of equals and of the community (assuming their respect is
based on reason rather than emotions). Concern about own
self-respect, that is, to avoid judging self as irrational, inconsistent,
non-purposeful.

Stage 6. Action is motivated by concern about self-
condemnation for violating one's own principles. (Differentiates
between community respect and self-respect). Differentiates
between self-respect for generally achieving rationality and self-
respect for maintaining moral principles.[18]

The progress of a student through the stages of cognitive
development can be more or less objectively tested by Kohlberg's
technique of presentation of simple cases, such as this one:

In Europe, a woman was near death from a very bad disease, a special
kind of cancer. There was one drug that the doctors thought might
save her. It was a form of radium that a druggist was charging ten
times what the drug cost him to make. He paid $200 for the radium and
charged $2,000 for a small dose of the drug. The sick woman's
husband, Heinz, went to everyone he knew to borrow the money, but
he could only get together about $1,000 which is half of what it cost.
He told the druggist that his wife was dying, and asked him to sell it
cheaper or let him pay later. But the druggist said, "No, I discovered
the drug and I'm going to make money from it." So Heinz got
desperate and broke into the man's store to steal the drug for his wife.

Kohlberg then asks: "Should the husband have done that? Why?"[19] The student is then asked to support his decision with reasoning which places the student in one of the six stages. The definition of each of the six stages becomes the decision of Kohlberg and his colleagues. They have made substantial efforts to base the stages on student reactions and on philosophical inquiry, but the decision about each of the stages is still more or less arbitrary.

A possible difficulty is that a student may be excluded from Kohlberg's Stage Six as a result of expressing a concern about maintaining respect for the community (as in Stage Five) or a respect for law and order (as in Stage Four). A very idealistic person might be graded down in Kohlberg's classification because his idealism included community respect and law and order as values of great and continuing importance. There, indeed, may be times in which those values rank ahead of philosophic consideration of the lives or welfare of particular individuals.

Kohlberg's cognitive-developmental theory clearly gives opportunity for the teaching of ethics. Kohlberg has himself taught Sunday School classes, both Christian and Jewish, with this method. He has evidence that teaching does advance classes through the various stages of ethical development.

The question to be asked about the Kohlberg technique is whether or not an advance in the stages of the Kohlberg scheme represents genuine progress in the development of character. Some authors have shown a linkage between the two, as well as the fact that Kohlberg's moral stages are tied in with other aspects of moral behavior, e.g. yielding to temptation in experimental tests was correlated with immature moral insight.[20]

However, there can be little doubt that the cognitive development group of psychologists have evidence which leads them to believe that ethics can be taught. Kohlberg's belief is stronger than Piaget's, but both believe in the possibility of ethical teaching.

Although Kohlberg is a professor in the Harvard School of Education, his work is not generally known by professional educators. This may be due to his emphasis on the philosophical justification and the psychological tests of objectivity to the exclusion of the preparation of teaching materials which classroom teachers could employ. The time is ripe for production of Kohlberg's materials in a form usable within the schools.

Methods of Teaching Ethics

Case Studies Approach

Shifting from psychological schools to specific methods of teaching ethics, we find several important means. Least dogmatic is the discussion of cases involving ethical questions. Jesus gave some good examples of it in the New Testament parables. He forced no conclusions on the crowd who wanted to stone to death the woman taken in adultery, but He certainly forced some thinking on the part of responsible members within the group.

The ambitious British Moral Education program referred to earlier is based entirely on class discussion of ethical problems, preferably cases which are drawn out of the environment surrounding the school. This program has been criticized as lacking a philosophical or religious basis, but it must stir some students to think about ethical problems. An American counterpart of it would raise no constitutional and very few political objections—an important consideration for a school administrator whose school must live in its community.

Moral Education in the Secondary School covers individual and social ethics, both pointing toward a greater concern for the feelings of others. Two examples indicate the effort to keep the cases close to home:

You belong to a crowd of "hard men" in your class who are always teasing others in the school about something or other—for being studious, for being fat and for many other things. One day when you are absent from school sick, your younger brother comes home and tells you that he was teased by them during a lunch-break.
What would you do?
How would your action affect everyone involved—yourself, your brother, the other hard men, others in the school?

You have come up from the country to live in the city: you feel strange among the boys in your class. A group of the noisier ones invite you at lunch-time to lift chocolates from a shop while they distract the shopkeeper's attention.
What would you do?
What would happen next?
Imagine that you are one of the group of noisy boys.
Explain why you have selected the new boy. Are you being fair?[21]

Professor Kohlberg's elaborate use of case studies for ethical instruction has been described. Other suggestions about the case studies approach include Miller's report on an experiment in the Tulsa public schools where law case materials were used for elementary and secondary schools. Students found the work interesting, the time well spent and productive of ideas which might be helpful in later life and worthy of more time. A high fraction of elementary children felt "more friendly" to the law and to the courts as a result, although the percentage of such attitudes was much lower in junior and senior high schools. The thirteen teachers who were involved evaluated the results favorably and thought the studies would be beneficial to the pupils as adults. Ten of the thirteen believed that the cases covered material which had been omitted in home training of many students. Eleven thought their students had shown increased ethical understanding.[22]

Several books published about "values" involve discussion of cases. They use the term "values" in the broad sense employed by sociologists. Personal ambition or the lack of it, aesthetic values, and psychological values are all included—as are individual ethical obligations to one's fellows, but only on a very minor basis.[23] Indeed, *Values and Teaching* goes out of its way to deprecate "moralizing."[24]

"Values clarification" has been well-received in the United States. Hundreds and perhaps thousands of school programs and teachers' workshops employ the clarification methodology, and ten states have value education programs modeled on this approach. A number of reasons account for this popularity, not the least of which is the basic sympathy between "values clarification" and democratic standards of education. European visitors to America have observed:

> My [parent] friend observed that the only thing to be done [in child rearing] is to avoid to the utmost the exercise of authority, and to make children friends from the very beginning. . . . They do not lay aside their democratic principles in this relation more than in others. . . . they leave as much as possible to natural retribution: they impose no opinions, and quarrel with none: . . . the children of America have the advantage of the best possible early discipline; that of activity and self-dependence.[25]

As early as the first quarter of the last century an English traveler wrote: "A close connection was made . . . between the republican form of government and the unlimited liberty which was allowed the younger generation. . . . They were rarely punished at home, and strict discipline was not tolerated in the schools."[26]

"Values clarification" continues this egalitarian/libertarian approach. "What seems to us of paramount importance is that the child be given a major freedom to exercise his intelligence and individuality, and increasingly larger amounts as he matures."[27] The method seeks to have students become aware of the values which they hold.

The teacher of "values clarification" is exhorted never to enforce his own views or to moralize; he or she is an agent who tries to remove the obstacles to a clear self-understanding. The ultimate goal is not to teach any particular values, but to present the "seven valuing processes": (1) prizing and cherishing, (2) publicly affirming, (3) choosing from alternatives, (4) choosing after considering consequences, (5) choosing freely, (6) acting, (7) acting with a pattern, repetition, and consistency.[28] The teaching methods employed are good and have been widely imitated.

One important consequence of this approach is an undue simplicity in dealing with children's development. For example, the designers of the method argue that it is wrong to believe that "children are not old enough or experienced enough or wise enough to choose values for themselves" and that "we [the adult educators] are responsible for starting them off on the right track."[29] Although there is controversy on this point, it seems that this "doctrinaire" statement of parental responsibility would be supported in part or in whole by the majority of those who have studied the developmental or social learning aspects of children's cognitive and affective behavior. Many authorities, therefore, have a more positive view of a non-aggressive heteronomy at some age levels and for some abilities than does "values clarification." John Wilson, Norman J. Bull, Jean Piaget, and Derek Wright would disagree with the fundamental rejection of heteronomy in the "values clarification" approach.[30] However, Kohlberg and McPhail would tend to accept it.[31]

The indifference of "values clarification" to performance criteria is partially revealed in the following statement: "It is not impossible to conceive of one going through the seven value criteria and deciding that he values intolerance or thievery. What is to be done? Our position is that we respect his right to decide upon that value."[32]

This statement carries the ideal of individuality to a point where one can no longer distinguish between the moral and the immoral, and therefore defeats the attempt to educate to values in even the broadest sense. Can an educational theory produce a dishonest person, and then merely say that the choice of dishonesty is a legitimate expression of individual preference?

Professors Donald W. Oliver and James P. Shaver[33] have one or two chapters dealing with values which may be more closely related to ethics than the books just discussed. These authors review bases of ethical theory without finding a satisfactory one, but finally conclude that human dignity is the basis of ethical values. They are also interested in the use of cases.

A "Public Issues Series" has been published by Xerox Corporation[34] under the direction of Professors Oliver and Newman. Each book of the series gives sample case studies of personal or family histories and asks many questions which may initiate class discussion. A few volumes have fairly clear-cut ethical problems developing from historical or literary cases, but the brunt of the series is on social problems, not on individual ethics.

The case study technique as a whole has the advantage of stimulating the student's curiosity and encourages role-playing by members of the class. It is subject to few legal difficulties since no point of view is being taught. The problem is whether or not—and at what point—the teacher's answer may be given. Obviously it should be long delayed. Perhaps it should wait for student request, but we believe that the teacher's own point of view must ultimately be indicated.

A major disadvantage of the case study method is that it may encourage some students to form their own opinions regardless of the accumulated experience of mankind or the insights of philosophic and religious thinkers.

Teachers who wish to employ the case study method may decide to develop their own cases, perhaps out of ethical problems raised by their students. The British publication, *Moral Education in the Secondary School*, can provide examples.[35] Professor Kohlberg's many publications are not designed specifically for the classroom teacher, but could be helpful. Of singular importance from the student's point of view is the need to make case studies which respect and are relevant to the student's mentality.

The case study method is clearly more useful in secondary than in elementary school. Secondary school students are more prepared for the discussion of cases, while those in elementary school may learn more from the individual virtues approach.

The Law as a Basis of Values

A recent California report on moral and civic education is explicitly based on a statutory requirement for teaching morality, truth, justice, patriotism, and citizenship.[36] It includes several references to teaching about the law, which is a time-honored means of teaching ethics. Much of the remarkable record of the Jews in economic and political operations is based on ethical traditions supported by centuries of rabbinical exposition of the Mosaic law and the several codifications of it by outstanding rabbis. Jewish writers and friends assure us that examination of the law has been very effective. It is true that less attention is being paid to it in the reformed Jewish tradition, but there are some signs of a return to such study.

The Jews are not alone in teaching ethics by analysis and discussion of the law. Many Christian groups followed the same tradition by continuous reading of the Ten Commandments in church services. Some studies of Greek city-states indicate that execution of the law was the major method of ethical instruction in those remarkable commonwealths. Teachers have successfully discussed legal cases in high school, and courses in law are gaining student favor.

The writers have often wondered at high school civics texts which describe the legislative and executive process in detail but tell nothing of the laws which our governmental bodies produce and enforce. Simple reading of the law would not be effective with American students. Although our laws are passed by demo-cratically-chosen representative bodies, students would resent the arbitrary language and the involved nature of the statutes themselves. But discussions of the reasons for statutory provisions, the problems of enforcing them, and the ethics involved in obeying or violating them could be useful to ethical education. The wisdom of judicial decisions—or those of rabbis in the Jewish law—can also be discussed.

Teaching the law has two advantages over the broader case study method discussed in the previous section. The law is concrete, and it is usually based on a standard of values. The disadvantage is that legal provisions are limited in scope and may be obsolete or unenforceable.

Conduct of the School

The California report on moral and civic education stresses the attitude and conduct of teachers, counsellors, administrators, secretaries, and custodians in presenting "daily lessons in morality." A survey of schools made by the English Moral Education group listed conduct of the school as the most important single existing factor in such education. The only method of ethical education which John Dewey approved in *Democracy and Education* (1916) and *School and Society* (1915) was that transmitted through the student's school experience, which certainly implied observation of school personnel. Later, in *Human Nature and Conduct* (1922), he indicated that people learn morals, as they do languages, by contact with those around them.[37]

In another section, however, he notes that these moral habits may be too deeply ingrained in emotion, thus accounting for "the mass of irrationalities that prevail among men of otherwise rational tastes."[38] It is desirable "that habits be formed which are more intelligent, more sensitively percipient, more informed with foresight, more aware of what they are about, more direct and sincere, more flexibly responsive than those now current."[39] Presumably, Dewey believed that the teacher should help the student develop these habits in the course of school experience.

Dewey placed such tremendous stress on this method of ethical education at the expense of all other methods that a few comments are needed. Its emphasis by the British in their so-called "public schools" sometimes sacrifices intellectual quality for character in teacher selection. American school administrators have not had so much freedom of choice and are not likely to have it in the future. Nevertheless, some efforts could be made. Character may be especially important in selecting administrative personnel and the coaching staff. The old adage that the young monkey does what he sees the old monkey doing applies to the importance of character in school personnel.

John Dewey's theory that all ethical development should come from the school experience overlooks those students who find little of importance in the school and its character-building activities. The sensitive student learns from his teacher's objective search for the truth; the activities-minded student develops character from working with his fellows under teacher or counsellor guidance. But what of the rest of the students?

If, as Dewey indicated, school experience is to be the only method of developing character through education, we are condemning many non-scholastic, non-activities students to ignorance of some of the basic aspects of human relationships. Therefore, if Dewey's ethical foundations—based as they are on the common morality of a common community experience—are to be successful for all, then the conduct of the school must stress the ethos of the entire school community, as the California report insists.

Individual Virtues

Throughout history efforts have been made to isolate individual ethic virtues, with the thought of then proceeding to teach them. Aristotle's *Nicomachean Ethics* is a good example. It discussed justice, liberality, courage, magnanimity, and other moral virtues. All of these are grounded on the fundamental necessity of temperance based on habit, and the ideal possessor of all such characteristics is a gentleman. But the learner who reads the book is taught how to secure the individual virtues.

Other writers have applied Aristotle's approach, if in more mundane ways. Castiglione, in *The Courtier*, lists virtues as well as vices for the Renaissance gentleman to follow. Lord Chesterfield's advice to his son includes many desirable attributes.

An effort to help younger children respect individual virtues has been developed by the American Institute for Character Education in San Antonio, Texas.[40] Emphasizing the right of the child to choose his own values, even if he selects values and behavior not acceptable to his peers, the Character Education Curriculum (CEC) goes one step further. It presents the pupil with values found in contemporary society, and tries to promote conditions in which children can understand their choiceworthiness. For example the CEC has modules aimed at promoting the values of generosity, kindness, helpfulness, honesty, honor, citizenship, and human rights, among others. The instructional sophistication of the CEC is second to none in this area. Role-play, case study discussion, story completion, art projects, and multi-media representations are all given effective use.

The individual virtue approach has several advantages. It breaks down the problem of ethical instruction into workable parts. Insofar as each virtue can be made appealing in itself, it decreases the necessity for an overall authoritative source of ethics, thus reducing the danger that some religious or political group can claim such teaching to be unconstitutional. The main disadvantage, of course, is that virtues may clash with one another. Telling the truth at times can be very cruel. The virtue of courage may be selfish. And how do we know the validity or importance of any one virtue? Skillful classroom teaching is indispensable at this point.

Teaching an individual virtue is perhaps a better technique for elementary school students, who may grasp it more readily. High school students are more likely to note the conflict between individual virtues and to reach for a consistent basis for morality, something they may develop from discussion of case studies or of the law.

Historical Examples

Using examples from history is a method of teaching ethics which has been widely used elsewhere but is little employed in American public schools—partly because John Dewey expressly opposed it in *Democracy and Education*. *Plutarch's Lives* includes comments on the virtues and vices of the subject of the biography; *The Lives of the Saints* has long been used in religious education. Military school curricula describe the courageous exploits of their alumni, and the British public schools in England's nineteenth-century revival of morality brought back "old boys" (alumni) to the campus to encourage students to higher and more courageous ideals of public service. Religious orders commemorate their more pious deceased members; the stories of Lincoln's moral deeds can inspire young people who are interested in politics; and Parson Weems's biography of George Washington was historically inaccurate, but the stories it told may have helped many Americans to live better lives. *McGuffey's Readers*, widely employed in American public schools in the last century, include a number of historical examples of courage, honesty, gentleness, and other moral qualities.

There are disadvantages to this method. A younger generation which believes that it knows more than its predecessors may take historical instruction lightly. The bravery of the martyrs, the humanity of St. Francis, or the tolerant fortitude of Lincoln may seem remote to the student. This is why stories of pre-Revolutionary American artisans constituted the only class of "anecdotes" from the "reservoir" of history not opposed by John Dewey in teaching ethics.

Taking a longer view of history than Dewey, one can imagine a number of students being inspired by courageous, merciful, or gentle deeds of compassion in the past. Socrates is still an inspiring example of a man who died for a purpose. The historical example can be an effective means of teaching ethics, and may simply be read and discussed as a normal lesson in history or in literature. Some examples can be used for discussion like case studies. Teachers may select examples for either affective or cognitive consequences, or for both.

Sociological Experience

The experience of all societies is another source of information on ethics. This is a less pedagogical technique, but one which provides more source material than the other methods. C. S. Lewis, in a non-theological work, *The Abolition of Man*, pointed out how our individual ethical responsibilities are recognized by all world civilizations. What he calls "The Law of General Beneficence" is backed up by quotations from ancient Egyptian, ancient Jewish, and Old Norse writings against murder. Babylonian and Hindu and Jewish writings oppose "bearing false witness." There are Roman, English, Chinese, Babylonian, Old Norse, ancient Jewish, and Christian injunctions to kindly treatment of one's fellow man. He includes quotations supporting the "Law of Special Beneficence," Duties to Parents and Elders, Duties to Children and Posterity, the Law of Justice, the Law of Veracity, and the Law of Magnanimity.

Lewis is careful not to say that the repetition of these injunctions in a wide variety of philosophic and religious views gives them a special authority. Rather, they are simply a sign of what constitutes civilization itself.[41]

Can these materials be taught? Certainly Supreme Court decisions, which allow comparative religious studies, would not cavil at comparative religious and philosophic studies. The problem is not constitutional but pedagogical. Who could teach such far-flung quotations in an effective manner?

Since recent Supreme Court decisions made it clear that teaching comparative religions is constitutional, there has been a slow development of such teaching in secondary schools throughout the country. Almost all religions help to create some of the climate for character development. If the teacher is alert to the repetition of the Golden Rule and to other ethical pronouncements in a wide variety of philosophies and religions, this study can give students an opportunity to appreciate the almost universal appearance of individual ethical rules.

Some teachers are concerned that emphasizing the ethical values in various religions may be interpreted as "laying down the law" of the Judeo-Christian tradition in an unconstitutional manner. But the comparative sociological method need not be dogmatic. Students can draw their own conclusions from the almost universal appearance of certain individual ethical concepts in every higher religion and philosophic system.

Patriotism and Ethics

Patriotism is not discussed here as a method of teaching ethics but as a closely-related field. The teaching of patriotism has been sharply criticized in the past as leading to chauvinistic and untruthful history and civics books.[42] More recent studies have indicated that today's textbooks are perhaps unduly critical of the United States.[43]

Without taking part in this controversy, the writers feel that patriotism, properly encouraged, can be a force for ethical improvement. It should help motivate us to throw out the corruption from our city governments, to help our fellow citizens in poverty areas who are the victims of organized crime, and to restore vitality to our state and national governments. Men must learn to work with one another toward a common end. This is the role of patriotism, and it is just as applicable to problems of ethics at home as it is to an enemy abroad. Real patriotism may lead to local pride, state pride, national pride, international pride or to a judicious mixture of two, three, or four such sentiments.

Most schools encourage patriotism with a flag salute and perhaps some other exercises which should be forces for ethics. They should not be excuses for braggadocio or narrow nationalism or for historical falsehoods. The flag salute should be explained and discussed in class from time to time. What does "liberty and justice for all" mean? Where have Americans achieved it? Why? "The public schools should foster informed and dedicated concern for America and its ideals."[44]

Private Schools

Since private schools include only 13 percent of America's school children,[45] no special study of them was made by the Center staff. However, one member of the staff serves on the Board of such a school and has researched and published a small amount on the subject of ethics in private schools, so this section is appended.[46]

Private schools seem to have much greater opportunity for ethical instruction than their public counterparts. Of necessity they draw their students from a socio-economic group which is prepared for higher ethical standards, and they do not face the constitutional and political objections to teaching ethics which are a hurdle for the public schools. They can maintain church ties and conduct religious services. They have a chance to develop a reputation in the building of character, and can more easily drop the student who proves to be a bad risk.

The counterparts of the American private school in Great Britain have distinguished themselves chiefly by character development. Since Thomas Arnold was appointed headmaster of Rugby in 1828, the independent schools of Great Britain—of which Eton, Harrow, and Rugby are best known—have built a reputation for teaching character to their students. Many place heavy emphasis on compulsory attendance at church services, usually of the Church of England. A system of student self-government in which most senior students participate stresses ethical training. Teachers, called masters, are selected both for their own character and for their ability to inspire emulation by the students. Graduates who distinguished themselves in public or military service are featured, and athletics are used as a means of developing sportsmanship and a sense of voluntary cooperation. Through the use of these and other devices the schools have made a real contribution to the moral standards of British politics, public service, and military service.

For several reasons, we cannot hope for as much leadership from independent schools in the United States. Ours is a society of much less class structure than is Britain, so independent schools are less in demand. A much smaller proportion of American leaders comes from independent schools, and their teachers are often taught the program of education intended for the public schools. The more Spartan life of the British independent schools would drive away American customers. There are many religious denominations in this country, so dependence on one upper-class church as in England would not be duplicated.

Nevertheless, there are steps which independent schools in the United States could take to establish a reputation for character development and perhaps to help them secure students. Athletics should emphasize sportsmanship; classes could discuss ethical values; student government could be an exercise in ethics. Church services, of an ecumenical nature, should be planned for ethical emphasis.

Today's independent schools in the United States overlook the chance to sell themselves by improving the character of the students in the sense that it is done in British independent schools.

11

Is There Room for Ethics in the Social Gospel?

The Continuing Importance of Organized Religion

Much has been written about the "crisis" in America's churches; there is a pervasive feeling that the churches are failing.[1] No longer relevant to life in a technological society, some say that the church has lost its self-confidence and is in the process of losing membership and its capacity to attract gifts.[2] Many persons in the church are speaking of the post-Christian age.

Analysis of surveys of church attendance and participant attitudes reveals some of the basis for the prevailing gloom. Church attendance has decreased. Only 40 percent of the respondents of the Gallup Poll reported attending church in an average week in 1972 versus 49 percent in 1958. Moreover, the percentage of respondents who felt that religion was losing its influence rose from 14 percent in 1957 to 75 percent in 1970.

While these figures are bad, they do not give the full story. If the church were in fact dead or dying, interest in its ethical functions would be only antiquarian. Further analysis of existing data reveals the continuing strength of religious institutions, encouraging a more hopeful view of the church's position. Economic support for religion has remained strong. Giving to churches has actually increased from $9 billion in 1960, to $14.5 billion in 1967, to $18.5 billion in 1970. Attitudinal studies show that large majorities of both Protestant and Catholic clergymen under forty "believe a person cannot be a good Protestant or Catholic if he does not attend church regularly." Finally, the fact that 40 percent of Americans attend church in an average week, while only 20 percent do so in Great Britain in spite of Britain's public support of religion, illustrates the continuing vitality of our churches.[3]

Speaking of religion in America, one should also consider its uniqueness. The separation of church and state, familiar to us all as a principle of government, has created an extraordinarily popular and competitive type of religious sectarianism. Without government support every church group has to compete for membership and financial sustenance. Formal government neutrality forces the churches to sink or swim in the tide of popular sentiment.

The separation of church and state was conceived by the founders as a solution to the problem of political tyranny and religious strife, not as a blow at religious belief. In fact, the founders thought that religious values were instrumental in encouraging public morality. Thomas Jefferson, one of the most radical of our early statesmen, said, "I must ever believe that religion substantially good which produces an honest life," while Washington added in his Farewell Address: "Let us with caution indulge the supposition that morality can be maintained without religion. Whatever may be conceded to the influence of refined education on minds of a peculiar structure, reason and experience both forbid us to expect that national morality can prevail in exclusion of religious principle."

Nearly a half-century later, Tocqueville made a similar observation regarding the necessity of religiously inspired values for individual and social stability:

> I have endeavored to point out in another part of this work the causes to which the maintenance of the political institutions of the Americans is attributable, and religion appeared to be one of the most promising among them. I am now treating the Americans in an individual capacity, and I again observe that religion is not less useful to each citizen than to the whole state. The Americans show by their practice that they feel the high necessity of imparting morality to democratic communities by means of religion.[4]

Because it must respect and cultivate the opinion of its voluntary members, American religion has always been largely non-dogmatic. There is probably less adherence to formal precepts and to rules of observance in the United States than in any other country. The power of the church in influencing the lives of its members comes about, according to Tocqueville, not from the weight of dogma but from its integral proximity to public opinion:

> Public opinion is therefore never hostile to them [the clergy]; it rather supports and protects them; and their belief owes its authority at the

same time to the strength which is its own and to that which it borrows from the opinion of the many.[5]

America has developed over the decades what various writers call a civil religion. This is a collection of beliefs about our institutions and their methods of operation which assumes a degree of divine guidance. It is usually enunciated in political speeches. Professor Bellah has given us some examples of it in Presidential inaugural addresses.[6] Civil religion has not tried to replace Christianity or Judaism. It tends to keep theological positions to a minimum— referring to God, not to Jesus Christ. But it does assume some religious sanction for our government and some religious urging for measures to improve the population.

Churches have responded to a limited extent to the appeal of civil religion. Some have prayers for all persons in "civil authority." Will Herburg, in *Protestant, Catholic, Jew*, thought all churches were becoming subdivisons of a national faith.[7] The last decade has shown us that the opposite danger—that of the churches becoming excessive critics of the nation—also existed.

What bearing does civil religion have on America's ethical problem? If the churches and political leaders could be persuaded to support individual ethical standards, the "civil religion" tradition might help tremendously. Presidents or governors could ask church support in the task of building better Americans. A national crusade against crime and corruption would be possible.

At the moment, however, neither churches nor the government seem greatly interested in improving America's ethics.

Modern Obstacles to Ethical Instruction

The quotation from Jefferson that religion was good which produced an honest life reveals the traditionally close association between religion and individual ethics. The faith of both the Christian and the Jew is in fundamental respects grounded on the law revealed to Moses which includes the absolute prohibition against theft, murder, and false witness. Public and private morality was benefitted, it was felt, by the transmission of these ethical precepts and of the belief in other worldly rewards and punishments.

The modern church, however, has to a large extent modified its concern with individual ethics. Judeo-Christian ethics have been replaced in the churches' interest by social action and psychological views of individual happiness. In so doing, the churches have followed the intellectual theories coming from the society around them—particularly from the universities. According to these views, individual unhappiness and criminality are consequences of social forces, and are not questions of spiritual or ethical choice. As long as there is racism, militarism, economic exploitation, etc., one should not be surprised—the argument goes—to find criminal reactions to these conditions.

Recently, Dean Joseph Fletcher developed an alternative to the ethical standards provided by the Mosaic (as well as the civil) law. According to Fletcher's new dispensation found in *Situation Ethics, A New Morality*,[8] morality is both more simple and more complex than simply following the old, oppressive Mosaic code. It is simpler because the numerous Mosaic laws are replaced by a single universal principle—*agapé*. It is more complex because the utilitarian judgments needed to foster *agapé* are, more often than not, subtle and elusive. In the course of *Situation Ethics*, Dean Fletcher tries to show how the law restricts, while arguing that murder, robbery, and many other actions normally considered unethical are permissible in certain, albeit rare, situations.

Fletcher, of course, is correct in anticipating that situational judgments are the desired goal of ethical instruction. But to throw away the rules at the beginning, and to teach only the exceptions to the rules, stands the Mosaic law on its head, leaving one's everyday ethical decisions without the necessary guideposts. Many ethical decisions are quite simple, often the result of habituation to simple rules. For example, is it necessary to decide what may produce the greatest *agapé* when one is tempted to steal some tools on the job or to keep the excess change which a cash register clerk hands you?

Freud and other psychologists-psychiatrists have also had a powerful influence on churchmen. If criminals are created by early childhood experience or other environmental influences, then it is superfluous to talk about ethical standards and individual responsibility. An extreme criticism is Anna Russell's humorous characterization of Freud's view of moral responsibility:

> At three I had a feeling of
> Ambivalence toward my brothers,

And so it follows naturally
I poison all my lovers.

But now I'm happy: I have learned
The lesson this has taught;
That everything I do that's wrong
Is someone else's fault.[9]

The views of Fletcher and Freud are complemented by the views of existential theorists who put no limits on human freedom and potential for change, and who thus tend to make religious education ethically valueless. W. F. O'Neal has described the existential approach to moral education as follows:

Moral education then is not the task of transmitting precepts, but teaching principles in terms of the ever changing exigencies of the contemporary society each child will face.

The church in this sense, and Christian education in this sense, aims not at transmission of moral values *per se*, but at providing a vehicle for responsible moral dialogue, and presenting children with a model for grappling with morality as an on-going existential process.[10]

New socially-oriented Christian theology, psychology, and existentialism have all played a part in reducing individual ethical instruction in church schools. These movements have not been impediments to other religious activities.

The History of the Sunday School

It is fair to say that the Sunday (or religious) school is the most misunderstood and underestimated institution in contemporary life. This is not simply by accident. As Lynn and Wright observe, "For over fifty years a hefty and vocal segment of the Protestant forces has preached and predicted its demise . . . and proposed alternatives for Christian education."[11] One might extend their time frame and recall Mark Twain's spoof on Sunday Schools in *Tom Sawyer*. Judge Thatcher's overblown encomium to that institution was a put-down, even in 1876: "You will be a great man and a good man yourself, some day, Thomas, and then you will look back and say, 'It's all owing to the precious Sunday School privileges of my boyhood—it's all owing to my dear teachers that taught me to learn—it's all owing to the good Superintendent, who encouraged me, and watched over me, and gave me a beautiful Bible.' ''

Generally, it is agreed that the Sunday School began in England near the end of the eighteenth century. Newspaper publisher and philanthropist Robert Raikes popularized the institution as a means of encouraging literacy and improving morality among urban youths. In this country the first large Sunday School league, American Sunday School Association, originated with the First Day Society of Philadelphia in 1790. According to Edwin Wilbur Rice, the ASSA's real purpose was to "improve the morals and the religious characters of the learners."[12]

The Sunday School in the United States quickly evolved from a primarily urban to a primarily rural institution; and from an institution designed to improve the manners and the morals of the poor to one in which it was felt that every young person should take a part. In 1830 the Sunday School Association, which counted 55,000 members in 1824, undertook the "Valley Campaign," enthusiastically committing itself to establish a "Sunday School in every destitute place where it is practicable, throughout the valley of the Mississippi" (over two-thirds of the current land mass of the nation).

The American Sunday School Union, the descendant of the Sunday School Association, built its schools around inexpensive books bought by local communities. By the late 1830s, the ASSU had developed a "Sunday School and family library" of "a hundred select volumes from 72 to 250 pages," which sold for just $10. One indication of the remarkable success of the Union can be found in an 1859 *Manual of Public Libraries*: out of the more than 50,000 public libraries in the states and territories, 30,000 were in Sunday Schools. Thus, in many hamlets and villages the Sunday School library was the only available source of reading material.[13]

These libraries contained some books of general interest, e.g., the Union speller and a description of the life of the Bedouin Arabs. However, their major subjects were ethics and Evangelicalism. The ethics of these early readers is, by modern standards, excessively rigid and their outlook is often morbid. High mortality rates and the general severity of living conditions may have accounted for the tone of their message; however, the pervasiveness of their ethical

message probably elevated general ethical levels. An example of
both the severity and the ethics of these early books can be found in
the "Sabbath School" song found in the 1838 *Union Melodies*:

> To Sabbath School, to Sabbath School,/ We'll haste, we'll haste
> away;
> We'll early be at Sunday School/ Nor ever stop to play.
>
> At Sunday School, at Sunday School,/ This precious holy day,
> We'll careful be at Sunday School/ Our lessons well to say.[14]

By mid-century Sunday Schools were a fixture in rural America.
However, their popularity and general lack of organization has from
the very beginning encouraged attempts to reform and improve
them. Shortly after the Civil War, one such attempt, the
International Lesson Series (ILS), successfully began to improve
instruction and control sectarian strife among the schools. The ILS,
which continues to this day, takes its lessons from the Bible, thus
continuing the trend away from catechisms begun in the 1830s.
Although the lessons remain "material centered," attempts have
been made, beginning in the early part of this century, to convert the
ILS approach to one where primary consideration is given to the
cognitive-emotive development of the student— but such changes
as have occurred have been largely cosmetic.

The International Lesson Series is still widely used in churches
across the country. Over the years, however, new reform demands
and social forces overtaxed the ILS's ability to act as a
comprehensive source for Protestant Sunday Schools. In the 1920s
and 1930s the evangelical denominations began to develop and
publish their own materials, which were less "high-brow" than the
ILS. Following World War II the landmark "Faith and Life"
curriculum, produced by the United Presbyterian Church (one of
the major supporters of both the ASSU and the ILS), initiated the
movement toward "modern" sectarian programs among the "main
line" denominations. Professional acceptance of these programs—
if not their grass roots popularity—is reflected in the fact that
contemporary Catholic CCD programs and reformed Jewish
religious schools now are based on similar child-centered curricula.

Up until World War II the emphasis on individual ethical
responsibility in religious education remained consistently high. An
extensive analysis of early publications of the ASSU, over one
hundred years of the International Lesson Series and Peloubet's

notes on the ILS, in addition to several decades of evangelical-fundamentalist material, suggest that they all assume that there is a relation between Christian faith and ethical activity.

Since World War II, however, the child-centered curricula of the liberal Protestants, Catholics, and Jews have moved away from the older view of Judeo-Christian ethics. Most significantly, they have posited that sin or criminality is not a product of choice but is socially and psychologically determined, as we shall see in the next section.

Religious School Curricula

How far have general intellectual trends affected the churches' activities in promoting ethical values in recent years? In order to determine the extent and kind of ethical instruction given in the churches today, we decided to analyse contemporary religious school curricula. By ethical instruction we mean the explicit attempt to foster individual ethical values—respect for others—beginning from the understanding that one does not rob, murder, or rape fellow human beings, and going on to the nuances which respect for one's fellow man implies. The writers reasoned that the religious school curriculum material would be the best place to begin. Here the church carefully composes or purchases material which it will use (usually on a national basis) to instruct and to recruit new members. An attitudinal study of pastors or religious schools might add depth to our results, but it could not ensure the same uniformity and "concreteness."

The analysis which we have made of many of the major religious school programs reveals a variety of views. There are four rough and frequently overlapping approaches to ethical instruction: (1) the indirect, (2) the hard-sell, (3) the integrated, and (4) some Jewish material, which combines 1 and 2. In addition, we analyze curricula from religious school programs in other Western nations.

The Indirect

The religious groups which deal with ethics indirectly usually feel that the development of ethically sensitive standards are much less important than the development of other values, e.g., self-awareness, social commitment, etc., or that ethical values are a consequence of or derivative from other values. These groups include the "main line" Protestant denominations—Presbyterian, Methodist, Episcopalian, and Congregationalists—the reform Jews, and the Roman Catholics. A brief description of the programs of one Protestant group (the Presbyterians) and the Catholics will illustrate this point of view.

The Presbyterian program, "The Christian Faith and Action,"[15] is devoted to an explicitly psychological end: "The most important thing about being a man is being one's own unique self." The curriculum is based on Bibical stories chosen to teach certain concepts such as family, motherhood, culture, and history, in addition to teaching the principles of scholarship itself. The main thrust of the Presbyterian program is directed toward developing a rational understanding of general ends of Christian life on a fairly high intellectual level.

The Catholic programs analysed were "Life, Love, and Joy"[16] and "The New Life."[17] In these series we examined the fourth and eighth grade levels for ethical content, for these were the years explicitly devoted to such teaching.

In the fourth grade (approximately ten years old), there is a section where the concept of Christian obedience is discussed. The Catholic writers clearly were influenced by the need for social action and the theories of the situation ethicists:

> Even for a fourth grader, obedience involves some sensitivity to the real demands and opportunities of a particular situation. . . . The ten-year-old is growing up in a society where young men actively resist the draft in order to be true to their consciences. . . . Civil disobedience is a part of a major civil rights strategy.

The "New Life" program for the eighth grade entitled "Free to Live," which is designed to teach ethical values, goes on in the same key. It centers on three important themes in the young teenager's life: "person, community, and church considered in the context of freedom." The starting point is that the young person must be accepted as he is, "faced with the reality of his own desire to live free and the problem of coping with the many implications of that freedom."

Both of these programs deal marginally with the question of personal ethical responsibility. In both programs it seems clear that the ethical message is psychological: live freely and creatively, with the unstated assumption that healthy, happy young persons aided by this program will not commit unethical acts. In their desire to have the students find their own values and reduce emotional conflict, they run the risk (which Hofstadter pointed out) of making their programs ethically haphazard. In this type of intellectual and ethical cloud there may be no authoritarianism, but there may also be no clear source or sense of the ethical dimension.

There is one noticeable exception to this general avoidance of direct ethical interest. The Presbyterians have a program for predominately black and Mexican-American churches, designed to be relevant to the special social experience of these groups. It addresses the questions of group self-identification, history, and the civil rights struggle. It also *directly* addresses ethical problems. One exercise called "What We Do" includes such topics as studying hard, knowing when Mother is tired, and returning something you have stolen.[18]

The Hard-Sell

The representative denominations we analyzed which practice "the hard-sell" are the Southern Baptist Convention and the Assembly of God. Their approach to teaching ethical responsibility is diametrically opposed to the first group—it is primary, direct, and assertive.

The emphasis in the Southern Baptist material is on the proper habits and attitudes toward sex, drug use, alcoholism, and the family. In particular, the material seeks to combat the swinging *Playboy* "philosophy" and the ethical relativism of situation ethics. The greatest difficulty which the Southern Baptists seem to face in their ethical instruction is pedagogical. To know what is "right" does not necessarily enable the student to wish to do it or, more importantly, know *how* to do it, i.e., apply his ethical precepts in the everyday world.

The material we analysed from the evangelical Assembly of God and the "*Bible* in Life" series tends to have the same approach as the Baptist. The *"Bible* in Life" explicitly handles ethical instruction from the Ten Commandments, discussing the significance of such moral precepts as "Thou shalt not steal."[19] This program faces the same difficulty as does the Baptist. How does one translate or make everyday "situational" judgments which will enable the students to practice their precepts in everyday life? A more contemporary case studies approach might be helpful.

The Integrated Ethical Program

There were two curricula which steered the middle course between ethical absolutism and ethical avoidance: those of the Church of Jesus Christ of Latter-Day Saints (the Mormons) and the First Church of Christ, Scientist (the Christian Scientists).

The Mormon instruction aims at completing the faith as well as the character of the students. It consists of stories and case studies explicitly designed to make students "better" members of their families, their country, and their church. Bible stories are used as case studies, i.e., they provide the basis for an open discussion. The educational principle of the Mormons is that "most people have a desire to improve if they have an example of something better."

The Christian Science material is harder to characterize. Nevertheless, it does maintain a balance between questions of personal character, faith, and social responsibility more closely than denominations in the other two categories. Two quotations are representative of the Christian Science view.

> Neither technology nor material strength can substitute for a living faith in God. Christianity has largely shaped the ethical, juridicial, and social concepts upon which our civilization is built. . . .

> From the viewpoint of the Christian Scientist, however, the solution does not lie either in viewing men as sinners or in reducing moral standards to a merely relative level. It lies in showing the individual that he can meet the demands of honesty, humanity, compassion, temperance, because it is in accord with his real nature to do so.[20]

The Jewish Program

The Jewish program we analyzed was prepared by the Rocky Mountain Curriculum Planning Workshop in 1972, "Le Havdil: To

Make a Difference." Because it is new and innovative "Le Havdil" cannot be considered simply as the Jewish norm; however, it is rapidly becoming the standard program in the Los Angeles Basin and is gaining acceptance nationally.

"Le Havdil" presents a union of the newest and the oldest. Its educational format is completely up-to-date, although many references were made to the traditional Jewish cultural and ethical values found in the great books of the Jewish heritage. The bulk of the instruction was oriented toward "freedom of choice." Encounter groups, role and game playing are standard pedagogical techniques; its reading list includes *Portnoy's Complaint* and *Soul on Ice*. "This material on Jewish ethics is an attempt to incorporate the Jewish tradition into a meaningful package so that students may choose their individual ethical systems with a firm understanding of the option which exists in the Jewish tradition."[21]

Our analysis showed that some significant attempt was made to reinforce the ethical intention of the older sources in assigned readings based on the *Chain of Tradition* series authored by Louis Jacobs. In particular, the volumes *The Jewish Law* and *Jewish Ethics, Philosophy and Mysticism* contained excellent discussions of ethical points drawn from the old Jewish heritage. This explicit material, when viewed in conjunction with the modern pedagogy of the teacher's program, would be, in our judgment, highly effective.[22]

Our divisions are obviously too neat. One wonders whether any simple basis of classifications is truly descriptive in as diverse a field as this. A history of religious school education clearly shows its polytrophic nature. "The Sunday School," Dr. John Vincent commented in the last century, " is strong at the heart and weak at the head."[23] Its history is marked by experimentation with curriculum, teacher training, class length, and value orientation, which—added to denominational friction—has produced in the past a sense of unease and concern similar to that felt by current participants in the religious education process.

Do churches of other countries have any better record in individual ethical instruction? Consideration of a number of European Sunday School programs being used in 1973–1974— including the Catholic and Presbyterian programs in Ireland and the Lutheran in Germany and Sweden—indicates that they do.[24] It is probably true that these advanced societies are also in transition from traditional ethical authority to more democratic, autonomous ethics. Religious ethics also experiences this transition. Church authority, founded on divine revelation, is no longer a satisfactory basis for instruction. Other Western democracies are making this transition more slowly than the United States; thus their religious school curricula generally pay more attention to ethical instruction than do American programs. The difference in ethical emphasis is more of degree than of kind, but it is enough to be noticeable.

Problems with Teaching Ethics

In spite of the large number of surveys which have been done, studies of delinquent youths are inconclusive on the question whether religious conviction has a modifying effect on delinquent behavior. Travers and Davis (1961) summarized the existing studies as follows: "Findings are in complete conflict and range from those investigators who view religion as a cure to those who seem to view it as a cause."[25] Their study of Catholic delinquent boys in the Boston area, however, yields the conclusion that youngsters with a high degree of religious intensity will be lower in juvenile delinquency than non-religious youth, a conclusion which is supported by Middleton and Wright (1941).[26] Two other studies, Allen and Sandhu, 1967, and Gannon, 1967, also support the conclusion that there is a favorable correlation between religious commitment and non-delinquency, although they found little correlation between church attendance or verbalized religious belief and delinquent behavior.[27] Another, reporting on a somewhat smaller sample than any of the above, reached the opposite conclusion; i.e., that "no evidence has been found here to support the idea that whether a youth adopts delinquent behavior patterns is critically related to his religious attitudes or beliefs."[28]

Several things may be inferred from these studies. First, that the separation between ethics and religion which was observed in some of the religious school material may be of comparatively long standing. Second, the validity of this method of testing procedure might be questioned, given the wide disparity of results. But most likely it would appear that Gannon's observations are correct. When juvenile delinquency arises in spite of substantial religious training, it may be concluded that "if other supporting controlling agencies are missing, this simply means that the church has encountered a difficulty in coping with factors in modern life which tend to neutralize the fundamental tenets of religious teaching. It also means that the church will have to develop a new dimension to its teaching, particularly for the lower class youngster.''[29]

Conclusion

It is our belief that the role of the church as a social institution able to help maintain public morality continues to be a viable one. Effective social reform also depends on the church's leadership in the ethical field. Although many intellectual currents are running against this concept of religious activity in a modern secular society, it seems that the Judeo-Christian ethical traditions, religious experience in America, and the availability of democratically and psychologically sound methods of teaching ethics are effective counterweights to intellectual objections. It is also important for American churches, lacking state support, to maintain the interest and the moral approval of their congregations.

In advocating a greater emphasis on explicit and integrated ethical programs using case studies and class discussion techniques, we do not expect, nor would it be desirable, for the church to abandon its present responsibilities—social action and spiritual solace.

Social action has helped to win important victories in the field of civil rights. Religious influence helped to bring about the eight-hour work day in the steel mills. The churches' social action regarding foreign policy, most notably the Vietnam War, has perhaps been of questionable value but was intended to be useful.

Spiritual solace, a sense of tradition, and belonging to a group are not unimportant benefits of church association. The psychological importance of religious sentiment is well-documented. A sense of the sacredness and significance of self formed in prayer and holy service gives individuals peace and a feeling of self-worth.[30] Moreover, the continuity provided by church tradition, be it only in hymns and the more external forms of worship, provides personal security in a world suffering from rapid technological change or "future shock." Finally, the role of the church as a social center where friendships can be made and maintained and where members can undertake personally meaningful tasks is vitally important.

Sociological studies have shown that churches are among the first institutions to develop in such new towns as Levittown, New Jersey.

These services the church has performed and probably should continue to perform. It is our belief, however, that such services would be enhanced—as would the popular standing of the church—if programs designed to renew a sense of the lost religious/ethical sphere were pursued in the pulpit, in adult education classes, and in the religious schools.

From the writers' viewpoint, the most important single reform would involve the main-line Protestant denominations and the Catholics in the reexamination of the role of Christian ethics in their religious school programs. As we have tried to demonstrate, ethics has an individual as well as a social aspect. It is just as important to consider what each person can do in his daily life to aid his family, his friends, and his neighbors with whom he comes in contact, as it is to improve social institutions and the status of the disadvantaged.

The next important reform would be for the "fundamentalist" denominations to adapt their curricula, which are strong in Christian ethics, to the improved teaching methods of "values clarification," the British Moral Education program, and the American Institute for Character Education discussed in Chapter Ten.

12

What Is the Media's Message?

Part of America's ethical problem can be traced to the change in methods of communicating ideology—including ethics—to the younger generation. In the last century, moral understanding was maintained by the traditional means of parental instruction and example, religious association, schools, and general reading. While there may have been differing parental attitudes toward their ethical responsibility, studies of church and school curricula and of the content of general reading material show that all three were major sources of ethical instruction. Today, existing evidence (examined in other chapters) shows that much less attention is given to individual ethics by schools, churches and families than formerly was the case. Moreover, the social importance of the family, the church, and to some extent the school, has decreased.

Major agents of this great change in our style of life are the new electronic media: television, radio, and films. Marshall McLuhan, a media guru, interprets his famous phrase, "the medium is the message," to mean that "in terms of the electronic age, a totally new environment has been created."[1] In the same vein, Paul Baran of the Institute for the Future says: "In our culture we tend almost completely to ignore the scope, effectiveness, and all-pervasiveness of social conditioning that occurs to the younger recipient of the constant barrage from the mass media."[2]

The introduction of mass media, Baran believes, has impoverished the traditional modes of communicating ethical values, substituting "alternative communications on morals" in their place:

> Communication developments also threaten the "middle management" of society's past value-setting organizations: the clergy and the teachers. Even today the local clergyman does not seem nearly so

all-knowing as he did during the last century. The diversity and often greater wisdom exhibited by a plurality of alternative commentaries on morals—on the radio and TV—is powerful competition. The work of a clergyman, as a distributor of moral wisdom, the teacher, as a dispenser of education, has to some degree already been displaced by electronic channels.[3]

Thus, America's youth is being reared in an environment which is radically different from that of any earlier age. Today's youth spends a quarter to a half of his waking hours before a TV screen.[4] It has been estimated that the average American—adults and youth alike—spends four-fifths of his leisure time on television.[5] TV has taken the place of farm work, house chores, general reading, and just loafing around town, which filled the out-of-school hours of earlier generations. In many families the parents are with their children less than is the television set. Television may very well have more to do with the character formation of the child than do the child's parents or his formal education.

This chapter will examine the extent and kind of the "moral wisdom," to use Baran's phrase, of the media. To anticipate our conclusions, we do not believe that the ethical basis of the media is adequate for the tremendous social role which it has created for itself. In all fairness, however, it should be added that the failure of the media to accept a limited sense of responsibility as our moral guides partly reflects the intellectual spirit of the modern age.

The primary medium of public communication is television, and it will command our major consideration. In addition, we will look at radio, films, comic books, and newspapers—each of which appears to have substantial effect on the ethical outlook of some percentage of the youth or of the population as a whole. Many of television's deficiencies are found in the other media, so they will be treated more cursorily. The chapter reviews each medium, seeking to discern its impact on ethical standards and its potentiality for improving them.

But before beginning our discussion of television, it would be best to point up one source of confusion. Except for the limited public broadcasting of television, all of these media are run for commercial reasons. By and large television, movies, radio, and comic books are designed to entertain Americans during their leisure hours. In comparison to the excitement of adventure stories filled with

violence, horror, or crime, stories which emphasize ethical principles may seem dull, thus losing part of the media's profits. Many
people argue that the commercial incentive points in the direction of
amorality; even in shows with a moral message, extravagant dis-
plays of violence may be eye-catching and incite imitation, particularly among some of the young.

Competitive Television

Television is especially subject to the market mechanism. The
three major networks and the independents are paid several billions
of dollars a year by commercial advertisers. These spoils are
distributed according to the numbers of viewers which programs and
shows can attract. If few viewers tune in to a show, advertisers
either pull out or pay less to sponsor it.

The market mechanism has many advantages for the commercial
world. It is quick, decisive, impersonal, and efficient. Most of the
economic transactions of society are well governed by it, although in
the media world where, except for radio, there is almost an oligopoly
control, the market may not produce the most desirable social
results. While this is a debatable point for policy-makers, it is
mooted by the fact that Americans seem sufficiently convinced of
the validity of the market and of the desirability of freedom of speech
that there has never been a serious movement in the country for the
public ownership or control of television found in most west
European countries.

It would be inappropriate here to go into a detailed analysis of the
complex problem of television regulation. In summary, however,
the federal government grants licenses to broadcasting stations.
These are reviewed periodically by the Federal Communications
Commission (FCC) for renewal. While the licenses have rarely been
revoked, the latent power of the government to withhold renewal
makes broadcasters listen more carefully to FCC officials. The
television industry, of course, would like to be completely free from
any regulation but has been reminded frequently by public officials
that it is a private industry granted special public privileges. By and
large the FCC has been kind to the industry but it has not been a
rubber stamp.[6]

In addition to the threat of direct FCC pressure, there have been cases where stations were forced, through public pressure on the licensing process, to change some program broadcasting. In late 1973 a licensee in the Los Angeles area (KTTV) agreed to drop three programs for children, to ban thirty nine others which were not in use, and to issue warnings to parents prior to broadcasting eighty-one additional series. The public pressure on the station was led by the National Association for Better Broadcasting, Action for Children's Television, the Mexican-American Political Association, and a local fair housing group. After the station's decision to drop programs and issue warnings, the aggrieved agreed to drop their petition opposing the station license renewal.

It is not clear whether such citizens' methods of controlling television in "the public interest" can or should be in general use. Should ad hoc citizen groups, which may be unrepresentative, be able to censor TV stations or networks by lobbying the FCC? In the absence of legislative guidelines the situation remains in flux.

Television and Violence

The most frequent charge against the television networks is that they too frequently show scenes of violence which encourage imitation by youthful audiences. The movies, perhaps more violent than TV, escape this criticism because they do not enter directly into the home. Children can be restricted from a X-rated movie house effectively, while it is virtually impossible to limit access to the family TV.

The Report of the National Commission on the Causes and Prevention of Violence (1969) was the first major analysis of televised violence: the Commission was against it. "It is a matter for grave concern that at a time when the values and the influence of traditional institutions such as family, church, and school are in question, television is emphasizing violent, anti-social styles of life. . . . Television," the Commission concluded, is a "contributing factor" to violence in our society.[7]

In formulating its report, the Commission and its staff reviewed a large quantity of social science research on televison violence. Great emphasis was placed on the amount of time devoted to the media. According to their estimates the average-income male watches TV two and one-half hours each weekday; he listens to the radio about two hours a day; he reads a newspaper for thirty minutes. Television is viewed even more by children and adults in lower income brackets.

In addition to available studies, the media task force conducted surveys which appraised a week of network prime-time shows for identical weeks in 1967 and 1968. In both years eight out of every ten dramatic programs contained some violence, although the rate of violent episodes declined slightly during the year. At the time of the study, virtually all the crime, western, and action-adventure programs contained some violence. In addition, cartoon programs on Saturday morning contained high proportions of violence in both years. In only two of ten acts of violence was the violence mitigated by humorous intent, such as slapstick or sham action. The staff estimated that in perhaps half the cases, "the violence is portrayed as a successful means of attaining the desired end."[8] It was rare that witnesses intervened, and only in 20 percent of the cases were lawful arrests and trials the result of violence. Violence was rarely presented as illegal or socially unacceptable. The cruel consequences of violence were minimized.

The Commission believed that televised violence has serious effects, particularly on young viewers; younger children between three and eight are highly susceptible to "observational learning" from television. Older children may consciously seek their "real-life roles" from it. For many children television becomes "the most accessible back door to the grown-up world." A larger proportion of poor children believe that television is true to life. A number of cited studies indicated that children do learn aggressive behavior from film or TV violence. The Commission concluded that "a constant diet of violent behavior on television has an adverse effect on human character and attitudes."[9]

Therefore, the Commission recommended abolishing children's cartoons containing serious non-comic violence, reducing violent episodes in the broadcast of crime, western, and adventure programs, making more effective efforts to "alter the basic context" in which violence is presented. They also recommended that members of the television industry become more seriously involved in research on the effects of violent programs and pay more attention to sociological evidence in planning their programs.

Some scholars have criticized the Commission's report. Professor James Q. Wilson has persuasively argued that the Commission presents no hard evidence to support its conclusion that television incites violence; in fact, he does not believe that it is possible to carry out an experiment which could determine whether television incites violence.[10]

In formulating his counter-charges, Wilson first re-analyzed the research reported to the Commission. In one experiment nursery school children watched an adult (in person or on film) strike a large inflated doll. After inducing some frustration among the children, the children were given a chance to kick or hit the doll themselves. Those who had seen the previous violence were more likely to strike the doll. Does this experiment prove the relationship between the observation of violence and the commission of violence? Wilson believes that it does not: the kicking of a doll is vastly different from crimes of violence.

In a second experiment, students who had seen a film of a knife fight gave slightly stronger electric shocks to another subject than those who had not seen the film. Analyzing this experiment, Wilson points out that the students were told to punish the subject with electric shock, so the experiment also measures obedience to authority and proves little about illegal violence itself.

Wilson concludes that the experiment required to prove the hypothesis relating TV and violent crime would be almost impossible to conduct. It would be a situation in which a group lived without television for several years while a comparable group lived with television. In the absence of truly adequate empirical data, Wilson concludes that it may be best to follow the opinion of the majority, i.e., normal political channels.

Because of dissatisfaction with the report of the National Commission on the Causes and Prevention of Violence, a second study was undertaken: The Surgeon General's Scientific Advisory Committee on Television and Social Behavior was composed of behavioral scientists and psychiatrists, nominated by various learned societies, and selected by the Surgeon General. The new Committee was more guarded than the Commission on Violence in its conclusion about the effect of television violence, perhaps because five of the twelve social scientists on the Committee were past or present employees of the broadcasting industry. Its report stated that only a small percentage of youth who were previously disposed to violence were incited by television. A few quotes may be the fairest means of presenting the Committee's findings:

> Studies of media content showed that violence is and has been a prominent component of all mass media in the United States. Television is no exception, and there can be no doubt that violence figures prominently in television entertainment. . . .

> It is sometimes asked if watching violent fare on television *can* cause a young person to act aggressively. The answer is that of course under some circumstances it can. . . . The question is faulty, for the real issue is how often it happens, what predispositional conditions have to be there, and what different undesirable, as well as benign, forms the aggressive reaction takes when it occurs. . . .

> . . . How much contribution to the violence of our society is made by extensive violent television viewing by our youth? The evidence (or, more accurately, the difficulty of finding evidence) suggests that the effect is small compared with many other possible causes, such as parental attitudes or knowledge of and experience with the real violence of our society.[11]

The Committee goes on to say that it does not know what changes should be made in television content and practices to reduce the tendency to "undesirable aggression among the audience."[12]

> There is evidence that among young children (ages 4 to 6) those most responsive to television violence are those who are highly aggressive to start with—who are prone to engage in spontaneous aggressive action against their playmates and, in the case of boys who display pleasure in viewing violence being inflicted on others.[13]

A number of surveys inquired into the relationship between violence viewing by young people and the tendency toward aggressiveness. The Committee concluded:

> There is a modest relationship between exposure to television violence and aggressive behavior or tendencies. . . .

> The experimental studies . . . contain indications that, under certain limited conditions, television viewing may lead to an increase in aggressive behavior. The evidence is clearest in highly controlled laboratory studies and considerably weaker in studies conducted under more natural conditions.[14]

It is the writers' impression that television has responded in a limited way to the conclusions of the National Commission on violence and the Surgeon General's committee's reports. "Gunsmoke," one of the longest running programs in TV history and frequently offered as an example of a program using excessive violence, was persuaded to reduce the violence in its stories. This trend is observable in several television series.

The electronic media also maintain an industry code which is much tighter than that of the movie industry. The National Association of Broadcasters forbids the encouragement of bad habits, the use of crude language and manners, unkind racial and ethnic references, and the details of murder and assault, in addition to excessive claims for products, and the mistreatment of animals.[15] It should be noted that this code is only negative; things should not be said or shown if particular groups might be offended.

In spite of the code and of the changes which have been made since the two reports, American television still apparently remains the most violent in the world.[16] A recent dispatch tells us that Chairman Richard E. Wiley of the FCC is determined to find some way to control video violence.[17] Thus there are many who continue to believe that television is a major contributing element to America's high rate of violent crime.

TV and American Ethical Values

Television's message, for commercial reasons, is geared to popular—and frequently violent—entertainment. Violence in and of itself is neither moral nor immoral, but what kind of values does television portray? TV viewing separates into two categories: the advertisements of the companies sponsoring the programs, and the programs themselves. Both present a wide range of subjects and of ethical standards.

The objective of all advertisers is to sell their products—a perfectly acceptable goal in a capitalist economy. But in their zeal to convince viewers to purchase their particular brand more than a few of them resort to exaggerated statements of questionable truth about the effectiveness or superiority of what they offer. Very few commercials portray violence; their ethical breach involves the validity of advertising claims, which leads to the possible belief that a successful sales record is the only valid standard. The integrity of those in charge of managing mass media is brought under suspicion by the recent movement toward advocacy journalism and by their use of the older trick of staged events.

Television programming itself offers a broad variety of situations. While a set of values which commonly employs excessive violence—as shown in many detective, western, and adventure shows—is undesirable, many of the best and longest-running television series have carried consistent ethical messages. The much criticized "Gunsmoke," "Bonanza," and such recent shows as "The Waltons" and "Apple's Way" are in themselves morality plays, as well as entertainment. Many people criticize programs like "All in the Family" and "Bridget Loves Bernie" because they deal with racial and religious differences in American society. One reason why "Bridget Loves Bernie" was cancelled was opposition to religious inter-marriage. But most observers must concede that both of these programs denigrate racial and religious prejudice, and thus indirectly support inter-racial tolerance. In addition to the foregoing, there are also some excellent public service programs. "Help Thy Neighbor" currently on every evening in the Los Angeles area, develops some much needed local charity. Television often gives alcohol or drug warning spots, and free time for important charities.

Chapter Seven's discussions of the family—the only real means of continuing ethical values today—noted that different kinds of child delinquency resulted from different kinds of parental mistakes in rearing children. The neurotic delinquent comes from overprotective family life; the aggressive delinquent from a home of hostility and rejection; the pseudo-social delinquent from a home of coldness and indifference. If this analysis is correct, could not television—which reaches far more homes than any other institution of society—try to help parents develop the type of loving but firm control that will help avoid delinquency in their children? Rodman and Grams have suggested a series of parent-education television messages to accomplish this purpose.[18]

Television is continuing to evolve as a communications medium. It has made mistakes, such as inadvertently aiding riots through TV exposure and publicity. When college rioters found that they were given live television coverage, riots became fashionable and acceptable and considerable imitation was encouraged. Simliar events may have taken place in race riots. As the television industry became aware of this problem, efforts were made to remedy it. Cameramen were less readily available at the telephone call of every would-be demonstration leader, and long-distance lenses were used in television coverage so that rioters would be less conscious of the presence of TV. Air time devoted to violent demonstrations was limited, and broadcasting was more likely to be delayed.

In other areas of public service the television medium has also had increasing success. Television documentaries have performed a needed service in informing the public about newsworthy events. Occasional muckraking has been unjust, such as the famous "Selling of the Pentagon" where questionable reporting techniques were employed. But on the whole, television documentaries and interviews, such as those of Walter Cronkite with Lyndon Johnson and Aleksandr Solzhenitsyn, contribute to their audiences' understanding of the world. The continuing broadcast of religious services also benefits significant portions of the community.

More important than the things which television currently does, however, are the things which it could do. With its constant presence in American homes, great public prestige, and financial power, the industry is in a unique position to influence the attitudes of Americans toward moral behavior. For example, television could portray the crime situation from the point of view of the victims and of the experience of the criminal and his family after he has committed the crime. The suffering of the victim and his or her family, the shame of the criminal's family, the years of languishing in jail, and the continuing negative influence of a criminal conviction on one's later possibilities of employment, are all significant detractions to a life of crime. This line of approach would increase the sympathy of society and of potential criminals for the victims of crime; in addition, it would augment the psychological fear of committing crimes because of the frightening consequences. The usually gritty cops and robbers or slick detective approach to crime now taken by television is largely two-dimensional and sensationally untrue to life. The real victim of crime, who is statistically more often a member of a minority group, is the "forgotten man" on television.

A similar idea was broached by the staff of the Surgeon General's Scientific Advisory Committee on Television and Social Behavior:

> Power tactics [police and penal force or threat of force] might become unnecessary if broad-scale identification with victims could be encouraged and reinforced, and television might be an important tool in such a movement. Thus television might be able to move people to be 'more human' on a plane where identification with victims would occur as readily as with aggressors and where the development of alliance would reduce divisiveness and conflict.
>
> Obviously, the utilization of television for this purpose involves some complex policy discussions by all society. Psychological sacrifices would be involved if audiences were carried along and obliged to identify with and suffer along with victims, seeing them as they are in real life. If violence were more realistically portrayed on television, it would not be so easy to watch, to accept, or to enjoy, and even less to participate in vicariously.[19]

The question, thus, is not the presence of television violence *per se*, but the context in which it is used. Television spokesmen frequently point out that great literature is filled with violence. They neglect to point out that great literature achieves distinction by making its frequently violent themes true to life, allowing the reader to feel compassion toward the powerless victim and usually, anger toward the unjust aggressor. For example, Shakespeare's *Macbeth* or *Hamlet* is bloodier than almost any televised shoot-'em-up, yet because of their basic humanism these plays entertain in a deeper sense than the vicarious violence of many media offerings.

It might involve greater expense and difficulty to re-orient exciting television shows or create new ones which focus on the consequences of crime. If properly done the effect, we believe, would be worth the effort. Perhaps for the first time, parts of our population would see the appalling consequences of crime and corruption, and would take action to minimize them throughout our public life.

Radio

The influence of the radio has been somewhat eclipsed by television; yet the average time devoted to listening is still substantial. Radio is available to car drivers, where television is not. It can also offer a much greater range of program choices, thus furnishing specialized services: news, good music, and talk shows.

Radio is governed by a self-regulating code which is considerably less detailed than that governing TV broadcasting, and is regulated by the FCC as is television.

Because of its specialized nature, radio is harder to analyze in reference to its effect on public morality than almost any other medium. However, one major interest in the last fifteen years has been in the ethical message of popular music—the varieties of rock, acid, hard, country, and the protest and folk songs. Although television has started moving into pop music, and live concerts are lucrative for pop groups, what makes or breaks stars and million-sellers is still radio air time.

The themes of most popular songs since the late 1960s involved love/sex, drugs, violence, and politics/society. These themes change over time, and the popularity of drugs has somewhat decreased. By the mid-1970s the greatest themes were the more enduring love/sex and politics/society. Analysis of song content suggests that the nature of sexual relations has changed from the romantic to a "possess and move on" approach.[20] Songs of protest and revolution were among the most popular at the end of the 1960s.[21]

Paul Hirsch, writing in the *American Behavioral Scientist*, documents the impression that "protest hits" were once very popular and that "unconventional messages about sex, drugs, and politics are recorded routinely now by major record companies and disseminated by widely listened-to radio stations across the land." However, Hirsch also cites studies which show that teenagers were not always able to interpret these references in the songs to which they listened.[22]

In relation to the amount of televised violence, the violence of pop artists and pop songs is considerably greater. One group smashes their instruments during the course of their performance. The Rolling Stones, one of the most important rock groups, reports that audiences at their concerts react in a variety of unconventional manners. At one concert in Altamont, California, the Stones hired the Hell's Angels as guards. The result was a widely publicized killing of a rock fan. However, many of the excesses of the hard rock popular in the late 1960s and 1970s are disappearing as modern music turns in the direction of the "country sound," which is considerably less violence-provoking in both lyrics and rhythm.

It would perhaps be an understatement to say that radio has been remiss in not curbing some of the excesses of the rock/drug music. However, in all fairness, given the intellectual climate of opinion, it is not surprising that radio stations and disc jockeys found it difficult to limit arbitrarily "freedom of expression." Nevertheless, it is a self-regulating industry and station managers and record company executives are called upon to make practical decisions about the likely impact of the songs which they broadcast. Although there is controversy on the basis of the United States Supreme Court decisions, a station manager who decides that a piece of music might potentially incite violence or illegal acts, or that it violates the mores of his listeners, would not be acting illegally to challenge its broadcast. At the least, a station manager could issue guidelines to his staff to indicate his understanding of the standards of ethics maintained by him and the community.

These are essentially checks on violent excess, checks which must continue to be maintained to restrain crime and violence. The positive efforts which radio could make are very similar to those recommended for television. Since radio has few dramatic or action programs, it would have to concentrate on short spots emphasizing the terrible human consequences of "middle class" crimes and crimes of violence.

Movies

There has been much public discussion of the sex and violence in recent films, although little research has been done on their impact. Audience surveys of the estimated twenty million moviegoers (1969) suggest that audiences tend to be affluent and under thirty, indicating that movies have a significant impact on teenagers and young adults. The increased affluence of the blacks has also given them the means to become frequent moviegoers.

Since movie audiences are a self-selected, paying group, there are fewer grounds for limiting film content. Nevertheless, the film industry maintains a rating system (G-all ages admitted; PG-all ages

admitted, parental guidance suggested; R-restricted to persons
under 17 unless accompanied by parents; and X-no one under 17
admitted. In addition to these there is the unofficial "triple X" rating
used to classify films dealing with explicit sex.)[23] There is no federal
regulation of the movie industry comparable to the FCC, and court
decisions defining pornography for the purpose of local prosecution
and distribution of explicit materials through the mails have been
sporadic.

Marshall McLuhan characterizes the film as a "hot medium,"
contrasted with television which is a "cool medium." In spite of
this, social scientists view television and films as quite similar, and
for the purposes of their studies often transpose the two. In one of
the few studies available, Leonard Berkowitz maintains that certain
frustrated children may withdraw into a world of violence in movies
or in television.[24] However, in the absence of adequate empirical
evidence of the effect of movies on violence, it is reasonable to
assume that many of the generalizations made by social scientists
about television, as problematic as they are, are also applicable to
films.

If television has reduced episodes of violence since its period of
criticism in the late 1960s, it seems that the movies have increased
theirs. Perhaps competition for audiences has persuaded them that
violence is popular, e.g., the success of Sam Peckinpah and Clint
Eastwood, as many competent observers believe.[25]

Unfortunately, to our knowledge no extensive studies of the new
trend toward violence are available. Observations indicate that
violence is no longer used in the traditional framework of crime and
punishment. Although in a majority of cases justice triumphs in the
end, in some cases it does not. There is also frequently a romance or
mystique of "gratuitous violence." This anti-social attitude of many
movie producers and directors, is, according to one critic, a major
element of the movie industry's thinking. "Today movies say that
the system is corrupt, that the whole thing stinks, and they've been
saying this steadily since the mid-1960s."[26]

To increase popular consciousness of the consequences of crime
and the public's role in reducing it, the movie industry—to a limited
extent—could produce films similar to those suggested for television
series: stories which emphasize the suffering of the victim and his
family, the guilt, remorse, and punishment of the criminal, the
anguish and frequent pauperization of the criminal's family.

Movies, because of their desire to glorify personalities ("stars"), can also stress the positive effects of ethical activity. Their heroes may no longer ride into the sunset and pass up the opportunity to kiss the leading lady, but they still can show the type of ethical acts which are possible in modern society.

However, the problem of securing the film industry's support is perhaps greater than it is in the case of television. The movie industry seems somewhat more faddish and perhaps more sensation-oriented. It will certainly support good causes such as better race relations, but usually they are causes which have great box office appeal.

Newspapers

Newspapers have a long and important history in our society. In the past, so-called yellow journalism distorted many features of American life and was blamed for our involvement in at least one war. Professional standards have dramatically increased in this century, with the possible additional consequence of increasing the "intellectual bias" in the news system. The constitutional guarantee of freedom of the press and the belief that this freedom promotes truth and accuracy in political affairs has helped, on the whole, to reduce political corruption. In recent years this belief allowed the press to focus on the crime problem.

While the amount of space devoted to violence is small, according to one analysis[27], the newspaper world apparently shares the common blindness toward the status of ethics in public life. Newspaper stories on crime are, of course, frequent; almost none analyze the problem from the point of view of ethical motivation or its lack. Journalists are more likely to write about the plight of criminals than the difficulties of crime victims and there are almost no news articles or editorials about the necessity of educating individuals to a sense of obligation to ethical conduct.

Comic Books

Comic books no longer hold the place which they once did for the entertainment of children and youths, primarily because of the impact of television. With a considerably smaller national population, over six hundred million comic books were sold in an average year in the 1940s; today's figure is still a high three hundred million. Through the 1950s comic books were frequently gory and sexy accounts of unbelievable life. Some comics were written in ways which explained how to commit crimes, and lurid advertisements appeared in each issue. In a number of cases juvenile offenders have stated that they took their cues directly from comic books.[28]

Because of public pressure, the Comic Code Authority was created to approve those comic books which are based on established standards of taste and ethical content. The code provides that crime shall not be presented in an encouraging manner; excessive violence and gruesome crimes shall be eliminated; narcotics shall not be presented except as a vicious habit; profanity, obscenity, and smut are forbidden; religion shall not be ridiculed; nudity is prohibited; and family situations depicted "should have as their ultimate goal the protection of the children and family life." Further, "in every instance good shall triumph over evil."[29] Advertising in comics is similarly controlled by the association. At this time, about 85 percent of comic books are controlled by the Code Authority.

We have read a dozen recently published comic books, all approved by the Authority. While they were filled with violence, being war and science fiction stories, there seemed little effort to glorify violence, to bring in unnecessary gore, or to show undue cruelty. For this reason it seems unlikely that comic books are a major contributor to violent behavior and may, indeed, have a salutary ethical effect. As it is, the comic book industry has made considerable strides in curtailing the sensationalism which formerly characterized their product.

Recommendations

We have briefly outlined some steps which the media could take in response to our ethical situation. They essentially involve adaptation to a presentation of ethics which emphasizes the terrible consequences of crime and corruption for all concerned. For example, there could be a TV documentary or a movie feature film depicting the psychological and economic load thrown on impoverished families by the prevalence of crime in core city areas.

Another documentary could trace the lives of several criminals—both lower and middle class—who ruin their chances and (with some) their consciences by injuring or robbing others. Still another program could show the effect of governmental corruption—like that of the New York City police force as exposed by the Knapp Commission—on many aspects of life in a major city, e.g., drug use in the high schools, mugging in order to acquire drug money, prostitution, the corruption of public officials, and so on. There might also be sketches of family life which would help parents to handle drug use and delinquency effectively.

A possibility for television or radio talk shows would be a program in which youths discussed problems of inter-personal relationships, going beyond the popular "Mind Your Manners" format of the 1940s to encourage the full expression of views, although criminologists, sociologists, and psychiatrists might give some helpful advice.

Neither television nor any other medium is likely to change without some external pressure. The National Commission on the Causes and Prevention of Violence and the Surgeon General's Committee gave television an impetus to reduce its level of violence, which has been done. What is now needed is a similar push in the direction of individual ethics. Another national commission or, more important, a change in the expressed attitudes of the major opinion-formers of the country, especially in the nationally prestigious newspapers and magazines, could have such an effect. If a half dozen of these should urge the television industry to increase the moral aspects of their programming, television writers and producers could find ways—as ingenious as those used in Sesame Street—to do so.

Another way in which television might get access to new ideas and to sources of information is through the creation of advisory boards composed of viewers. The networks would, of course, be free to accept or reject the board's proposals.

A more drastic alternative to help bring about greater ethical responsibility might be to nationalize television or to greatly expand the influence of public broadcasting. This could produce more problems than benefits, and we do not believe that it is a reasonable course of action. However, given the rather poor performance record of the industry which in many respects continues to be a comparatively unresponsible attempt at mass entertainment, many people will continue to advocate much greater regulation.

The dangers of nationalized TV, however, are great.

Nationalized television may easily become political television. There are many indications that this has happened in France and Sweden. In this country, where politics is largely a way of life and passions run high, it is likely that television would become a greater political football than it is at present.

This great danger is not offset by any guaranteed benefit. There is great doubt whether publicly-owned television in Europe is either more ethically responsible or more entertaining than it is in the U.S. The British Broadcasting Company has been criticized for its excessive presentation of violence.[30] By and large European television is dull; governmental cultural activities are rarely exceptional. Is there any reason to believe that nationalization would improve the quality of broadcasting either culturally or ethically?

While public ownership of television does not seem desirable, there is much to be said for the kind of supervision implied in the report of the National Commission on the Causes and Prevention of Violence and the Surgeon General's research. Apparently it has had beneficial effects on television programming. Also, the Public Broadcasting Service (PBS) could be extended into the ethical area. PBS has had some limited success in cultural broadcasts and a great success with special educational programs such as "Sesame Street," "Mister Rogers," and "The Electric Company." If PBS has been more responsive to social needs than is the private sphere in the area of education, it does not necessarily follow that an increase in its budget and programming would bring about increased interest in ethics. In many respects, PBS administrators seem to reflect the bias of the intellectuals—who have been hostile to ethical instruction—more than do the average television executives.

All of the media need to understand that their social responsibilities include individual ethical values. If they continue to provide only amoral entertainment with a diffuse social concern, leaving ethics to other areas of society, they will do society a great injustice. The other agencies of society—home, schools, churches—are largely unable at this time to maintain ethical standards, in great measure because of the electronic media's increasing influence. If the media has become the schoolmaster of the nation, it has a responsibility to maintain the ethical standards of the nation. Being unaware of its influence and responsibilities is no long-term excuse.

— 13 —

Government—Corruption or Reform?

This chapter discusses the role of governments (local, state, and national) in helping to improve or corrupt American ethics. The first section deals with the responsibilities of government in executing the law well and fairly and in improving the social/material conditions of its citizens. We believe that the ability of the government to do these two things well will help to eliminate many of the causes of crime. The second section deals with the substantive actions (legislative, regulatory) which the government can take to improve ethical education and general attitudes. The third section treats the symbolic and ceremonial functions of government which can affect general ethical attitudes.

Governments have a profound effect on their populace. In spite of its general protestations of ethical rearmament, the Nazis' thorough corruption, venality, and calculated disregard of accepted standards of ethical behavior hurt the ethics of German society. Aleksandr Solzhenitsyn has written of the corrosion of moral standards created by the failure of Russian society to punish the agents of state repression:

> We have to condemn publicly the very *idea* that some people have the right to repress others. In keeping silent about evil, in burying it so deep within us that no sign of it appears on the surface, we are *implanting* it, and it will rise up a thousandfold in the future. When we neither punish nor reproach evildoers, we are not simply protecting their trivial old age, we are thereby ripping the foundations of justice from beneath new generations. It is for this reason, and not because of the 'weakness of indoctrinational work,' that they are growing up 'indifferent.' Young people are acquiring the conviction that foul deeds are never punished on earth, that they always bring prosperity.
>
> It is going to be uncomfortable, horrible, to live in such a country![1]

213

Britain's government helped to improve British ethical standards in the nineteenth century. Of course, no government, especially in a democratic society, can be too far removed from the opinions of its citizenry. Therefore, professional leaders in business, the unions, academics, and many other fields, will need to play important roles in shaping government policy in the area of ethics.

While this book explores the thesis that lack of adequate instruction is one reason for America's ethical difficulties, we do not believe that it is alone. Two other reasons—the lack of adequate execution of the law and persistent poverty areas which "breed" certain types of crime—were discussed in Chapter Three. We will recur to them here because they fall within the purview of government action. They have not been discussed at greater length in this book because many other writers have done so comprehensively.

Government Policy Indirectly Related to Ethics

There is perhaps no more controversial subject in American government today than law enforcement. Liberals frequently argue that America is becoming a police state; minority groups believe that they are the victims of "police brutality"; conservatives maintain that high crime rates demonstrate that the law is not being adequately enforced. Frequently a single law enforcement unit may be simultaneously labelled "fascistic," "racist," and "bleeding heart" by its critics.

As noted earlier, American law enforcement is a patchwork, particularly in contrast to the more centralized police agencies of Western Europe. Like local governments in the United States, the law enforcement agencies are broken up into thousands of small units. Many local police forces—both urban and rural—are poorly trained and poorly disciplined. Also, the prosecuting attorneys in many areas, especially county officials, may be ill-prepared for their crucial tasks. Finally, police in some areas are accepting pay-offs to ignore crimes or are actually committing crimes themselves.

Of course, some cities, both large and small, have good police and prosecutors. A few states have effective state police. The Federal Bureau of Investigation is a well-run agency, although as a matter of policy it has limited the coordination of its functions with other law enforcement units.

Even the better-organized police agencies suffer from court procedures which, especially in the last decade, seem to encourage delays. Fred P. Graham, a news reporter for CBS and former Supreme Court correspondent for the *New York Times* and a supporter of the Warren Court, has described the situation:

> When the panorama of crime and punishment of the later Warren years is parsed, it is evident that the uneasy feelings among the public were justified, if for the wrong reasons. The criminal justice system *was* eroding. Crime was increasing and there was a decline in the system's capacity to deal with each crime. For each 100 serious crimes reported at the end of the Warren era, fewer were solved by the police than had been the case in 1961. Thus there were fewer arrests, few convictions. For law-abiding citizens, the chances of becoming crime victims had increased; for criminals the prospects of punishment had declined.[2]

Bank robbers robbed more banks while they were awaiting trial. Witnesses forgot or disappeared. The slowness of American justice was made worse by the new changes in the judicial process.[3] It has been estimated that it took twice as long to try a federal criminal case in 1970 as in 1960.[4]

The problem of paralyzing court delays could be helped by the establishment of unified state court systems and by the selection of judges according to a merit plan, as recommended by the Advisory Commission on Intergovernmental Relations. It is surprising that the powerful bar associations of our states and cities have done so little to try to improve the processes of justice to which they are so closely related.

In sum, our society's law enforcement is remarkably shoddy. In Appendix B we discuss some desirable improvements of law enforcement which could help to improve it and, we believe, the overall ethical condition of our society.

Corrupt and inefficient law enforcement affects the citizen's perception of the law. In our essentially libertarian society, the law continues to be the only generally accepted standard and regulator of individual ethical behavior. Since the churches, the schools, and mass entertainment have dropped individual ethics as a major focus of concern, the penal and civil statutes remain as the only point of reference for them. A description of the law as an ethical force is given by Professor Edmund Cahn:

> In the system of law, statutes and judicial principles mark off the edges with a sharpness which—though by no means invariable or exact—is at least sufficient to unite the community behind the enforcement official and thus to serve warning on all concerned that this specific precept defined in these terms cannot be transgressed with impunity. It is in this fashion that the *sense of wrong* makes its appearance in the law courts and legislatures as the firmer and more precise *sense of justice*.[5]

Most professional discussions of the crime problem by criminologists emphasize the amelioration of conditions in the slum areas where there is a high crime rate. The criminologists tend to advocate more generous welfare policies, more and better housing (slum clearance), better education and recreational facilities, and better job training and job placement services.[6]

These recommendations are observed by many with considerable skepticism. They point out that there is little or no correlation between welfare measures and the decrease of crime; in fact, the federal "war on poverty" was accompanied by large crime-rate increases. Many criminologists answer that the increase in crime came from other factors and could have been higher if the social welfare programs had not been in existence. There are few objective studies which permit us to appraise the truth of this controversy.[7]

In spite of the inadequacy of existing evidence, we do not believe that it is in the best interests of our society to abandon social welfare programs. These measures are presumed to be useful in combatting crime and they increase the possibility of bringing all American citizens into an active role in the economic, social, and political life of the country. A well-conceived and well-administered social welfare program would benefit society as a whole—economically, socially, and ethically.[8]

It seems apparent that in order to secure effective reformation of our ethical standards, all three approaches—improvement in law enforcement, poverty conditions, and ethical instruction—need to be pursued. It frequently happens that in order to bring about a desirable social goal a variety of approaches may ultimately prove most successful. In terms of "cost/benefit analysis," we believe that our society can afford all three approaches to ethical reform, especially since the recommended changes in ethical teaching would cost very little.

Direct Governmental Action

There are a number of things government can do in the area of ethics. Two major steps would be (1) efforts to improve education in ethics and (2) direct legislation in the ethical area. Action in either area is problematic. First, both school boards and teachers, not to mention students, are resentful of efforts to dictate school policy. In the states where legislatures have passed bills requiring courses in values or ethics, little or nothing has been done by the local boards to implement them in 50 percent of the cases.

While new curriculum requirements do not seem to be the answer, there are other options open for schools. For one thing, cooperation between education and justice agencies at all levels of government can be extended. State Attorneys General could ask Superintendents of Public Instruction for joint conferences or joint committees to work on problems of basic ethical instruction. Mayors could bring chiefs of police, prosecutors, judges, and local school superintendents together to discuss ethical issues. It would be highly desirable if the United States Department of Justice and the Office of Education could agree on policies of ethical education—as has been done in Sweden through a joint committee of Ministers of Education and Justice—but it is more likely that state and local offices will learn to cooperate with one another.

In spite of good intentions on both sides there will be friction in this arrangement. Teachers and students may again oppose "outside" interference with what they teach. The Justice agency will need to have a representative who is qualified to explain the place of ethical education in the schools. As we have pointed out, schools are just beginning to turn away from John Dewey's strictures against ethical education. School officials need reasoned analysis about ethics, not orders from legal authorities.

Legislating in the ethical area is also extremely sensitive. In recent years the pendulum which originally began to swing away from ethical legislation with the repeal of Prohibition has completed its arc. Not only has there been no further legislation in fields related to ethics, but laws governing such things as sex and drug use are less frequently enforced. Also, the penalties for many crimes have apparently become less severe (e.g., the virtual abolishment of capital punishment and increased ease of parole).

Fortunately there is no major disagreement concerning such offenses as embezzlement, robbery, armed assault, rape, murder, or similar crimes. In these areas the government has a great deal to do with maintaining a conception of individual ethical responsibility.

Unfortunately, politicians, legislators, and bureaucrats are generally not too highly respected professionals in our society. This may be due to the tradition of self-service, not self-sacrifice, in American public life. For example, Tocqueville thought that in comparison to aristocratic societies American public servants were more corrupt and incapable.[9] He was more laudatory about the long-run tendency of American laws. Thus, although legislators and politicians generally may rhetorically attempt to elevate ethics, and may pass ethical legislation, rarely are they or their legislation given much public weight.

One of the greatest sources of ethical controversy in America today centers around the ethics of the legislators themselves, that is, the tendency toward conflict of interest. The basic problem is whether a legislator should vote for a law which will affect his own economic interest. It is generally accepted—indeed one cannot see how democratic government could operate otherwise—that representatives usually vote for the economic interests of what they view to be the most significant part of their constituency. We expect representatives from strong union areas to vote with the unions, and representatives from farm or business areas to act in a similar fashion. Of course, there are situations where the legislator's interest may be considerably more divided. However, it is inevitable that in United States politics, as in other constitutional democracies, the political parties are themselves to some extent pressure groups for economic interests. This is a reflection of cultural and economic pluralism in our society. But when a legislator becomes the tool of a specific economic group which financed his campaign, or accepts financial support in exchange for a vote, or votes for a bill which will benefit him directly, then an ethical trust has been violated.

Except for the last, each of these cases of legislative influence can be justified. Frequently the only substantial source of campaign support in one district is a union, and in another is a corporation—both of which have specific legislative goals. Sometimes the financial support—such as a lobbyist's payment of a fee to a member of the representative law firm—does not benefit the legislator directly. Occasionally a legislator may conscientiously vote for a bill which benefits him personally; for example, a banker-representative may reasonably support legislation strengthening the banking industry, and presumably strengthening the economy as a whole.

While there may be legitimate conflict of interest, too many of our legislators' financial transactions appear to be suspicious. Therefore, a legislative code of ethics which would preclude direct or indirect bribes for votes and would require a full statement of sources of financial interests affected by a vote including a full statement of financial support, seems desirable. In general, our legislative bodies have shown a greater willingness to set ethical requirements for administrative officials than for elected officials.

Many representatives may be unconscious of the effect which questionable legislative practices can have upon the ethical conduct of other citizens. We know of no studies which measure the effect of legislative or administrative corruption on public ethical attitudes, although studies have been made which have shown a connection between police corruption and ghetto riots. The popular reaction to Watergate and the attendant corruption scandals is reassuring from the view that good political practice is still the socially-accepted standard.

In addition to cleaning up the electoral process, governments can use their powers of the purse and of regulation to encourage greater ethical behavior. As examples, cities and counties where widespread corruption exists could lose state and national funds (revenue sharing, block grants) if they did not take steps to ameliorate the situation; the FCC can encourage more ethical radio and TV broadcasting; the Department of Labor with the cooperation of the National Labor Relations Board (given some changes in its powers) could make it more difficult for corrupt unions to organize and operate. Needless to say, these kinds of sweeping changes could only be undertaken after exhaustive analysis of their likely impact.

Symbolic and Ceremonial Functions of Government

Conflict of interest and other legislative and executive misconduct are of paramount importance, not only because of waste and inefficient use of public resources, but because of the examples of illegality which are presented to the members of society. Why obey the law if the representatives who make the laws do not? Why serve the country or community if the elected servants only serve themselves? Perceiving corruption in their representatives, "there comes about" in the minds of the general populace "an odious mingling of the conceptions of baseness and power, or unworthiness and success, and of profit and dishonor."[10] Tocqueville also said:

> While the rulers of aristocracies sometimes seek to corrupt, those of democracies prove corruptible. . . . As the men at the head of the state in democracies are almost always subject to suspicion, in some sense they give government support to the crimes of which they are accused. They thus provide dangerous examples to still struggling virtue and furnish glorious comparisons for hidden vice.[11]

There can be no doubt that major public figures influence the characters and attitudes of the populace. Several studies of political socialization (education of children for citizenship) indicate the impact of the President on younger children. After President Kennedy's assassination, parents in particular handed on to their children a good deal of knowledge of politics.[12]

The lives of great political leaders continue to interest those whom they lead, for obvious and intelligible reasons. They also serve as "ideals" worthy of emulation. For example, Daniel Webster glorifies the ethics of Adams and Jefferson in this famous commemorative speech:

> No men, fellow citizens, ever served their country with more entire exemption from every imputation of selfish and mercenary motives, than those to whose memory we are paying these proofs of respect. A suspicion of any disposition to enrich themselves or to profit by their public employments never rested on either. No sordid motive approached them. The inheritance which they have left to their children is of their character and their fame.[13]

In recent years, David Packard gave away several million dollars to avoid the possibility of conflict of interest while he was Secretary of Defense. Averell Harriman's public career cost him large sums. The press may not emphasize such meritorious actions as much as they deserve, but when they are the accepted standards of conduct they strengthen both the reputation of the man and, also importantly, set an example for other men.

On the negative side, public officials may also serve as a counter example to ethical behavior, as Tocqueville indicated. Speaker James G. Blaine set a poor example through passage of the Crédit Mobilier bill. President Harding eroded confidence in the integrity of men in high office by being too easy on the delinquencies of his Attorney General and Secretary of the Interior. Although it is too early to tell if Watergate and other scandals of the Nixon administration will have a lasting impression on American political life, it is not easy to see how this corruption may have helped to educate citizens in ethical behavior.

Public officials may also provide ethical leadership for society. For example, Abraham Lincoln's personal example was matched by his eloquent attack on the institution of slavery, and Theodore Roosevelt's attack on the "malefactors of great wealth" was some help in encouraging needed social reform. F.D.R.'s criticism of the "economic royalists" was a continuation of this phenomenon which was perhaps less needed. In the last two cases their attacks may have been discounted because the President assaulted an interest which had relatively few votes. Greater credit is reserved for leaders who attack urban machines, union dynasties, or corporate-sponsored legislative machines which have substantial votes at their disposal.

If public leaders of reputation—whether executive, legislative, or judicial—should endorse efforts to make America more ethically conscious, such efforts would be worthwhile. It is true that the public has a not unreasonable suspicion of political hucksterism. But, as Professor Marvin Meyers observes: "Characteristically, a commanding presidential voice and figure—Jefferson, Jackson, Lincoln, Theodore Roosevelt, Wilson, F.D.R.—immediately works a change by giving moral direction, programmatic purpose to conventional rhetoric."[14] For an example of the power of moral leadership, consider Lord Charnwood's analysis of Lincoln:

> He had been able to save the nation, partly because he saw that unity was not to be sought by way of base concession. He had been able to free the slaves, partly because he would not hasten to the object at the

sacrifice of what he thought a larger purpose. This most unrelenting enemy to the project of the Confederacy was the one man who had quite purged his heart and mind from hatred or even anger toward his fellow countrymen of the South. That fact came to be seen in the South too, and generations in America are likely to remember it when all other features of his statecraft have grown indistinct. . . . For perhaps not many conquerors, and certainly few sucessful statemen, have escaped the tendency of power to harden or at least to narrow their human sympathies, but in this man a natural wealth of tender compassion became richer and more tender while in the stress of deadly conflict he developed an astounding strength.[15]

Another important activity of government is ceremonial. On public holidays, such as inaugurations, commemorative days, public works dedications, and other important achievements, national, state, and local governments have the occasion to appeal to their constituents. These functions are perhaps not as important as they were in the last century when they were also almost the only occasion for community entertainment. Nevertheless, many millions of people, in person or by radio and television, attend presidential and gubernatorial inaugurations and large national celebrations.

The political rhetoric of the last century seems pompous and perhaps chauvinistic to modern ears, but it is nevertheless instructive as a model of what ceremonial rhetoric can be. For example:

We celebrate the return of the day on which our separate national existence was declared; the day when the momentous experience was commenced, by which the world, and posterity, and we ourselves were to be taught, how far a nation can be trusted with self-government—how far life, and liberty, and property are safe, and the progress of social improvement is secure, under the influence of laws made by those who are to obey them; the day when, for the first time in the world, a numerous people was ushered into the family of nations, organized on the principle of the political equality of all the citizens.[16]

Perhaps the great seriousness and high moral tone of such rhetoric would strike us today as preachy and moralistic. If carried to excess it might even lose votes. On the other hand, one should not cynically dismiss the importance of democratic principles and ethical standards in public life.

Summary

American governments have a checkered record of corruption. Our national government was seriously corrupt in the last half of the nineteenth century, although now it is considerably reformed. State governments have generally improved, but striking examples of misconduct continually come to light. Local governments seem to be especially subject to domination by business and organized crime interests, and in many areas police are systematically corrupted.

As was suggested in Chapter Three, for government to serve as an effective ethical agent it must first remove the general impression connecting it and its representatives with unethical practices. Second, there needs to be a greater consciousness among public officials regarding ethical leadership potential in their public offices and private lives. As we have tried to suggest, more can be done by government both directly (statute and regulatory proceedings) and indirectly (through example and rhetoric).

Epilogue

If the reader has followed our discussion this far, he has little more to do. We only ask him to bear with us while we summarize our argument and make a few policy and research recommendations.

Contemporary Western society, and especially American society, suffers from inadequate training in individual ethics. Personal honesty and integrity, appreciation of the interests of others, non-violence, and abiding by the law are examples of values insufficiently taught at the present time. Lack of instruction in individual ethics can be seen in many ways, from public vandalism, verbal abuse, and a general lack of civility to pervasive criminal activity and corruption. When we argue that individual ethical instruction is related to criminality, we *are not saying* that it is the sole or even major cause of crime. Poverty, poor law enforcement, and social injustice are also important factors which must be dealt with in order to have an effective public policy.

As political scientists we have not been merely content to trace the course of the decline in ethical instruction and its correlation with increased crime. We are also interested in analyzing methods by which ethics can be encouraged and applying that analysis to the various institutions which can help or hinder the formation of ethical values. Our chapters on family, peers, church, school, media, intellectuals, and government are designed to analyze existing patterns of ethical education and to make suggestions regarding its improvement.

The most important single change which could possibly be made would be in the intellectual attitude toward ethical responsibility. In many cases this would involve no more than an examination by leading intellectuals of recent research in the field of ethical education, permitting them to re-think existing stereotypes and to see that there are many things which can be done to improve value learning.

Because family and peer groups are not "institutions" in any normal sense, our recommendations are very general. The family—weakened by the increasing influence of the mass media and by peer groups—nevertheless does a reasonably good job of ethical education. The family's position would be strengthened if other institutions, e.g., the schools, churches, and television, strengthened their position on ethical education. The peer groups are almost always derivative groups depending for their structure, habits, and attitudes on influences around them. To improve peer groups requires the active cooperation of community agencies and good individual adult leadership.

The schools and the churches are well situated to teach individual ethical responsibility, but do not do so. A reform of their ethical education would involve a recommitment to ethical instruction and a re-training of instructional staff. A great deal of developmental research applicable to the schools and the churches is being done. It is an understatement to say that the leaders of public education and of the churches must reappraise their ethical instruction in light of the increasing need for ethically sensitive members of society.

A change in the media approach might perhaps have the greatest immediate effect on national ethical attitudes. The television industry, which has been reasonably conscientious about limiting excessive violence and sex—more so that the movies—has not taken advantage of many of the situations available to it to get an ethical message across. The argument that these shows, or spots, are not commercially competitive is not ultimately valid. Television has been so successful, has fashioned such a large place for itself in contemporary society, that it must take on a greater social responsibility. If it does not do so there may very well be increasing pressure to tighten FCC regulations.

Government must make sure that it escapes the taint of corruption before it can become an effective part of ethical reform. There are not too many statutory actions which it can take, but it can play a significant role through regulation and through some ceremonial activities. The Office of Education and the Federal Communications Commission are two good examples of bodies which can have significant impact on our major institutions. The ceremonial and exemplary role of governments, particularly great national and state leaders, is always important for ill or for good.

It is important that the institutions of our society take up ethical reform because the long-run maintenance of our democracy depends upon a citizen body which is politically and ethically responsible. It is reasonable to suppose that as the crime situation continues to worsen the strain on our society will continue to grow. Not only will the freedom which comes from a secure environment disappear, as has partially occurred already, but the respect for individual rights, both of crime victims and crime offenders, will also disappear. Finally, and inescapably, democratic procedures will fall into disrepute, and increasingly centralized, authoritarian measures will be necessarily employed to handle the crime problem as well as other problems.

This is not a pretty picture, but it seems to be a highly likely one if our society does not voluntarily seek to transmit minimal individual ethics through its educational process. Societies, after all, are not formed by propinquity, or economy, or history, but by a shared set of beliefs and experiences—one large part of which, particularly in a democratic society, is the acceptance of ethical responsibility for one's actions.

We believe that in light of the severity of this social problem, new thought and study on ethics is imperative. Much needed work is now being done in education and psychology to understand the educational/developmental process involved. A major problem lies in transmitting this knowledge to the general society, so that non-academics can be informed about the possibilities of ethical instruction. This seems to be the case because practitioners of several of the major disciplines do not consider general social ethical attitudes, and therefore ethical education, to be part of their field. These include most political scientists, sociologists, and psychologists, especially when they are quantitatively-oriented.

The direction of future research should then be in these areas, enabling them to contribute to a much-needed national ethical dialogue. Our society needs to provide an education which will enable each of its members to have a deep ethical regard for fellow citizens.

Appendix A

Criminal Statistics

Ruth Aura Ross

Although statistical comparisons are widely used by social scientists, students of criminal justice largely have ignored the potential of this form of analysis in their research. Criminologists have a parochial focus and usually limit themselves to case studies of a single geographic area or to the data in the Uniform Crime Reports (UCR) of the Federal Bureau of Investigation (FBI). In the first instance, one cannot extrapolate beyond the immediate area of study. In the second case, the published information is fragmentary.

Comparative criminal studies, however, have the potential to lead to sound generalizations which might apply across cultures. Such research could increase the body of knowledge about the relative volume of crime and the deterrence procedures which seem important. Optimally, a comparative focus might provide an understanding of the causes of crime and lead to specific government policy recommendations to reduce the volume of unlawful behavior.

Because there is a gap in comparative criminal literature, it seems important to illustrate the utility of a statistical analysis from available data, and to present examples of the kinds of things to be learned from such comparisons. Two major sources will be discussed, the Uniform Crime Reports and the Annual Reports of Criminal Activity from the International Criminal Police Organization (INTERPOL).

FBI Data

The UCR are the basic continuing source of the nature and volume of criminal activity in the United States. Each month local

227

law enforcement agencies submit their crime tabulations to the FBI, which provides reporting forms and a guide book to aid police in the classifications. The FBI collects the greatest detail for the Crime Index offenses—murder, forcible rape, robbery, aggravated assault, burglary, larceny-theft ($50 and over through 1972, and $200 and over since 1973), and auto theft. It concentrates on these offenses because "they are the most likely to be reported and occur with sufficient frequency to provide an adequate basis for comparison."[1] Arrest records provide more specific information about the age, sex, and race of the offender.

Unfortunately, UCR information is incomplete for a number of reasons. First, law enforcement agencies in some states do not report to the FBI. In 1973, for example, the FBI received arrest reports from 6,004 law enforcement agencies representing 154,995,000 people—or only 73% of the population. From the printed reports it is impossible to learn which jurisdictions are not included. The overall rates of crime are based upon projections from the reported figures. Second, the United States data reflects only reported crime. A former chief of the FBI criminal statistics division feels that certain crimes are nearly always reported. These include bank robberies because of their significance, murder because a body is found, and assault by gun because by law physicians must file a report.[2] Figures for the volume of other crimes are very likely to be inaccurate.

As a check on the accuracy of crime data, the Katzenbach Commission in 1967 and the Law Enforcement Assistance Agency (LEAA) in 1973 surveyed victims of crime. In the first six months of 1973 LEAA interviewed approximately 60,000 households and 15,000 businesses to measure the extent that persons twelve and older, households, and businesses have been victimized by certain types of crimes. The preliminary reports indicated that the volume of rape, robbery, aggravated assault, and burglary is three times higher than the amounts reported to the police; larceny is nearly five times higher; and auto theft 50% higher.[3] LEAA readily admits that direct comparisons with FBI data are impossible. The LEAA unit of measure is the victim and more than one victim may be involved in a crime incident, which is the FBI unit of measure. Further, some sampling error may result from the procedure used to select respondents, as well as from the use of a survey rather than a complete census. Nevertheless, the victimization studies reveal a much higher volume of crime than the amount actually reported and support the view that U.S. criminal statistics are inaccurate.

Two further problems may contribute to incomplete police records. Many victims do not report to the police. The LEAA survey discovered that the most common reason for not reporting a crime was the feeling that nothing could be accomplished by reporting an incident. Some victims felt the incident was too trivial; others feared retaliation if the crime were reported. The survey also discovered that the highest rates of personal victimization occurred among the young (ages 12 to 19), an age group that might not be as likely to report to the police.[4]

Finally, police officials suspect that some agencies underreport the volume of crime, perhaps for reasons of community pride or of political advantage. In the decentralized United States law enforcement system, there is no higher authority than the local police or sheriff and no auditing of records. Even the process of reporting to the FBI is voluntary, and some small departments resent the amount of paperwork necessary to fill out the UCR forms.

Fred Graham cites two other reasons for underreporting. Much of the crime occurs in black neighborhoods among blacks and "there has sometimes been an easy-going tolerance of it by police."[5] City administrations want to keep crime "under control" and for political expediency "complaints sometimes get 'lost.' "[6]

In addition to the problems of measurement, FBI reports are criticized because they sensationalize crime. They dramatize crime waves. The Bureau prints crime clocks showing the utterly useless measure of the decreasing time intervals between crime incidents. To establish crime rates for jurisdictions they lump property crimes with violent crimes. Graham charges that "The FBI with its flare for publicity, has managed five times a year to wring the maximum amount of public terror out of a statistical system that was conceived as a technique for keeping lawmen informed of the trends of their trade."[7]

Both the FBI and LEAA recognize the need for improved data, and the latter group funds some states to collect criminal statistics. The California Attorney General's office in 1974 received $276,000 to gather the Uniform Crime Reports from local agencies, and in 1975 this office expects to receive complete reports from all local law enforcement bodies in the state.

INTERPOL Data

Criminal statistics of other countries can be obtained from three sources: a nation's statistical yearbook, special government publications on criminal activity (England, West Germany, and Canada, for example, publish extremely detailed reports), and from the International Criminal Police Organization, headquartered near Paris. In the most recent published volume, titled *International Crime Statistics, 1969–1970*, INTERPOL reports criminal data for seventy-four countries. Each nation annually completes standard forms which detail the volume of crime and the sex and age of offenders. The forms provide definitions for grouping the statistics, which are indexed into the following categories: murder and attempted murder, sex offenses, two classifications of larceny (major theft or robbery with dangerous aggravating circumstances, and minor theft or all other forms of larceny), fraud (including swindling, embezzlement, and forgery), counterfeit currency offenses, and drug offenses. INTERPOL selects these offenses because the categories are broad enough to permit countries to use their own crime data with minimal adjustments.

Crime indices are not exactly comparable for each country. A nation will use definitions which apply locally, so some variations occur in defining juvenile or sex offenses, for example. These data do provide, however, an indication of crime trends, and the relative degree of the rate of crime, but not a precise measure of the amount of crime. The INTERPOL staff in an interview with Salvatori staff agreed that the murder figures probably are comparable although national statutes may differ about what constitutes intent to murder.

Although the United States is an active member, it does not submit criminal data to INTERPOL. This may be for several reasons. First, the U.S. representative comes from the Treasury Department, rather than the Justice Department, and a lack of inter-departmental communication seems to exist. Second, the FBI data are not complete, and may not be as accurate as that from Western European countries, for example.

Certainly the inclusion of United States crime figures would be an extremely useful contribution to potential comparative criminal research. American criminologists could well make use of INTERPOL data for some comparisons of crime rates because these data are relatively standardized. More precise checks on the meaning of the numbers can be made from the detailed reports of individual countries.

One further question must be raised, however. Are the criminal data from the various countries reliable? For the purposes of the comparisons made in Chapter One, the Western European data are more likely to be accurate than the United States information. Law enforcement is more centralized in these countries, and the respective Ministries of Justice probably secure more accurate reports from local agencies. In England, for example, half the police budget is supplied by the Home Office and local departments are subject to periodic inspection and a cut in their funds if standards are not maintained. In France police are rotated every five years to help maintain police honesty. Lacking these central controls, United States data are probably less accurate, and certainly the recent victimization studies indicate excessive underreporting of crime.

Research Utility

Comparative criminal justice should have as a goal the production of theory generated from the data. Admittedly a thorough study must involve knowledge of the language of each country, knowledge of the history and culture, a detailed background in the criminal codes, and familiarity with indigenous research on the subject. Nevertheless, some analysis is possible using available crime data.

As an illustration of the research potential of comparative crime statistics we will use two offenses which can be defined precisely—murder and auto theft—and compare these crimes in the United States, England, Canada, and Australia. The actual numbers are converted into the rates of crime per 100,000 population for each country. Data for the United States and England come from the 1972 UCR and 1972 *Criminal Statistics*, respectively.[8] Data for Canada come from *Crime and Traffic Enforcement Statistics, 1972–73* and for Australia come from the 1973 statistical yearbook.[9] It is essential to remember that the data for England, Canada, and Australia are likely to be more accurate than the U.S. data.

By all definitions murder is a heinous crime. As Table 1 indicates, the rate of murders known to the police in the United States in 1972, 8.9 per 100,000 population, is nearly eighteen times higher than the rate in England for the same year, six times the rate in Australia, and four times the rate in Canada. The volume of murder in America is enormous in comparison with these other English-speaking countries.

TABLE 1

Murder in Four English-Speaking Democracies
(Offenses known to authorities)

	U.S. (1972)	England (1972)	Australia (1971)	Canada (1972)
Number	18,515	251	185	479
Rate per 100,000	8.9	0.5	1.45	2.22
% offenses cleared	82.2	94.4	96.2	87.9

A frequent reaction to the high U.S. murder rate is a reference to the proportion of ethnic minorities and the extremely high incidence of crime among some groups. Using the 1972 UCR Arrests by Race table (based upon an estimated population of 150,922,000), the murder rate for whites only is 3.4 per 100,000—still nearly seven times the rate for England, and higher than the rates for Canada and Australia.

TABLE 2

Auto Theft in Four English-Speaking Democracies
(Offenses known to authorities)

	U.S. (1972)	England (1972)	Australia (1971)	Canada (1972)
Number	880,983	184,158	45,795	79,775
Rate per 100,000	423.1	375.54	352.26	369.87
% cleared	16.6	34.46	22.69	21.08
Rate of cars per 1,000	46.6	23.2	31.79	34.3

These sources can also indicate the effectiveness of law enforcement agencies in the four countries by comparison of the arrest data for murder suspects in the most recent available year. Australian forces were most efficient, clearing by arrest more than 96% of the murders. England cleared more than 94%. Canada and the United States have similar arrest percentages, indicating that one out of six murders was unsolved.

Table 2 uses recent statistics for auto theft in the same four countries based upon the rate of theft per 100,000 people. Although the differences between countries are not as distinct as the murder rates, the U.S. volume is considerably higher than that in the other three countries. In this area of property crime, Australia ranks lowest, followed by Canada and England.

Since the rate of this theft may well be associated with the number of automobiles in a country, the U.N. passenger car data per 1,000 people is included in this table. Clearly, the United States has more cars to steal. The English figures are interesting, though, when one considers that England has half the number of passenger cars of the United States per 1,000 people, but a theft rate approaching that in the United States.[10]

Police effectiveness in solving this crime can be compared from the arrest information. England solved more than one-third of its cases, Australia and Canada nearly one-fourth, but the United States only one-sixth.

TABLE 3[11]

Police Forces in Four English-Speaking Democracies

	U.S.* (1971)	England (1972)	Australia (1971)	Canada (1970)
Number	472,066	98,560	20,990	40,295
Rate per 100,000	228.9	202.8	164.9	216.5

*U.S. figures: uniformed city, state police; excludes university police and county sheriffs.

Tables 1 and 2 indicate that the proportion of murder and auto theft cleared by arrest in England and Australia is higher than in the United States. This measure of law enforcement effectiveness might be associated with the overall number of uniformed police in each country. Table 3, however, reveals that the proportion of police to the population is greater in the United States than in the other three countries. Crime detection efficiency, therefore, probably has little association with the sheer numbers of police.

Appendix B

Suggestions for Improved Law Enforcement

Ruth Aura Ross

Law enforcement is one of the most decentralized government functions in the United States federal system. The fifty states possess the policing powers, but historically have entrusted their implementation to cities and counties and to the law enforcement agencies local governments create. Therefore, more than 40,000 agencies are responsible for preserving the peace and detecting and prosecuting criminal violations, but nearly 90% employ less than ten full time personnel.[1]

The extreme decentralization of criminal justice creates numerous administrative problems which may exacerbate crime. Since 1931 a series of commissions and private studies have critiqued the system and have suggested major organizational changes. This study will discuss several of these governmental issues and their impact on crime levels and a number of proposed administrative changes.

The fragmentation of American federalism contributes to criminal activity in at least four ways. First, thousands of small cities and rural areas cannot finance professional police. In 1931, the Wickersham Commission noted that "the multitude of police forces in any state and the varying standards of organization and service have contributed immeasurably to the general low grade of police performance in this country."[2] More than forty years later, the Advisory Commission on Intergovernmental Relations (ACIR) reported that "the average police department is undermanned and over-worked; its personnel are recruited by outdated methods and inadequately trained. Where a highly professional service is needed, a politically oriented system rooted in the Middle Ages frequently is offered."[3]

Second, criminal elements are mobile and insensitive to government boundaries. Offenders find it advantageous to change locations frequently. The Federal Bureau of Investigation Uniform Crime Reports indicate that nearly two-thirds of the persons arrested for the more serious crimes have arrest records in two or more states.

Third, organized crime exploits the thousands of police agencies. Syndicate boundaries depend upon the size of the area they can control, and frequently they operate in more than one state. The ACIR comments that syndicates seek "crime havens" and near monopoly control of narcotics, gambling, prostitution, and stolen goods within their area.

Fourth, police corruption and complicity of police with syndicates in narcotics, gambling, vice, and prostitution is facilitated by the thousands of jurisdictions and a lack of inspection by larger units of government. As the Knapp Commission discovered in New York City, "the underlying problem is that the climate of the Department is inhospitable to attempts to uncover acts of corruption, and protection of those who are corrupt."[4]

In addition to the problems of policing which are related to federalism, separation of powers also fragments criminal justice. Policing and prosecution are administrative functions, sentencing a judicial function, and incarceration or probation are administrative functions. The dilemma this can create was illustrated recently by the arrest of 211 narcotics "pushers" in the Los Angeles schools after several months of undercover work. The Los Angeles Police Department, however, had not coordinated its efforts with the District Attorney's office, and most of the youths were released to their parents' custody and were back in school the next day.[5]

The political process also fragments law enforcement. The election in many states of certain personnel, especially sheriffs, constables, prosecutors, judges, and attorneys general, leaves these officials relatively "independent" of other components in the system and responsible theoretically to the "will of the people" rather than to organizational needs.

States structurally splinter criminal justice agencies, especially the courts and correctional systems. Most state court systems lack clear jurisdictional patterns. Thirty-three states in 1972 still maintained Justice of the Peace courts, usually staffed with poorly trained part-time jurists. Correctional responsibility is scattered in most states through health, welfare, youth, and correctional agencies and is administered by city, county, and state levels, with no government level holding coordinating responsibility.

Admittedly, jurisdictional fragmentation is not the major cause of crime. Sociologists, psychologists, and criminologists usually discuss a number of deep societal and family problems which contribute to crime, such as urban crowding and poverty, community and family instability, and peer group values. Such factors, however, cannot be remedied by direct government action. The Katzenbach Report comments: "They are strands that can be disentangled from the fabric of American life only by the concerted action of all society."[6]

On the other hand, some of the crime problems can be alleviated by government action. Political corruption, white collar crime, and organized crime are serious issues, and systemic reforms may reduce these activities. Courts are congested, criminal codes are outdated, and prisons overcrowded. All three contribute to crime levels and require political changes.

Three major recent studies recommend a comprehensive reorganization of the police and judicial structures: the Advisory Commission on Intergovernmental Relations (ACIR), the Committee for Economic Development (CED), and the National Advisory Commission on Criminal Justice Standards and Goals. CED charges that: "A total, all-embracing 'systems' overhaul of the present 'non-system' of criminal justice is an absolute necessity."[7] The three studies would like to see the states assume more responsibility, especially in providing centralized records, crime laboratory facilities, and a centralized reporting system on crimes known to the police and on arrest records. The CED additionally supports state supervision over law enforcement by establishment of a Department of Justice with direct control of law enforcement, prosecution, juvenile problems, drugs, and rehabilitation.

For example, California state government already cooperates to some degree with local agencies. The state established minimum standards in 1960 for police recruitment and training, and local agencies which participate are reimbursed for portions of salaries and expenses they incur.[8] Community colleges operate training programs, and some state colleges and universities provide middle management level programs for police. The Justice Department has centralized information systems for such things as gun registrations, stolen vehicles, and wanted persons, and it plans automation of finger-print files. An organized crime and intelligence unit coordinates law enforcement activities which cross government jurisdictions.

All three studies recommend more coordination in planning. Since 1969 each state wishing federal funds for law enforcement assistance must create a planning agency and develop an annual combined interest comprehensive plan. Similar coordination, however, should be utilized for state and local resources, particularly in metropolitan regions where crime prevention needs area-wide cooperation.

Contract law enforcement is another interesting example of metropolitan coordination. This began in 1954 as the Lakewood Plan. The Los Angeles County Sheriff provides police service for twenty-nine cities in the county. Similar contracting systems have been established in other states.

The CED recommends even greater centralization of law enforcement by creation of a national judicial body with broad statutory powers and supervised by a Presidentially-appointed board. The proposed agency would function to create and administer policies and planning, to evaluate programs, to advise and provide liaison to state and local law enforcement procedures, to collect dependable and comprehensive data, and to enforce standards governing large federal grants in criminal justice.[9]

The proposed federal judicial board, however, would not nationalize law enforcement functions. Two European examples illustrate the process of national centralization. The French police are an agency of the central government, and salaries, training, and duty assignments are controlled in Paris. Great Britain's police are locally controlled but trained and supervised by the Home Office, with Parliament paying half the salaries. This uniformity creates standardized pay, qualifications, and enforcement criteria.

The three studies also recommend structural reforms for several other sections of the criminal justice system. Court congestion is excessive in all states, and particularly in large cities. Delays of more than a year are common. According to CED, some courts are releasing prisoners who were held for unreasonably long periods without a trial.[10] Administrative changes can relieve the backlog. First, state courts need to be unified, with final authority residing in the state supreme court. Second, judges must be flexibly assigned by a court administrator based upon case load. This management change in New York City reduced the court backlog by 58%.[11] Third, certain offenses, such as gambling and prostitution, can be decriminalized to reduce both court and police activity. Fourth, where court delays still exist the state can create more judgeships.

Correctional institutions are criticized for corrupting more people than they rehabilitate—two-thirds of all released prisoners commit another crime.[12] Many of the larger prisons are century-old buildings with grossly inadequate facilities. Most studies recommend an emphasis on rehabilitation in the community rather than punishment in jail, in an effort to reduce recidivism.

Finally, the prosecuting function needs reordering Most prosecutors are part-time public servants who receive poor compensation. The studies recommend consolidation of prosecution at the state level, with the chief prosecutors and their staffs serving full-time.

Implementation of these suggestions will tend to centralize criminal justice systems in the United States in the interests of greater efficiency and effectiveness. More centralized law enforcement, however, need not weaken local government. Most of the reforms suggest greater state control to eliminate some of the current fragmentation. Population growth, concentrated living patterns, and high urban crime rates necessitate a more centralized form of criminal justice.

Notes

Introduction

1. See Joseph Fletcher, *Situation Ethics: The New Morality* (Philadelphia: Westminster Press, 1966).

2. James Q. Wilson, "Crime and Criminologists," *Commentary* 58 (July 1958); idem., "Violence, Pornography, and Social Science," *The Public Interest*, no. 22 (1971), pp. 45–61.

3. Aristotle, *Nicomachean Ethics*, 102a 7–23, in *Introduction to Aristotle*, Richard M. McKeon, ed. and trans. Modern Library College edition (New York: Random House, 1947).

4. Ibid., 1095b 3–7.

5. John Dewey, *Human Nature and Conduct*, Modern Library edition (New York: Random House, 1930 and 1957), p. 42.

6. Alexis de Tocqueville, *Democracy in America*, J. P. Mayer, ed., George Lawrence, trans. (New York: Doubleday Anchor Books, 1969), pp. 308, 291.

7. Leonard D. White, *The Republican Era* (New York: Free Press paperback, 1965); Paul H. Douglas, *Ethics in Government* (Cambridge: Harvard University Press, 1952).

8. Edwin M. Schur, *Our Criminal Society* (Englewood Cliffs, N.J.: Prentice-Hall, 1969), p. 234.

9. Carl J. Friedrich, *The Pathology of Politics* (New York: Harper and Row, 1972).

10. Irving Kristol, *On the Democratic Idea in America* (New York: Harper and Row, 1972).

11. Walter E. Schafer and Kenneth Polk, "Delinquency and the Schools," in *Task Force Report: Juvenile Delinquency and Youth Crime*, The President's Commission on Law Enforcement and the Administration of Justice (Washington, D.C.: U.S. Government Printing Office, 1967), p. 273.

1: America's Ethical Malaise

1. Henry Steele Commager, *The American Mind* (New York: Bantam Books, 1970).

2. *Max Weber*, edited by Girth and Mills, p. 307, cited in Seymour Martin Lipset, *The First New Nation* (Garden City, N.Y.: Doubleday Anchor Books, 1967), p. 177.

3. Dennis W. Brogan, *The American Character* (New York: Alfred A. Knopf, 1944), p. 102.

4. Lipset, *First New Nation*, pp. 166–67.

5. Tocqueville, *Democracy in America*, p. 291.

6. Fletcher, *Situation Ethics*, pp. 18–21; Paul Ramsey, *Basic Christian Ethics* (New York: Charles Scribner's Sons, 1950), pp. 46–91.

7. Tocqueville, *Democracy in America*, pp. 544–45.

8. Neil G. McCluskey, *Public Schools and Moral Education* (New York: Columbia University Press, 1958).

9. Commager, *American Mind*, p. 87.

10. McCluskey, *Public Schools*, pp. 109–54.

11. Otto F. Krauschaar, "Kant," in *Dictionary of Philosophy*, Dagobert D. Runes, ed. (New York: Philosophical Library, 1942), pp. 158–60.

12. John Rawls, *A Theory of Justice* (Cambridge, Mass.: Harvard University Press, 1971).

13. Harold Laski, *The American Democracy* (New York: Viking Press, 1948).

14. William K. Frankena, "Utilitarianism," in *Dictionary of Philosophy*, p. 327.

15. Fletcher, *Situation Ethics*; idem, *Moral Responsibility: Situation Ethics at Work* (Philadelphia: Westminster Press, 1967).

16. See Commager, *American Mind*, pp. 203–6.

17. Martin Diamond, Winston Mills Fisk, and Herbert Garfinkel, *The Democratic Republic* (Chicago: Rand McNally, 1971), p. 21.

18. Edmund Cahn, *The Moral Decision: Right and Wrong in the Light of American Law* (Bloomington, Ind.: Indiana University Press, 1955), p. 3.

19. Lord Charnwood, *Abraham Lincoln* (New York: Henry Holt and Company, 1917), p. 162.

20. Lee Coleman, *What Is an American?: A Study of Alleged American Traits*, quoted in *The Character of Americans*, M. McGiffert, ed. (Homewood, Ill.: Dorsey Press, 1964), p. 28.

21. Arthur Schlesinger, Sr., *Paths to the Present* (New York: Macmillan Company, 1949).

22. Richard Hofstadter and M. Wallace, *American Violence: A Documentary History* (New York: Alfred A. Knopf, 1970), "Introduction."

23. Tocqueville, *Democracy in America*, p. 264.

24. Abraham Lincoln, Lyceum speech, 1838.

25. William K. Frankena, *Ethics* (Englewood Cliffs, N.J.: Prentice-Hall, 1961), p. 90.

26. William Barrett, *Irrational Man* (Garden City, N.Y.: Doubleday Anchor Books, 1961).

27. Sigmund Freud, *Totem and Taboo* (New York: Vintage Books, 1946), p. 102.

28. Idem, *Civilization and Its Discontents* (New York: W. W. Norton, 1962), p. 42.

29. Seymour Halleck, *Psychiatry and the Dilemma of Crime* (New York: Harper and Row, 1967), p. 42.

30. Paul Roazen, *Freud: Political and Social Thought* (New York: Alfred A. Knopf, 1968), p. 103.

31. Nathan Hale, *Freud in America* (Oxford: Oxford University Press, 1971), p. 431.

32. B. F. Skinner, *Beyond Freedom and Dignity* (New York: Alfred A. Knopf, 1971).

33. Idem, *Walden II* (New York: Macmillan Company, 1948), p. 200.

34. Thomas A. Harris, *I'm OK . . . You're OK: A Practical Guide to Transactional Analysis* (New York: Harper and Row, 1967), p. 200.

35. Commager, *American Mind*, p. 118.

36. Ibid., p. 101.

37. John Dewey, *Democracy and Education* (New York: Free Press paperback, 1966), p. 234.

38. Commager, *American Mind*, pp. 42, 50.

39. Richard deCharms and Gerald H. Moeller, "Values Expressed in American Children's Readers, 1800–1950," *Journal of Abnormal and Social Psychology* 64 (1962): 136–42.

40. Margaret P. Foster, "A Study of the Content of Selected Third Grade Basic Readers Used in the United States from 1900 to 1953" (Master's thesis, Wesleyan University, Conn., 1956).

41. Cited in Harry C. McKown, *Character Education* New York: McGraw-Hill, 1935), p. 74.

42. Celia Stindler, "Sixty Years of Child Training Practice," *Journal of Pediatrics* 36 (January 1950).

43. Durant Drake, *Problems of Conduct* (Boston: Houghton Mifflin, 1921), pp. 357–58.

44. L. Wittgenstein, "A Lecture on Ethics," *Philosophical Review* 74 (1965), pp. 11–12, quoted in W. D. Hudson, *Modern Moral Philosophy* (Garden City, N.Y.: Doubleday Anchor, 1970), p. 108.

45. Examples of texts used in such courses are: R. N. Beck and J. B. Orr, eds., *Ethical Choice: A Case Study Approach* (New York: Free Press, 1970); a more contemporary and advocacy approach is A. K. Bierman and James A. Gould, eds., *Philosophy for a New Generation* (New York: Macmillan, 1970).

2: Crimes: Street and White Collar

1. National Commission on the Causes and Prevention of Violence, *Final Report* (Washington, D.C.: U.S. Government Printing Office, 1969), p. xv.

2. British Home Office, *Criminal Statistics, England and Wales, 1971* (London: Her Majesty's Stationery Office, 1971).

3. *Los Angeles Times*, 14 January 1973.

4. James Q. Wilson, *Varieties of Police Behavior* (Cambridge, Mass.: Harvard University Press, 1968), pp. 161, 298.

5. The President's Commission on Law Enforcement and the Administration of Justice, *Task Force Report: Crime and Its Impact* (Washington, D.C.: U.S. Goverment Printing Office, 1967).

6. George Won and George Yamamoto, "Social Structure and Deviant Behavior: A Study of Shoplifting," *Sociology and Social Research* 53 (October 1968): 44–45. See also Paula Newburg, "A Study in Deviance: Shoplifting," *International Journal of Comparative Sociology* 9 (June 1968): 132–36.

7. Mary Owen Cameron, *The Booster and the Snitch* (Glencoe, Ill.: Free Press, 1964).

8. Commission on Law Enforcement, *Task Force Report: Crime and Its Impact*, p. 48.

9. Mark Lipman, *Stealing* (New York: Harper's Magazine Press, 1973).

10. William W. Wattenberg and James Balistrieri, "Auto Theft: A Favored Group Delinquency," *American Journal of Sociology* 57 (May

1952): 75–79. See also, Fred J. Shanley, "Middle Class Delinquency as a Social Problem," *Sociology and Social Research* (July 1967), especially footnote 32; and John P. Clark and Eugene P. Wenneger, "Socio-Economic Class and Area as Correlates of Illegal Behavior among Juveniles," *American Sociological Review* 27 (1962): 826–34.

11. J. Edgar Hoover, "Embezzlements: Their Causes and Conse-quences," *New York Certified Public Accountant* (July 1968).

12. Donald R. Cressey, *Other People's Money* (Glencoe, Ill.: Free Press, 1953), p. 30.

13. Glenn R. Winters, "What Can Be Done about Pettifoggery and Legal Delays?" *Annals of the Academy of Political and Social Science* 363 (January 1966), p. 55.

14. Jerome E. Carlin, *Lawyer's Ethics* (New York: Russell Sage Foun-dation, 1966).

15. William T. Fitts, Jr., and Barbara Fitts, "Ethical Standards of the Medical Profession," *The Annals* 297 (January 1955): 17–36.

16. Seymour Martin Lipset and Philip G. Altbach, eds., *Students in Revolt* (Boston: Beacon Press, 1970).

17. The President's Commission on Campus Unrest, *Report* (Washington, D.C.: U.S. Government Printing Office, 1970), p. 38.

18. Ibid., pp. 37–39.

19. F. Ivan Nye, James F. Short, Jr., and Virgil J. Olson, "Socioeconomic Status and Delinquent Behavior," *American Journal of Sociology* 63 (January 1958): 338, 383.

20. Hyman Rodman and Paul Grams, "Juvenile Delinquency and the Family," in *Task Force Report: Juvenile Delinquency and Youth Crime*, Commission on Law Enforcement, p. 195.

21. Albert J. Reiss, Jr., and Albert Lewis Rhodes, "The Distribution of Juvenile Delinquency in the Social Class Structure," *American Sociological Review* 26 (October 1961): 720–32.

3: Reasons for America's High Crime Rate

1. Commission on Violence, *Final Report*, p. xv.

2. Charles Tilly, "Collective Violence in European Perspective," and Ben C. Roberts, "On the Origins and Resolution of English Working Class Protest," in *Violence in America, Historical and Comparative Perspec-tives*, Staff Report, Commission on Violence (Washington, D.C.: U.S. Government Printing Office, 1969).

3. See the comparison of crime rates in Canada and in America in Seymour Martin Lipset, *Revolution and Counterrevolution* (New York: Basic Books, 1968), Chapter Two.

4. Marshall B. Clinard, "A Cross-Cultural Replication of the Relation of Urbanism to Criminal Behavior," *American Sociological Review* 25 (April 1960): 253–57.

5. Interpol, *International Crime Statistics, 1969–1970* (St. Cloud, France: International Criminal Police Organization).

6. Edwin H. Sutherland and Donald Cressey, *Criminology* (Philadelphia: J. B. Lippincott, 1970), pp. 176–80.

7. Walter D. Connor, *Deviance in Soviet Society* (New York: Columbia University Press, 1972).

8. Vance Packard, *A Nation of Strangers* (New York: David McKay, 1972), p. 7.

9. Ibid., pp. 6–7.

10. Ibid., p. 243.

11. Ibid., p. 244.

12. Ibid., p. 269.

13. C. R. Shaw and H. D. McKay, *Juvenile Delinquency and Urban Areas* (Chicago: University of Chicago Press, 1942).

14. Jackson Toby, "Affluence and Adolescent Crime," in *Task Force Report: Juvenile Delinquency and Youth Crime*, Commission on Law Enforcement, pp. 132–44.

15. Sutherland and Cressey, *Criminology*, pp. 71–91.

16. Albert K. Cohen, *Delinquent Boys* (Glencoe, Ill.: Free Press, 1955).

17. Richard A. Cloward and Lloyd E. Ohlin, *Delinquency and Opportunity* (New York: Free Press, 1960).

18. W. C. Kvaraceus and W. B. Miller, *Delinquent Behavior: Culture and the Individual* (Washington, D.C.: National Education Association, 1959).

19. Rodman and Grams, "Juvenile Delinquency and the Family," in *Task Force Report: Juvenile Delinquency and Youth Crime*, Commission on Law Enforcement, pp. 210–11.

20. Federal Bureau of Investigation, *Crime in the United States* (Washington, D.C., 1973).

21. Fred P. Graham, *The Due Process Revolution* (New York: Hayden Book Company, 1970), Chapter Five.

22. Walter B. Miller, quoted in Graham, *Due Process Revolution*, p. 94.

23. Edward C. Banfield, *How Many and Who Should Be Set At Liberty?* Public Affairs Conference Center, Kenyon College, 1970, p. 4.

24. Committee for Economic Development, *Reducing Crime and Assuring Justice* (New York, 1972).

25. National Advisory Commission on Intergovernmental Relations, *State-Local Relations in the Criminal Justice System* (Washington, D.C.: U.S. Government Printing Office, 1971).

26. Graham, *Due Process Revolution*, p. 293.

27. Ibid., Chapter Twelve.

28. James Q. Wilson, "If Every Criminal Knew He Would Be Punished if Caught," *New York Time Magazine*, 28 January 1973.

29. See Jethro K. Lieberman, *How the Government Breaks the Law* (Baltimore: Penquin Books, 1972); Theordore L. Becker and Vernon G. Murray, eds., *Government Lawlessness in America* (London: Oxford University Press, 1971). For a worse picture of forty years ago, see Ernest Jerome Hopkins, *Our Lawless Police* (New York: Viking Press, 1931).

30. Sir Robert Peel, quoted in D. Chappell and P. R. Wilson, *The Police and the Public in Australia and New Zealand* (St. Lucia: University of Queensland Press, 1969).

31. United Nations, *Practical Results and Financial Aspects of Adult Probation in Selected Countries* (New York, 1954).

32. Sutherland and Cressey, *Criminology*, p. 48.

33. Edwin M. Schur, *Crimes Without Victims* (Englewood Cliffs, N.J.: Prentice-Hall, 1965).

34. James Q. Wilson, Mark H. Moore, and I. David Wheat, Jr., "The Problem of Heroin," *The Public Interest*, no. 29 (1972), pp. 3–28.

35. See Alfred R. Lindesmith, *The Addict and the Law* (Bloomington, Ind.: Indiana University Press, 1965).

36. Wilson et al., "The Problem of Heroin," *The Public Interest*, no. 29 (1972), pp. 3–28.

37. Ibid., p. 20.

38. Donald R. Cressey, *Theft of the Nation: The Structure and Operations of Organized Crime in America* (New York: Harper and Row, Harper Colophon Book, 1969), p. 294.

4: The Payoff in Business, Unions, and Government

1. John C. Burton, ed., *Corporate Financial Reporting: Ethical and*

Other Problems (New York: American Institute of Certified Public Accountants, 1972).

2. Raymond L. Dirks and Leonard Gross, *The Great Wall Street Scandal* (New York: McGraw-Hill, 1974).

3. Commission on Law Enforcement, *Task Force Report: Crime and Its Impact*, Chapter Three.

4. Edwin H. Sutherland, *White Collar Crime* (New York: Holt, Rinehart and Winston, 1949), Part 2.

5. Commission on Law Enforcement, *Task Force Report: Crime and Its Impact*, p. 103.

6. Ibid.

7. Marshall B. Clinard, *The Black Market* (New York: Rinehart and Company, 1952).

8. Ari Hoogenboom, *Outlawing the.Spoils* (Champaign, Ill.: University of Illinois Press, 1968).

9. John Hutchinson, *The Imperfect Union* (New York: E. P. Dutton, 1972), p. 389.

10. Lipset, *First New Nation*, p. 230. See also idem, *Political Man* (Garden City: Doubleday, 1963), Part 4.

11. Hutchinson, *Imperfect Union*, Chapter Two.

12. Ibid., Chapter Four.

13. Ibid., Chapter Six.

14. Ibid., Chapter Seven.

15. Ibid., Chapter Eight.

16. Ibid., Chapter Nine.

17. Ibid., Chapter Fourteen.

18. Ibid., Chapter Fifteen.

19. Ibid., Chapter Eighteen.

20. Ibid., Chapter Nineteen.

21. Ibid., p. 362.

22. Ibid., p. 374.

23. Ibid., pp. 382–83.

24. Lipset, *First New Nation*, Chapter Five.

25. Estes Kefauver, "Past and Present Standards of Public Ethics in America: Are We Improving?" *The Annals* 280 (March 1952): 1.

26. Leonard D. White, *The Federalists* (New York: Free Press, 1965), p. 283.

27. Ibid., pp. 295–96.

28. Ibid., p. 310.

29. Quoted in idem, *The Jeffersonians* (New York: Free Press, 1965), pp. 157–58.

30. Ibid., pp. 229–30.

31. Ibid., pp. 406–8, 415–18.

32. Ibid., pp. 419–22.

33. Idem, *The Jacksonians* (New York: Free Press, 1965), p. 27.

34. Ibid., p. 176.

35. Ibid., p. 204.

36. Ibid., p. 220.

37. Ibid., p. 252.

38. Ibid., p. 259.

39. Ibid., pp. 291–92.

40. Ibid., pp. 334–35.

41. Ibid., p. 413.

42. Ibid., pp. 421–23.

43. Ibid., p. 426.

44. Idem, *Republican Era*, pp. 12–14.

45. Ibid., pp. 9–10.

46. Ibid., p. 188.

47. Ibid., p. 205.

48. Ibid., p. 217.

49. Ibid., p. 271.

50. Ibid., p. 273.

51. David A. Frier, *Conflict of Interest in the Eisenhower Administration* (Baltimore: Penquin Books, 1970).

52. H. H. Wilson, *Congress: Corruption and Compromise* (New York: Rinehart and Company, 1951).

53. Robert S. Getz, *Congressional Ethics* (Princeton: D. Van Nostrand, 1966).

54. Ibid., Chapter Eight.

55. *Los Angeles Times*, 14 November 1974.

56. Getz, *Congressional Ethics*, pp. 117–39.

57. M. R. Werner, *Tammany Hall* (Garden City, N. Y.: Doubleday, Doran, 1928), pp. 161–69.

58. Ibid., p. 164.

59. Ibid., p. 162.

60. Ibid., p. 161.

61. Ibid., pp. 177–85.

62. Ernest S. Griffith, *Modern Development of City Government*, 2 vols. (London: Oxford University Press, 1927), 1:139–40. See also idem, *A History of American City Government* (New York: Praeger, 1974), Chapter Eight.

63. Idem, *Modern Development of City Government*, 1:27.

64. Lincoln Steffens, *The Shame of the Cities* (New York: Hill and Wang, 1966). See also idem, *The Struggle for Self-Government* (New York: McClure, Phillips and Company, 1906).

65. Griffith, *Modern Development of City Government*, 1:283.

66. A. James Reichley, "Getting at the Roots of Watergate," *Fortune*, July 1973, p. 91.

67. See also Peter Maas, *Serpico* (New York: Bantam Books, 1973).

68. John A. Gardiner, *The Politics of Corruption* (New York: Russell Sage Foundation, 1970).

69. Albert J. Reiss, *The Police and the Public* (New Haven, Conn.: Yale University Press, 1971), Chapter Three.

70. Michael Dorman, *Payoff* (New York: David McKay Company, 1972).

71. The President's Commission on Law Enforcement and the Administration of Justice, *Task Force Report: Organized Crime* (Washington, D.C.: U.S. Government Printing Office, 1967), p. 5.

72. Dorman, *Payoff*, p. 126.

73. Cressey, *Theft of the Nation*, p. xi.

74. Friedrich, *Pathology of Politics*, p. 136. See also Sidney D. Bailey, *British Parliamentary Democracy* (Boston: Houghton Mifflin, 1971), pp. 98–103, 166–72; Alexis de Tocqueville, Letter to Henry Hallam, 29 May 1835, in *Democracy in America*.

75. Hiram Stout, *British Government* (New York: Oxford University Press, 1953), p. 278.

76. Alvin Schuster, "Graft Charges Rare in Western Europe's Judiciary," *New York Times*, 8 October 1972.

77. Roland Huntford, *The New Totalitarians* (New York: Stein and Day, 1972), p. 129.

78. Arnold J. Heidenheimer, *The Governments of Germany* (New York: Thomas Y. Crowell, 1971), pp. 210–16.

79. Hans Rosenberg, *Bureaucracy, Aristocracy, and Autocracy* (Boston: Beacon Press, 1958).

80. H. A. Brasy, "Administrative Corruption in Theory and Dutch Practice," in *Political Corruption*, Arnold J. Heidenheimer, ed. (New York: Rinehart and Winston, 1970). The Heidenheimer collection is very valuable.

81. Denis de Rougement, *La Suisse* (Paris: Hachette, 1965), p. 120; G. A. Chevallaz, *La Suisse ou Le Sommeil du Juste* (Lausanne: Payot, 1967), Chapter Twelve.

82. William L. Shirer, *The Collapse of the Third Republic* (New York: Pocket Books, 1971), pp. 57, 187.

83. National Advisory Commission on Civil Disorders, *Supplemental Studies* (Washington, D.C.: U.S. Government Printing Office, July 1968), p. 146.

84. Friedrich, *Pathology of Politics*, p. 168.

85. Samuel Huntington, *Political Order in Changing Societies* (New Haven, Conn.: Yale University Press, 1968), p. 59.

86. Ibid., p. 67.

87. Ibid., pp. 68–69.

88. Griffith, *Modern Development of City Government*, 2:614.

89. Lipset, *Revolution and Counterrevolution*, Chapter Two.

90. Walter Bean, *Boss Ruef's San Francisco* (Berkeley, Cal.: University of California Press, 1968), p. 195; Steffens, *Shame of the Cities*, p. 3.

91. Douglas, *Ethics in Government*.

92. White, *Republican Era*, p. 366.

93. Henry Jones Ford, "Municipal Corruption: A Comment on Lincoln Steffens," *Political Science Quarterly* 19 (1904): 673–86, reprinted in *Political Corruption*, Heidenheimer, ed.

94. James Q. Wilson, "Corruption: The Shame of the States," *The Public Interest*, no. 6 (1966), pp. 30–32.

95. Nathan Glazer and Daniel P. Moynihan, *Beyond the Melting Pot*, 2nd ed. (Cambridge, Mass.: M. I. T. Press, 1970).

96. White, *Republican Era*, p. 380.

97. William A. Clebsch, "American Religion and the Cure of Souls," in *Religion in America*, William G. McLoughlin and Robert N. Bellah, eds. (Boston: Beacon Press, 1968), p. 255.

98. Richard M. Merelman, *Political Socialization and Educational Climates* (New York: Holt, Rinehart, and Winston, 1971), pp. 6–7.

5: You Can Teach Ethics

1. William Ball, "Religion and Public Education: the Post-*Schempp* Years," in *Religion and Public Education*, Theodore R. Sizer, ed. (New York: Houghton Mifflin, 1967), pp. 144–64.

2. Daniel Patrick Moynihan, *The Negro Family: The Case for National Action*, p. 8, in Lee Rainwater and William L. Yancey, *The Moynihan Report and the Politics of Controversy* (Cambridge, Mass.: M. I. T. Press, 1967), p. 54.

3. Edith Hamilton and Huntington Cairns, eds., *Meno*, 70a 1–3, in *The Collected Dialogues of Plato*, W. K. C. Guthrie, trans., Bollingen Series (New York: Random House, Pantheon Books, 1961), p. 354.

4. Friedrich, *Pathology of Politics*, p. 136.

5. Gertrude Himmelfarb, *Victorian Minds* (New York: Harper Torchbooks, 1968), p. 291. Italics added.

6. Ibid.

7. Friedrich, *Pathology of Politics*, p. 136.

8. George LaPiana, "Doctrinal Background of Moral Theology," quoted in *Moral Principles of Action*, Ruth N. Anshen, ed. (New York: Harper and Row, 1952), pp. 378–409.

9. Max Weber, *The Protestant Ethic and the Spirit of Capitalism* (New York: Charles Scribner's Sons, 1958), p. 165.

10. Ernst Troeltsch, *The Social Teaching of the Christian Churches*, 2 vols. (New York: Macmillan Company, 1931), 1:324.

11. W. E. H. Lecky, *History of European Morals*, 2 vols. (New York: D. Appleton and Company, 1879), vol. 2; L. Rabinowitz, "France in the Thirteenth Century," in *The Feudal Period in Judaism and Christianity*, G. C. Coulton and A. C. Adcock, eds. (New York: Ktav Publishing House, 1969).

12. James Breasted, *The Dawn of Conscience* (New York: Charles Scribner's Sons, 1935).

13. See Gordon Tullock, "Does Punishment Deter Crime?" *The Public Interest*, no. 36 (1974), pp. 103–11.

14. Aristotle, *Nicomachean Ethics*, 1103a.

15. Lawrence Kohlberg, "Education for Justice: A Modern Statement of the Platonic View," in *Moral Education: Five Lectures* (Cambridge, Mass.: Harvard University Press, 1970).

16. John Dewey and James H. Tufts, *Ethics*, rev. ed. (New York: Henry Holt and Company, 1932), p. 173.

17. Dewey, *Democracy and Education*, p. 356.

18. C. S. Lewis, *The Abolition of Man* (New York: Macmillan Paperback Edition, 1965).

19. Clyde Kluckhohn, "Ethical Relativity: Sic et Non," *Journal of Philosophy* 52 (1955).

20. Ralph Linton, "Universal Ethical Principles: An Anthropological Point of View," in *Moral Principles of Action*, Anshen, ed.

21. Paul Taylor, "Social Science and Ethical Relativism," *Journal of Philosophy* 55 (1958).

6: Ethical Reform: An Opportunity for the Intellectuals

1. For example, books: David Halberstam, *The Best and the Brightest* (Greenwich, Conn.: Fawcett Publications, 1972); David Riesman, *The Lonely Crowd* (Garden City, N.Y.: Doubleday Anchor, 1955); Marshall McLuhan, *The Medium is the Message* (New York: Random House, 1967); and magazines: *Harper's, Saturday Review, The Public Interest, The New York Review*, in addition to a few others.

2. Charles Kadushin, "Who Are the Elite Intellectuals?" *The Public Interest*, no. 29 (1972), pp. 109–25.

3. J. S. Nye, "Corruption and Political Development: A Cost Benefit Analysis," *American Political Science Review* 61 (June 1967): 417; James C. Scott, "Corruption, Machine Politics, and Political Change," *American Political Science Review* 63 (December 1969): 1142.

4. Robert K. Merton, *Social Theory and Social Structure* (New York: Free Press, 1968), p. 127.

5. Friedrich, *Pathology of Politics*, pp. 170–71, 168.

6. Richard Hofstadter, "Commentary: Have There Been Discernible Shifts in American Values during the Past Generation?" in *The American Style*, E. E. Morison, ed. (New York: Harper and Row, 1958), p. 355.

7. Skinner, *Beyond Freedom and Dignity*, is a striking example of this "reductionism."

8. Edward Shils, *The Intellectuals and the Powers* (Chicago: University of Chicago, 1972); Thomas Molnar, *The Decline of the Intellectual* (New York: World Publishing Company, 1961), pp. 116–17.

9. Lionel Trilling, quoted in Kluckhohn, "Discernible Shifts in American Values?" in *The American Style*, Morison, ed., p. 196.

10. Irving Kristol, " 'When Virtue Loses All Her Loveliness'—Some Reflections on Capitalism and the 'Free Society,' " *The Public Interest*, no. 21 (1970), pp. 3–15.

11. D. W. Oliver and J. P. Shaver, *Teaching Public Issues in the High School* (Boston: Houghton Mifflin, 1966).

12. Kristol, *Democratic Idea in America*, p. 125.

13. Edmund E. Day, *Education for Freedom and Responsibility* (Ithaca, N.Y.: Cornell University Press, 1952), p. 25.

14. Derek Wright, ed., *The Journal of Moral Education* (London: Pemberton Publishing Company, n.d.).

15. Alexander Bickel, *The Least Dangerous Branch* (New York: Bobbs-Merrill, 1962), p. 268.

7: Bringing Them Up Right

1. George Gilder, "In Defense of Monogamy," *Commentary* 58 (November 1974): 31–36.

2. Alex Inkeles and Raymond Bauer, *The Soviet Citizen* (New York: Atheneum, 1968), pp. 190–91.

3. Herbert McCloskey and Harold E. Dahlgren, "Primary Group Influence on Party Loyalty," *American Political Science Review* 53 (September 1959): 757–76.

4. Herbert H. Hyman, *Political Socialization* (Glencoe, Ill.: Free Press, 1959), pp. 69–73.

5. Kent Jennings and Richard S. Niemi, "The Transmission of Political Values from Parents to Child," *American Political Science Review* 53 (March 1968): 169–84.

6. Norman J. Bull, *Moral Education* (Beverly Hills, Cal.: Sage Publications, 1969), p. 11.

7. Idem, *Moral Judgment from Childhood to Adolescence* (Beverly Hills, Cal.: Sage Publications, 1969), p. 38.

8. Idem, *Moral Education*, p. 109.

9. Ibid., p. 111.

10. Ibid., p. 113.

11. Ralph H. Turner, *Family Interaction* (New York: John Wiley and Sons, 1970), p. 169.

12. Joan McCord and William McCord, "The Effects of Parental Role Model on Criminality," *Journal of Social Issues* 14 (1958): 66–75.

13. Turner, *Family Interaction*, p. 144.

14. Erik H. Erikson, *Childhood and Society* (New York: W. W. Norton and Company, 1950), pp. 275–77.

15. Rodman and Grams, "Juvenile Delinquency and the Family," in

Task Force Report: Juvenile Delinquency and Youth Crime, Commission on Law Enforcement, p. 196.

16. Ibid.

17. Ibid., pp. 210–11.

18. Derek Wright, *The Psychology of Moral Behavior* (London: Penguin Books, 1971), pp. 90–91.

19. Turner, *Family Interaction*, pp. 217–18.

20. Jean Piaget, *The Moral Judgment of the Child* (New York: Free Press, 1965), pp. 191–92.

21. Oscar Lewis, *La Vida* (New York: Vintage Books, 1965), p. xlvi.

22. F. Ivan Nye, *Family Relationships and Delinquent Behavior* (New York: John Wiley and Sons, 1958), pp. 58–59.

23. Moynihan, "The Negro Family," in Rainwater and Yancey, *Politics of Controversy*, p. 51.

24. Andrew Billingsley, *Black Families in White America* (Englewood Cliffs, N.J.: Prentice Hall, 1968).

25. R. H. Peck and R. J. Havighurst, *The Psychology of Character Development* (New York: John Wiley and Sons, 1960), p. 197.

8: Gang Leader or Eagle Scout?

1. Boyd McCandless, "Childhood Socialization," in *Goslin Handbook of Socialization Theory and Research* (Chicago: Rand McNally, 1969), pp. 808–9.

2. F. L. K. Hsu, B. G. Watrous, and E. M. Lord, "Culture Pattern and Adolescent Behavior," *International Journal of Social Psychiatrists* 7 (1960): 33–35; A. H. Maslow and R. Diaz-Guerrero, "Delinquency as a Value Disturbance," in *Festschrift for Gardner Murphy*, J. G. Peatman and E. L. Hartley, eds. (New York: Harper, 1960), pp. 228–40, cited by John D. Campbell, "Peer Relations in Childhood," in *Review of Child Development Research*, Martin Hoffman and Lois Hoffman, eds., (New York: Russell Sage Foundation, 1964), 1:295.

3. D. P. Ausubel, *Theory and Problems of Child Development* (New York: Grune and Stratton, 1958), p. 393.

4. Talcott Parsons and Winston White, "The Link between Character and Society," in *Culture and Social Character*, Seymour Martin Lipset and Leo Lowenthal, eds. (Glencoe, Ill.: Free Press, 1961), p. 125.

5. Lyle Larson, "The Influence of Parents and Peers during Adolescence: The Situation Hypothesis Revisited," *Journal of Marriage and the Family* 34 (February 1972): 71.

6. Clay Brittain, "Adolescent Choices and Parent-Peer Cross Pressures," *American Sociological Review* 28 (June 1963): 389.

7. Clay Brittain, "An Exploration of the Bases of Peer-Compliance and Parent-Compliance in Adolescence," *Adolescence* 2 (Winter 1967): 477, 455.

8. Hyman, *Political Socialization*, pp. 107–9.

9. Kenneth Langton, *Political Socialization* (New York: Oxford University Press, 1969).

10. Urie Bronfenbrenner, *Two Worlds of Childhood: U.S. and U.S.S.R.* (New York: Russell Sage, 1970), p. 102.

11. Charles Bowerman and John Kinch, "Changes in Family and Peer Orientation of Children between the Fourth and Tenth Grades," *Social Forces* 37 (March 1959): 211.

12. Ibid., p. 208.

13. E. C. Devereux, "Socialization in Cross-Cultural Perspective: A Comparative Study of England, Germany, and the United States," and idem, "Authority, Guilt, and Conformity to Adult Standards among German School Children: A Pilot Experimental Study"; unpublished manuscripts, Cornell University, 1965 and 1966, cited by Willard Hartup, "Peer Interaction and Social Organization," in *Carmichael's Manual of Child Psychology,* Paul Mussen, ed., 3rd ed. (New York: John Wiley and Sons, 1970), 2:434.

14. M. L. Kohn, "Social Class and Parent-Child Relationships: An Interpretation," *American Journal of Sociology* 64 (January 1959): 337–51; G. Psathas, "Ethnicity, Social Class, and Adolescent Independence from Parental Control," *American Sociological Review* 22 (1957): 415–23.

15. James Coleman, *The Adolescent Society* (New York: Free Press, 1961), p. 9.

16. This section is largely drawn from Schafer and Polk, "Delinquency and the Schools," in *Task Force Report: Juvenile Delinquency and Youth Crime,* Commission on Law Enforcement; Cloward and Ohlin, *Delinquency and Opportunity*; and Cohen, *Delinquent Boys*.

17. Walter Miller, "Lower Class Culture as a Generating Milieu of Gang Delinquency," *Journal of Social Issues* 14 (1959): 5–19; Larry Karacki and Jackson Toby, "The Uncommitted Adolescent: Candidate for Gang Socialization," *Sociological Inquiry* 32 (Spring 1962): 203–15.

18. Paul Lerman, "Individual Values, Peer Values, and Subcultural Delinquency," *American Sociological Review* 33 (April 1968): 233–34.

19. Martin Gold, *Status Forces in Delinquent Boys* (Ann Arbor, Mich.: University of Michigan, Institute for Social Research, 1963); James F.

Short, Jr., and Fred L. Strodtlick, *Group Process and Gang Delinquency* (Chicago: University of Chicago, 1965); James F. Short, Jr., "Social Structure and Group Processes in Explanations of Gang Delinquency," in *Problems of Youth: Transition to Adulthood in a Changing World*, Muzafer Sherif and Carolyn W. Sherif, eds. (Chicago: Aldine Publishing Company, 1965).

20. Melford Spiro, "Education in a Communal Village in Israel," *American Journal of Orthopsychiatry* 23 (1955): 283–93.

21. Urie Bronfenbrenner, "The Split-Level American Family," *Saturday Review*, 7 October 1967.

22. T. W. Bamford, *Rise of the Public Schools* (London: Thomas Nelson and Son, 1967), Chapter Four, especially pp. 65–73.

23. Daniel P. Moynihan, *Maximum Feasible Misunderstanding* (New York: Free Press, 1969), pp. 150, 163, 197.

24. Bertram Beck, "Recreation and Delinquency," in *Task Force Report: Juvenile Delinquency and Youth Crime*, Commission on Law Enforcement, pp. 331–43.

25. William Golding, *Lord of the Flies* (New York: Capricorn Books, 1954).

26. Coleman, *Adolescent Society*, p. 9.

27. Ibid., p. 322.

28. Bronfenbrenner, *Two Worlds of Childhood*, p. 156.

29. Ibid., pp. 157–58.

30. Idem, "Split-Level American Family," *Saturday Review*, 7 October 1967.

9: Ethics K–12, I

1. Walter Lippmann, *A Preface to Morals* (New York: Time-Life Books, 1964), p. 212.

2. Ibid., p. 214.

3. McCluskey, *Public Schools and Moral Education*, p. 170.

4. John Dewey, *Reconstruction in Philosophy* (Boston: Beacon Press, 1948), p. xiii.

5. Richard J. Bernstein, "John Dewey," *Encyclopedia of Philosophy* (New York: Macmillan Company and Free Press, 1967), Vol. 2.

6. Dewey, *Democracy and Education*, p. 354.

7. Ibid., p. 359.

8. Ibid., p. 346.

9. Ibid., p. 122.

10. Ibid., p. 217.

11. Ibid.

12. Ibid., p. 234.

13. Idem, *The School and Society*, rev. ed. (Chicago: University of Chicago, 1971), p. 137.

14. Ibid., pp. 152–53.

15. Ibid., pp. 107–8.

16. Idem, *Democracy and Education*, pp. 356–57.

17. George Herbert Palmer, *Ethical and Moral Instruction in Schools* (Boston: Mifflin, 1908); E. Hershey Sneath and George Hodges, *Moral Training in the School and Home* (New York: Macmillan, 1913); Henry Neumann, *Education for Moral Growth* (New York: D. Appleton and Company, 1928); Percival M. Symonds, *The Nature of Conduct* (New York: Macmillan, 1928); Charles E. Germane and Edith Gayton Germane, *Character Education* (New York: Silver, Bendett and Company, 1929); Dennis C. Troth, *Selected Readings in Character Education* (Boston: Beacon Press, 1930); Harold S. Tuttle, *Character Education by State and Church* (New York: Abingdon Press, 1930); McKown, *Character Education*; Ellis Ford Hartford, *Moral Values in Public Education* (New York: Harper and Brothers, 1958); McCluskey, *Public Schools and Moral Education*.

18. McKown, *Character Education*, p. 129.

19. Hartford, *Moral Values in Public Education*.

20. McKown, *Character Education*, Chapter Four.

21. Germane and Germane, *Character Education*.

22. Neumann, *Education for Moral Growth*, p. 185.

23. P. R. May, "Teachers' Attitudes to Moral Education," *Educational Research* 11 (June 1969): 215.

10: Ethics K–12, II

1. Connor, *Deviance in Soviet Society*.

2. Bronfenbrenner, *Two Worlds of Childhood*.

3. Charles P. Ridley, Paul H. B. Godwin, Dennis J. Doolin, *The Making of a Model Citizen in Communist China* (Stanford, Cal.: Hoover Institution Press, 1971).

4. See Caspar Kuhmann, *Schulreform und Gesellschaft in der Bundesrepublik Deutschland* (Stuttgart: Ernst Klett Verlag, 1970).

5. See "Religious Education in a Pluralistic Society," Addresses and Papers of the National Conference, Ecumenical Study Commission on Religion in Public Education, Toronto, Canada. *Religious Education* 68 (July–August 1973).

6. British Department of Education and Science, *Reports on Education*, no. 58, September 1969 (London: Her Majesty's Stationery Office).

7. Peter McPhail, J. R. Ungoed-Thomas, Hilary Chapman, *Moral Education in the Secondary School* (London: Longman Group, Ltd., 1972), p. 216.

8. See, for example Christopher Macy, ed., *Let's Teach Them Right* (London: Pemberton Books, 1969).

9. See note 7 above.

10. Peter McPhail, "Schools Council Moral Education Curriculum Project 13–16—Some Notes on the Work of the Project," unpublished descriptive paper, p. 2.

11. McPhail, Ungoed-Thomas, and Chapman, *Moral Education in the Secondary School*, p. 25.

12. Ibid., p. 63.

13. Each of these is in a series of booklets in the *Lifeline Series* prepared by the Schools Council Moral Education Curriculum Project (London: Longman Group, Ltd., 1972).

14. Harris, *I'm OK . . . You're OK*; Karl Menninger, *Whatever Became of Sin?* (New York: Hawthorn Books, 1973).

15. A. Bandura and R. W. Walters, *Social Learning and Personality Development* (New York: Holt, Rinehart, and Winston, 1963).

16. Piaget, *The Moral Judgment of the Child*; Lawrence Kohlberg, "Moral Development and Identification," in *Child Psychology, 62nd Yearbook of the National Society for the Study of Education*, H. W. Stevenson, ed. (Chicago: University of Chicago, 1963); Lawrence Kohlberg, "The Development of Children's Orientations toward a Moral Order: I. Sequence in the Development of Moral Thought," *Vita Humana* 6 (1963): 11–33.

17. Piaget, *Moral Judgment of the Child*, pp. 404–6.

18. Lawrence Kohlberg, "From Is to Ought," reprint of chapter in forthcoming book, idem and E. Turiel, *Moralization Research, the Cognitive-Developmental Approach* (New York: Holt, Rinehart, and Winston, in press).

19. Lawrence Kohlberg quoted in *Moral Education, Interdisciplinary Approaches*, C. M. Beck, B. S. Crittenden, and E. V. Sullivan, eds. (Toronto: University of Toronto Press, 1971), p. 33.

20. S. H. Schwartz et al., "Some Personality Correlates of Conduct in Two Situations of Moral Conflict," *Journal of Personality* 37 (1969): 41–57; Moshe M. Blatt and Lawrence Kohlberg, "The Effects of Classroom Moral Discussion," *Journal of Moral Education* 4 (February 1975): 129–61.

21. McPhail, Ungoed-Thomas, and Chapman, *Moral Education in the Secondary School*, p. 210.

22. Lebern N. Miller, "A Law Case Approach to Ethical Education," *Educational Forum* 21 (May 1967): 421–28.

23. Sidney B. Simon, Leland W. Howe, and Howard Kirschenbaum, *Values Clarification* (New York: Hart Publishing Company, 1972); Louis E. Raths, Merrill Harmin, Sidney B. Simon, *Values and Teaching* (Columbus, Ohio: Charles E. Merrill, 1966).

24. Raths, Harmin, and Simon, *Values and Teaching*, p. 109.

25. Harriet Martineau, *Society in America* (New York: Saunders and Otlay, 1837), pp. 168, 177, quoted in Lipset, *First New Nation*, p. 136.

26. Jane L. Mesick, *The English Traveller in America, 1785–1835* (New York: Columbia University Press, 1922), pp. 83, 84, quoted in Lipset, *First New Nation*, p. 137. Many Americans question whether child rearing was already so democratic as is suggested by these quotations. Lipset, however, based on admittedly scanty evidence, generalizes that this appears to have been the case; ibid., pp. 135–38.

27. Raths, Harmin, and Simon, *Values and Teaching*, p. 228.

28. H. Kirschenbaum and S. B. Simon, "Values and the Future Movement in Education," in *Learning for Tomorrow*, Alvin Toffler, ed. (New York: Random House, Vintage Books, 1974).

29. Raths, Harmin, and Simon, *Values and Teaching*, p. 41.

30. John Wilson, *Moral Thinking* (London: Heineman Educational Books, 1970); Bull, *Moral Education;* Piaget, *Moral Judgment of the Child*; Wright, *The Psychology of Moral Behavior*.

31. Lawrence Kohlberg, "Education for Future," in *Moral Education: Five Lectures* (Cambridge, Mass.: Harvard University Press, 1970); McPhail, Ungoed-Thomas, and Chapman, *Moral Education in the Secondary School*.

32. Raths, Harmin, and Simon, *Values and Teaching*, p. 227.

33. Oliver and Shaver, *Teaching Public Issues in the High School*.

34. D. W. Oliver and Fred M. Newman, *Public Issues Series* (Middletown, Conn.: American Education Publications, n.d.).

35. McPhail, Ungoed-Thomas, and Chapman, *Moral Education in the Secondary School*.

36. *Moral and Civic Education and Teaching about Religion* (Sacramento, Cal.: California State Board of Education, 1973).

37. Dewey, *Human Nature and Conduct*, Part 1, Section 5.

38. Ibid., Part 2, Section 2.

39. Ibid., Part 2, Section 4.

40. *Character Education Curriculum* (San Antonio, Texas: American Institute for Character Education, Character Education Project, n.d.).

41. Lewis, *Abolition of Man*.

42. Bessie Louise Pierce, *Civic Attitudes in American School Textbooks* (Chicago: University of Chicago, 1930).

43. Mark M. Krug, "History Textbooks in England and in the United States," *Education Digest* 29 (March 1964): 41–44; "Citizenship Courses" *Scholastic Teacher* 84 (31 January 1964): 1T-2T. For a discussion of the situation in other countries, see Alan Barcan, "The Decline of Citizenship as an Educational Aim," *Quadrant*, April 1972, pp. 42–47.

44. *Moral and Civic Education and Teaching About Religion*, p. 4.

45. Otto F. Kraushaar, *American Non-Public Schools* (Baltimore: Johns Hopkins University Press, 1972), p. 13.

46. George C. S. Benson, "American Ethics and Independent Schools" *Independent School Bulletin* 33 (May 1974): 13–15.

11: Is There Room for Ethics in the Social Gospel?

1. Jeffrey Hadden, *The Gathering Storm in the Churches* (Garden City, N.Y.: Doubleday and Company, 1969).

2. Dean M. Kelly, *Why Conservative Churches Are Growing* (New York: Harper and Row, 1972).

3. *Yearbook of American Churches for 1973* (New York: Council Press, 1973).

4. Tocqueville, *Democracy in America*, Phillips Bradley, trans., 2 vols. (New York: Random House, Vintage Books, 1945), 2:152–53.

5. Ibid.

6. Robert N. Bellah, "Civil Religion in America," in *Religion in America*, McLoughlin and Bellah, eds.

7. Will Herburg, *Protestant, Catholic, Jew* (Garden City, N.Y.: Doubleday and Company, 1955).

8. Fletcher, *Situation Ethics*.

9. Quoted in O. Hobart Mowrer, *The Crisis in Psychiatry and Religion* (New York: D. Van Nostrand Company, 1961), p. 49.

10. W. F. O'Neal, "Existentialism and Education for Moral Choice," *The Phi Delta Kappan*, 44 (October 1964). See also E. Mansell Pattison, "The Development of Moral Values in Children," *Pastoral Psychology* 20 (February 1969).

11. Robert W. Lynn and Elliott Wright, *The Big Little School* (New York: Harper and Row, 1971), p. xi.

12. Edwin Wilbur Rice, *The Sunday School Movement and the American Sunday School Union, 1780–1917* (Philadelphia: The American Sunday School Union, 1917), p. 47.

13. Lynn and Wright, *Big Little School*, p. 131.

14. Ibid., p. 48.

15. *The Christian Faith and Action*, rev. ed. (n.p.: Board of Christian Education, United Presbyterian Church, 1972).

16. *Life, Love, and Joy* (Morristown, N.J.: Silver Burdett Company, 1971).

17. *The New Life* (New York: William H. Sadlier, 1972).

18. *God Lives in His City* (Philadelphia: Geneva Press, 1968).

19. *Bible in Life* (Elgin, Ill.: David C. Cook Publishing Company, n.d.).

20. DeWitt John, *The Christian Science Way of Life* (Boston: The Chrstian Science Publishing Society, 1962), pp. 38, 185.

21. *Le Havdil: To Make a Difference* (Denver, Col.: The Rocky Mountain Curriculum Planning Workshop, 1972).

22. Louis Jacobs, *Chain of Tradition*, 3 vols.: 1. *Jewish Law* (1968), 2. *Jewish Ethics, Philosophy, and Mysticism* (1969), 3. *Jewish Thought Today* (1970) (New York: Behrman House, Inc., 1968–1970).

23. Quoted in Arlo Ayres Brown, *A History of Religious Education in Recent Times* (New York: Abington Press, 1923), p. 83. See also Robert Ulich, *A History of Religious Education* (New York: New York University Press, 1968).

24. Material from the Board of Education and Youth of the Presbyterian Church in Ireland: *Saved in Christ* and *Christ With Us*, the *Irish Catechetical Programme*, the *Sabbath School Soceity for Ireland* (Dublin: Veritas Publications, n.d.); *Curriculares Lehrplan für den Evangelischen Religiös Unterricht an der Grundschule in Bayern* (Augsberg: E. Kieser K. G., 1972); *Mannen Från Nasaret*, Utgivet i samarbete med, Svenska Kyrkans Centralråd, söndagsskolnämnden (Stockholm: A. B. Tryckmans, 1972); and other material.

25. John F. Travers and Russell G. Davis, "A Study of Religious Motivation and Delinquency," *Journal of Educational Sociology* 20 (January 1961).

26. Warren C. Middleton and Robert R. Wright, "A Comparison of a Group of Ninth and Tenth Grade Delinquent and Non-Delinquent Boys and Girls on Certain Attitude Scales," *Journal of Genetic Psychology*, no. 58 (1941).

27. Donald E. Allen and Harjit S. Sandhu, "A Comparative Study of Delinquents and non-Delinquents: Family Affect, Religion, and Personal Income," *Social Forces* (December 1967); Thomas M. Gannon, S. J., "Religious Control and Delinquent Behavior," *Sociology and Social Rsearch* 31 (July 1967).

28. Mason E. Scholl and Jerome Beker, "A Comparison of the Religious Beliefs of Delinquent and Non-Delinquent Protestant Adolescent Boys," *Religious Education* 59 (May 1964): 250–53.

29. Gannon, "Religious Control and Delinquent Behavior," *Sociology and Social Research* 31 (July 1967).

30. Eric Fromm, *The Art of Loving* (New York: Harper and Row, 1956).

12: What is the Media's Message?

1. Marshall McLuhan, *Understanding Media: The Extensions of Man* (New York: McGraw-Hill Book Company, 1964), p. 7.

2. Paul Baran, "On the Impact of the New Communication Media upon Social Values," *Law and Contemporary Problems* 34 (Spring 1969): 244–54.

3. Ibid., p. 252.

4. National Commission on the Causes and Prevention of Violence, *Final Report*, p. 190.

5. William F. Buckley, Jr., *Los Angeles Times*, 16 August 1973.

6. Erwin G. Krasnow and Lawrence D. Langley, *Politics of Broadcast Regulation* (New York: St. Martin's Press, 1973).

7. National Commission on the Causes and Prevention of Violence, *Final Report*, p. 199.

8. Ibid., p. 197.

9. Ibid., p. 199.

10. Wilson, "Violence, Pornography, and Social Science."

11. Scientific Advisory Committee on Television and Social Behavior,

Television and Growing Up: The Impact of Televised Violence, Report to the Surgeon General, United States Public Health Service (Washington, D.C.: U.S. Government Printing Office, 1972), pp. 4–7.

12. Ibid., pp. 8–9.

13. Ibid., p. 12.

14. Ibid., pp. 14, 16.

15. Charles Winick, "Censor and Sensibility: A Content Analysis of the Television Censor's Comments," in *Violence and the Mass Media*, Otto N. Larsen, ed. (New York: Harper and Row, 1968), p. 252.

16. Michael Gurevitch, "The Structure and Content of Television Broadcasting in Four Countries: An Overview," in Reports and Papers, Vol. 1: *Media Content and Control*, Scientific Advisory Committee on Television and Social Behavior, p. 383.

17. *Los Angeles Times*, 20 December 1974.

18. Rodman and Grams, "Juvenile Delinquency and the Family," in *Task Force Report: Juvenile Delinquency and Youth Crime*, Commission on Law Enforcement, pp. 216–17.

19. Scientific Advisory Committee on Television and Social Behavior, *Impact of Televised Violence*, p. 209.

20. James T. Carey, "Changing Courtship Patterns in the Popular Song," *American Journal of Sociology* (May 1969), pp. 720–31.

21. R. Serge Denisoff and Mark H. Levine, "The Popular Protest Song: The Case of 'Eve of Destruction,' " *Public Opinion Quarterly* (Spring 1971), pp. 117–22.

22. Paul M. Hirsch, "Sociological Approaches to the Pop Music Phenomenon," *American Behavioral Scientist* 14 (August–September 1971): 371–86.

23. *Report of the Commission on Obscenity and Pornography* (New York: Bantam Books, 1970), p. 86.

24. Leonard Berkowitz, *Aggression* (New York: McGraw-Hill Book Company, 1962), p. 234.

25. Joseph Morgenstern, "The New Violence," *Newsweek*, 14 February 1972. See also Charles Thomas Samuels, "Doing Violence," *American Scholar* 40 (August 1971): 695–700; and Roger Edert, "Just Another Horror Movie, or Is It?" *Reader's Digest*, June 1969.

26. Pauline Kael, "The Current Cinema," *The New Yorker*, 1 October 1973, p. 113.

27. Herbert A. Otto, "Sex and Violence on the American Newsstand," in *Violence and the Mass Media*, Larsen, ed.

28. Frederick Wertham, "Comic Books: Blueprints for Delinquency," *Reader's Digest*, May 1954, pp. 24–29.

29. Jane Clapp, comp., *Professional Ethics and Insignia* (Metuchen, N.J.: Scarecrow Press, 1974), pp. 190–95.

30. See *The Economist* 29 (January 1972): 25; *Encounter*, April 1972, p. 59.

13: Government: Corruption or Reform?

1. Aleksandr Solzhenitsyn, *The Gulag Archipelago* (New York: Harper and Row, 1973), pp. 177–78.

2. Graham, *Due Process Revolution*, p. 285.

3. Ibid., pp. 290–91.

4. Ward Elliott, "Crime, Punishment, and Professional Paradigms," a paper presented to the American Political Science Association, Washington, D.C., September 1972.

5. Cahn, *The Moral Decision: Right and Wrong in the Light of American Law*, p. 53.

6. For example, see Schur, *Our Criminal Society*, Chapter Four.

7. For some general appraisals of crime and the welfare programs, see Moynihan, *Maximum Feasible Misunderstanding*, and Elliott, "Crime, Punishment, and Professional Paradigms."

8. For more discussion of policies which the federal, state, and local governments could pursue with profit, the reader should consult Appendix B.

9. Tocqueville, *Democracy in America*, Lawrence, trans., pp. 232–33.

10. Ibid., p. 221.

11. Ibid., pp. 220–221.

12. Karren Orren and Paul Peterson, "Presidential Assassination: A Case Study in the Dynamics of Political Assassination," *Journal of Politics* 29 (May 1967): 388–404.

13. B. F. Tefft, *Speeches of Daniel Webster* (New York: A. L. Burt Company, n.d.), p. 233.

14. Marvin Meyers, *The Jacksonian Persuasion: Politics and Belief* (Stanford, Cal.: Stanford University Press, 1966), p. vii.

15. Charnwood, *Abraham Lincoln*, pp. 454–55.

16. From a speech by Edward Everett on 4 July 1828.

Appendix A

1. Federal Bureau of Investigation, *Uniform Crime Reporting Handbook* (Washington, D.C., January 1974), p. 3.

2. Jerome Daunt, quoted in Graham, *Due Process Revolution*, p. 79.

3. U.S. Department of Justice, Law Enforcement Assistance Agency (LEAA) News Release, 27 November 1974.

4. U.S. Department of Justice, LEAA, "Criminal Victimization in the United States—January to June 1973," *Report No. SD-NCP-N-1* (November 1974), p. 4.

5. Graham, *Due Process Revolution*, p. 78.

6. Ibid.

7. Ibid., p. 75.

8. British Home Office, *Criminal Statistics: England and Wales, 1972* (London: Her Majesty's Stationery Office, 1973).

9. Statistics Canada, *Crime and Traffic Enforcement Statistics, 1972–73* (Ottawa: Information Canada, August 1974); and *Official Yearbook of the Commonwealth of Australia, No. 58, 1972* (Canberra: The Commonwealth Bureau of Census and Statistics, 1972).

10. Another possible explanation for the relatively high auto theft rate in Great Britain could be England's more accurate statistical reports on their crime incidence.

11. United States police strength is reported in U.S. Department of Commerce, Social and Economic Statistics Administration, Bureau of the Census, *Statistical Abstract of the United States: 1973*. Strength of the police forces in England, Australia, and Canada is reported in their annual statistical yearbooks.

Appendix B

1. Advisory Commission on Intergovernmental Relations (ACIR), *American Federalism: Into the Third Century* (Washington, D.C.: U.S. Government Printing Office, May 1974), p. 24.

2. Commission on Law Enforcement and Administration of Justice, *Task Force Report: The Police* (Washington, D.C.: U.S. Government Printing Office, 1967), p. 42.

3. ACIR, *American Federalism*, p. 24.

4. The Knapp Commission, *Report on Police Corruption* (New York: George Braziller, 1973), p. 274.

5. Los Angeles Police Department press release, 3 December 1974.

6. Commission on Law Enforcement and Administration of Justice, *The Challenge of Crime in a Free Society* (Washington, D.C.: U.S. Government Printing Office, 1967), p. 1.

7. Committee for Economic Development (CED), *Reducing Crime and Assuring Justice*, p. 13.

8. John Kenney, "California's Integrated Police System," *Crime Prevention Review*, 2:5.

9. CED, *Reducing Crime and Assuring Justice*, p. 70.

10. Ibid., p. 18.

11. Ibid., p. 19.

12. ACIR, *American Federalism*, p. 26.

Bibliography

Advisory Commission on Intergovernmental Relations. *American Federalism: Into the Third Century.* Washington, D.C.: U.S. Government Printing Office, 1974.

Allen, Donald E., and Sandhu, Harjit S. "A Comparative Study of Delinquents and Non-Delinquents: Family Affect, Religion, and Personal Income." *Social Forces,* December 1967.

Anshen, Ruth N., ed. *Moral Principles of Action.* New York: Harper and Row, 1952.

Aristotle. *Nicomachean Ethics.* In *Introduction to Aristotle,* edited and translated by Richard M. McKeon. Modern Library College edition. New York: Random House, 1947.

Ausubel, D. P. *Theory and Problems of Child Development.* New York: Grune and Stratton, 1958.

Bailey, Sidney D. *British Parliamentary Democracy.* Boston: Houghton Mifflin, 1971.

Ball, William. "Religion and Public Education: the Post-Schempp Years." In *Religion and Public Education,* Theodore R. Sizer, ed. New York: Houghton Mifflin, 1967.

Bamford, T. W. *Rise of the Public Schools.* London: Thomas Nelson and Son, 1967.

Bandura, A., and Walters, R. W. *Social Learning and Personality Development.* New York: Holt, Rinehart, and Winston, 1963.

Banfield, Edward C. *How Many and Who Should Be Set at Liberty?* Public Affairs Conference Center, Kenyon College, 1970.

Baran, Paul. "On the Impact of the New Communication Media upon Social Values." *Law and Contemporary Problems* 34 (Spring 1969): 244–54.

Barcan, Alan. "The Decline of Citizenship as an Educational Aim." *Quadrant,* April 1972, pp. 42–47.

Barrett, William. *Irrational Man.* Garden City, N.Y.: Doubleday Anchor Books, 1961.

Bean, Walter. *Boss Ruef's San Francisco.* Berkeley: University of California Press, 1968.

Beck, Bertram. "Recreation and Delinquency." In *Task Force Report: Juvenile Delinquency and Youth Crime.* The President's Commission on Law Enforcement and the Administration of Justice. Washington, D.C.: U.S. Government Printing Office, 1967.

Beck, C. M.; Crittenden, B. S.; and Sullivan, E. V., eds. *Moral Education, Interdisciplinary Approaches.* Toronto: University of Toronto Press, 1971.

Beck, R. N., and Orr, J. B., eds. *Ethical Choice: A Case Study Approach.* New York: Free Press, 1970.

Becker, Theodore L., and Murray, Vernon G., eds. *Government Lawlessness in America.* London: Oxford University Press, 1971.

Bellah, Robert N. "Civil Religion in America." In *Religion in America,* William G. McLoughlin and Robert N. Bellah, eds. Boston: Beacon Press, 1968.

Benson, George C. S. "American Ethics and Independent Schools." *Independent School Bulletin* 33 (May 1974): 13–15.

Berkowitz, Leonard. *Aggression.* New York: McGraw-Hill Book Company, 1962.

Bernstein, Richard J. "John Dewey." In *Encyclopedia of Philosophy,* vol. 2.

Bible in Life. Elgin, Ill.: David C. Cook Publishing Company, n.d.

Bickel, Alexander. *The Least Dangerous Branch.* New York: Bobbs-Merrill, 1962.

Bierman, A. K., and Gould, James A., eds. *Philosophy for a New Generation.* New York: Macmillan, 1970.

Billingsley, Andrew. *Black Families in White America.* Englewood Cliffs, N.J.: Prentice Hall, 1968.

Blatt, Moshe M., and Kohlberg, Lawrence. "The Effects of Classroom Moral Discussion." *Journal of Moral Education* 4 (February 1975): 129–61.

Board of Education and Youth, the Presbyterian Church in Ireland. *Catechetical Programme.* Dublin: Veritas Publications, n.d.

———. *Christ with Us.* Dublin: Veritas Publications, n.d.

———. *Sabbath School Society for Ireland.* Dublin: Veritas Publications, n.d.

———. *Saved in Christ.* Dublin: Veritas Publications, n.d.

Bowerman, Charles, and Kinch, John. "Changes in Family and Peer Orientation of Children between the Fourth and Tenth Grades." *Social Forces* 37 (March 1959).

Brasy, H. A. "Administrative Corruption in Theory and Dutch Practice." In *Political Corruption,* Arnold J. Heidenheimer, ed. New York: Rinehart and Winston, 1970.

Breasted, James. *The Dawn of Conscience.* New York: Charles Scribner's Sons, 1935.

British Department of Education and Science. *Reports on Education,* no. 58, September 1969. London: Her Majesty's Stationery Office.

British Home Office. *Criminal Statistics, England and Wales, 1971. London: Her Majesty's Stationery Office,* 1971.

————. *Criminal Statistics: England and Wales, 1972.* London: Her Majesty's Stationery Office, 1973.

Brittain, Clay. "Adolescent Choices and Parent-Peer Cross Pressures." *American Sociological Review* 28 (June 1963): 389.

————. "An Exploration of the Bases of Peer-Compliance and Parent-Compliance in Adolescence." *Adolescence* 2 (Winter 1967).

Brogan, Dennis W. *The American Character.* New York: Alfred A. Knopf, 1944.

Bronfenbrenner, Urie. "The Split-Level American Family." *Saturday Review,* 7 October 1967.

————. *Two Worlds of Childhood: U.S. and U.S.S.R.* New York: Russell Sage, 1970.

Brown, Arlo Ayres. *A History of Religious Education in Recent Times.* New York: Abington Press, 1923.

Bull, Norman J. *Moral Education.* Beverly Hills, Cal.: Sage Publications, 1969.

————. *Moral Judgment from Childhood to Adolescence.* Beverly Hills, Cal.: Sage Publicatiohs, 1969.

Burton, John C., ed. *Corporate Financial Reporting: Ethical and Other Problems.* New York: American Institute of Certified Public Accountants, 1972.

Cahn, Edmond. *The Moral Decision: Right and Wrong in the Light of American Law.* Bloomington, Ind.: Indiana University Press, 1955.

Cameron, Mary Owen. *The Booster and the Snitch.* Glencoe, Ill.: Free Press, 1964.

Campbell, John D. "Peer Relations in Childhood." In *Review of Child Development Research,* Martin Hoffman and Lois Hoffman, eds., vol. 1. New York: Russell Sage Foundation, 1964.

Carey, James T. "Changing Courtship Patterns in the Popular Song." *American Journal of Sociology,* May 1969, pp. 720–31.

Carlin, Jerome E. *Lawyer's Ethics.* New York: Russell Sage Foundation, 1966.

Chappell, D., and Wilson, P. R. *The Police and the Public in Australia and New Zealand.* St. Lucia: University of Queensland Press, 1969.

Character Education Curriculum. San Antonio, Texas: American Institute for Character Education, Character Education Project, n.d.

Charnwood, Lord. *Abraham Lincoln.* New York: Henry Holt and Company, 1917.

Chevallaz, G. A. *La Suisse ou le Sommeil du Juste.* Lausanne: Payot, 1967.

The Christian Faith and Action. Rev. ed. N.p.: Board of Christian Education of the United Presbyterian Church, 1972.

"Citizenship Courses." *Scholastic Teacher* 84 (31 January 1964): 1T–2T.

Clapp, Jane, *Professional Ethics and Insignia.* Metuchen, N.J.: Scarecrow Press, 1974.

Clark, John P., and Wennenger, Eugene P. "Socio-Economic Class and Area as Correlates of Illegal Behavior among Juveniles." *American Sociological Review* 27 (1962): 826–34.

Clebsch, William A. "American Religion and the Cure of Souls." In *Religion in America,* William G. McLoughlin and Robert N. Bellah, eds. Boston: Beacon Press, 1968.

Clinard, Marshall B. *The Black Market.* New York: Rinehart and Company, 1952.

―――. "A Cross-Cultural Replication of the Relation of Urbanism to Criminal Behavior." *American Sociological Review* 25 (April 1960): 253–57.

Cloward, Richard A., and Ohlin, Lloyd E. *Delinquency and Opportunity.* New York: Free Press, 1960.

Cohen, Albert K. *Delinquent Boys.* Glencoe, Ill.: Free Press, 1955.

Coleman, James. *The Adolescent Society.* New York: Free Press, 1961.

Coleman, Lee. *What Is an American?: A Study of Alleged American Traits.* In *The Character of Americans,* M. McGiffert, ed. Homewood, Ill.: Dorsey Press, 1964.

Commager, Henry Steele. *The American Mind.* Reprint ed. New York: Bantam Books, 1970.

Commission on Law Enforcement. See The President's Commission on Law Enforcement and the Administration of Justice.

Commission on Violence. See National Commission on the Causes and Prevention of Violence.

Committee for Economic Development. *Reducing Crime and Assuring Justice*. New York: Committee for Economic Development, 1972.

Connor, Walter D. *Deviance in Soviet Society*. New York: Columbia University Press, 1972.

Coulton, G. C., and Adcock, A. D., eds. *The Feudal Period in Judaism and Christianity*. New York: Ktav Publishing House, 1969.

Cressey, Donald R. *Other People's Money*. Glencoe, Ill.: Free Press, 1953.

———. *Theft of the Nation: The Structure and Operations of Organized Crime in America*. New York: Harper Colophon Book, Harper and Row, 1969.

Curriculares Lehrplan für den Evangelischen Religiös Unterricht an der Grundschule in Bayern. Augsberg: E. Kieser K. G., 1972.

Day, Edmund E. *Education for Freedom and Responsibility*. Ithaca, N.Y.: Cornell University Press, 1952.

DeCharms, Richard, and Moeller, Gerald H. "Values Expressed in American Children's Readers, 1800-1950." *Journal of Abnormal and Social Psychology* 64 (1962): 136–42.

Denisoff, R. Serge, and Levine, Mark H. "The Popular Protest Song: The Case of 'Eve of Destruction.' " *Public Opinion Quarterly* (Spring 1971), pp. 117–22.

Devereux, E. C. "Authority, Guilt, and Conformity to Adult Standards among German School Children: A Pilot Experimental Study." Cornell University, 1966.

———. "Socialization in Cross-Cultural Perspective: A Comparative Study of England, Germany, and the United States." Cornell University, 1965.

Dewey, John. *Democracy and Education*. 1916. New York: Free Press Paperback, 1966.

———. *Human Nature and Conduct*. 1922. Reprint. New York: Random House, The Modern Library, 1930 and 1957.

———. *Reconstruction in Philosophy*. Boston: Beacon Press, 1948.

———. *The School and Society*. Rev. ed. Chicago: University of Chicago, 1971.

Dewey, John, and Tufts, James H. *Ethics*. Rev. ed. New York: Henry Holt and Company, 1932.

Diamond, Martin; Fisk, Winston Mills; and Garfinkel, Herbert. *The Democratic Republic*. 1966. Reprint. Chicago: Rand McNally, 1971.

Dirks, Raymond L., and Cross, Leonard. *The Great Wall Street Scandal.* New York: McGraw-Hill, 1974.

Dorman, Michael. *Payoff.* New York: David McKay Company, 1972.

Douglas, Paul H. *Ethics in Government.* Cambridge, Mass.: Harvard University Press, 1952.

Drake, Durant. *Problems of Conduct.* Rev. ed. Boston: Houghton Mifflin, 1921.

The Economist 29 (January 1972).

Edert, Roger. "Just Another Horror Movie, or Is It?" *Reader's Digest,* June 1969.

Elliott, Ward. "Crime, Punishment, and Professional Paradigms." Paper presented to the American Political Science Association, Washington, D.C., September 1972.

Encounter, April 1972.

Encyclopedia of Philosophy. Vol. 2. New York: Macmillan Company and Free Press, 1967.

Erikson, Erik H. *Childhood and Society.* New York: W. W. Norton and Company, 1950.

Federal Bureau of Investigation. *Crime in the United States.* Washington, D.C., 1973.

―――. *Uniform Crime Reporting Handbook.* Washington, D.C.: U.S. Government Printing Office, 1974.

Fitts, William T., Jr., and Fitts, Barbara. "Ethical Standards of the Medical Profession." *The Annals* 297 (January 1955): 17–36.

Fletcher, Joseph. *Moral Responsibility: Situation Ethics at Work.* Philadelphia: Westminster Press, 1967.

―――. *Situation Ethics: The New Morality.* Philadelphia: Westminster Press, 1966.

Ford, Henry Jones. "Municipal Corruption: A Comment on Lincoln Steffens." *Political Science Quarterly* 19 (1904): 673–86.

Foster, Margaret P. "A Study of the Content of Selected Third Grade Basic Readers Used in the United States from 1900 to 1953." Master's thesis, Wesleyan University, Connecticut, 1956.

Frankena, William. *Ethics.* Englewood Cliffs, N.J.: Prentice-Hall, 1961.

Frankena, William K. "Utilitarianism." In *Dictionary of Philosophy,* Dagobert D. Runes, ed. New York: Philosophical Library, 1942.

Freud, Sigmund. *Civilization and Its Discontents.* New York: W. W. Norton, 1962.

―――. *Totem and Taboo.* 1913. Reprint. New York: Vintage Books, 1946.

Friedrich, Carl J. *The Pathology of Politics*. New York: Harper and Row, 1972.

Frier, David A. *Conflict of Interest in the Eisenhower Administration*. Baltimore: Penquin Books, 1970.

Fromm, Eric. *The Art of Loving*. New York: Harper and Row, 1956.

Gannon, Thomas M. "Religious Control and Delinquent Behavior." *Sociology and Social Research* 31 (July 1967).

Gardiner, John A. *The Politics of Corruption*. New York: Russell Sage Foundation, 1970.

Germane, Charles E., and Germane, Edith Clayton. *Character Education*. New York: Silver, Bendett and Company, 1929.

Getz, Robert S. *Congressional Ethics*. Princeton, N.J.: D. Van Nostrand, 1966.

Gilder, George. "In Defense of Monogamy." *Commentary* 58 (November 1974): 31–36.

Glazer, Nathan, and Moynihan, Daniel P. *Beyond the Melting Pot*. 2nd ed. Cambridge, Mass.: M. I. T. Press, 1970.

God Lives in His City. Philadelphia: Geneva Press, 1968.

Gold, Martin. *Status Forces in Delinquent Boys*. Ann Arbor, Mich.: University of Michigan, Institute for Social Research, 1963.

Golding, William. *Lord of the Flies*. New York: Capricorn Books, 1954.

Goslin Handbook of Socialization Theory and Research. Chicago: Rand McNally, 1969.

Graham, Fred P. *The Due Process Revolution*. New York: Hayden Book Company, 1970.

Griffith, Ernest S. *A History of American City Government*. New York: Praeger, 1974.

———. *Modern Development of City Governemnt*. 2 vols. London: Oxford University Press, 1927.

Gurevitch, Michael. "The Structure and Content of Television Broadcasting in Four Countries: An Overview." In *Reports and Papers,* vol. 1: *Media Content and Control,* Surgeon General's Scientific Advisory Committee on Television and Social Behavior. Washington, D.C.: U.S. Government Printing Office, 1972.

Hadden, Jeffrey. *The Gathering Storm in the Churches*. Garden City, N.Y.: Doubleday and Company, 1969.

Halberstam, David. *The Best and the Brightest*. New York: Random House, 1969; Greenwich, Conn.: Fawcett Publications, 1972.

Hale, Nathan. *Freud in America*. Oxford: Oxford University Press, 1971.

Halleck, Seymour. *Psychiatry and the Dilemma of Crime.* New York: Harper and Row, 1967.

Hamilton, Edith, and Cairns, Huntington, eds. *Meno.* W. K. C. Guthrie, trans. In *The Collected Dialogues of Plato,* Bollingen Series. New York: Random House, Pantheon Books, 1961.

Harper's.

Harris, Thomas A. *I'm OK . . . You're OK: A Practical Guide to Transactional Analysis.* New York: Harper and Row, 1967.

Hartford, Ellis Ford. *Moral Values in Public Education.* New York: Harper and Brothers, 1958.

Hartup, Willard. "Peer Interaction and Social Organization." In *Carmichael's Manual of Child Psychology,* Paul Mussen, ed. 3rd ed., vol. 2. New York: John Wiley and Sons, 1970.

Heidenheimer, Arnold J. *The Governments of Germany.* New York: Thomas Y. Crowell, 1971.

————, ed. *Political Corruption.* New York: Rinehart and Winston, 1970.

Herburg, Will. *Protestant, Catholic, Jew.* Garden City, N.Y.: Doubleday and Company, 1955.

Himmelfarb, Gertrude. *Victorian Minds.* 1952. Reprint ed. New York: Harper Torchbooks, 1968.

Hirsch, Paul M. "Sociological Approaches to the Pop Music Phenomenon." *American Behavioral Scientist* 14 (August-September 1971): 371–86.

Hoffman, Martin, and Hoffman, Lois, eds. *Review of Child Development Research.* New York: Russell Sage Foundation, 1964.

Hofstadter, Richard. "Commentary: Have There Been Discernible Shifts in American Values during the Past Generation?" In *The American Style,* E. E. Morison, ed. New York: Harper and Row, 1958.

Hofstadter, Richard, and Wallace, M. *American Violence: A Documentary History.* New York: Alfred A. Knopf, 1970.

Hoogenboom, Ari. *Outlawing the Spoils.* Champaign, Ill.: University of Illinois Press, 1968.

Hoover, J. Edgar. "Embezzlements: Their Causes and Consequences." *New York Certified Public Accountant,* July 1968.

Hopkins, Ernest Jerome. *Our Lawless Police.* New York: Viking Press, 1931.

Hsu, F. L. K.; Watrous, B. G.; and Lord, E. M. "Culture Pattern and Adolescent Behavior." *International Journal of Social Psychiatrists* 7 (1960): 33–35.

Hudson, W. D. *Modern Moral Philosophy.* Garden City, N.Y.: Doubleday Anchor, 1970.

Huntford, Roland. *The New Totalitarians.* New York: Stein and Day, 1972.

Huntington, Samuel. *Political Order in Changing Societies.* New Haven: Yale University Press, 1968.

Hutchinson, John. *The Imperfect Union.* New York: E. P. Dutton, 1972.

Hyman, Herbert H. *Political Socialization.* Glencoe, Ill.: Free Press, 1959.

Inkeles, Alex, and Bauer, Raymond. *The Soviet Citizen.* New York: Atheneum, 1968.

Interpol. *International Crime Statistics, 1969–1970.* St. Cloud, France: International Criminal Police Organization, n.d.

Jacobs, Louis. *Chain of Tradition.* 3 vols.: 1968, 1969, 1970. New York: Behrman House, Inc., 1968–1970.

Jennings, Kent, and Niemi, Richard S. "The Transmission of Political Values from Parents to Child." *American Political Science Review* 53 (March 1968): 169–84.

John, DeWitt. *The Christian Science Way of Life.* Boston: The Christian Science Publishing Society, 1962.

Kadushin, Charles. "Who Are the Elite Intellectuals?" *The Public Interest,* no. 29 (1972), pp. 109–25.

Kael, Pauline. "The Current Cinema." *The New Yorker,* 1 October 1973.

Karacki, Larry, and Toby, Jackson. "The Uncommitted Adolescent: Candidate for Gang Socialization." *Sociological Inquiry* 32 (Spring 1962): 203–15.

Kefauver, Estes. "Past and Present Standards of Public Ethics in America: Are We Improving?" *The Annals* 280 (March 1952): 1.

Kelly, Dean M. *Why Conservative Churches Are Growing.* New York: Harper and Row, 1972.

Kenney, John. "California's Integrated Police System." *Crime Prevention Review,* 2:5.

Kirschenbaum, H., and Simon, S. B. "Values and the Future Movement in Education." In *Learning for Tomorrow,* Alvin Toffler, ed. New York: Random House, Vintage Books, 1974.

Kluckhohn, Clyde. "Discernible Shifts in American Values?" In *The American Style,* E. E. Morison, ed. New York: Harper and Row, 1958.

———. "Ethical Relativity: Sic et Non." *Journal of Philosophy* 52 (1955).

The Knapp Commission. *Report on Police Corruption.* New York: George Braziller, 1973.

Kohlberg, Lawrence. "The Development of Children's Orientations toward a Moral Order: I. Sequence in the Development of Moral Thought." *Vita Humana* 6 (1963): 11–33.

―――. "Education for Future." In *Moral Education: Five Lectures;* Introduction by Nancy F. Sizer and Theodore R. Sizer. Cambridge, Mass.: Harvard University Press, 1970.

―――. "Education for Justice: A Modern Statement of the Platonic View." In *Moral Education: Five Lectures;* Introduction by Nancy F. Sizer and Theodore R. Sizer. Cambridge, Mass.: Harvard University Press, 1970.

―――. "From Is to Ought." In *Moralization Research, the Cognitive-Developmental Approach,* Lawrence Kohlberg and E. Turiel. New York: Holt, Rinehart, and Winston, in press.

―――. "Moral Development and Identification." In *Child Psychology, 62nd Yearbook of the National Society for the Study of Education,* H. W. Stevenson, ed. Chicago: University of Chicago, 1963.

Kohlberg, Lawrence, and Turiel, E. *Moralization Research, the Cognitive-Developmental Approach.* New York: Holt, Rinehart, and Winston, in press.

Kohn, M. L. "Social Class and Parent-Child Relationships: An Interpretation." *American Journal of Sociology* 64 (January 1959): 337–51.

Krasnow, Erwin G., and Langley, Lawrence D. *Politics of Broadcast Regulation.* New York: St. Marin's Press, 1973.

Kraushaar, Otto F. *American Non-Public Schools.* Baltimore, Md.: Johns Hopkins University Press, 1972.

―――. "Kant." In *Dictionary of Philosophy,* Dagobert D. Runes, ed. New York: Philosophical Library, 1942.

Kristol, Irving. *On the Democratic Idea in America.* New York: Harper and Row, 1972.

―――. " 'When Virtue Loses All Her Loveliness'—Some Reflections on Capitalism and the 'Free Society.' " *The Public Interest,* no. 21 (1970), pp. 3–15.

Krug, Mark M. "History Textbooks in England and in the United States." *Education Digest* 29 (March 1964): 41–44.

Kuhmann, Caspar. *Schulreform und Gesellschaft in der Bundesrepublik Deutschland.* Stuttgart: Ernst Klett Verlag, 1970.

Kvaraceus, W. C., and Miller, W. B. *Delinquent Behavior: Culture and the Individual.* Washington, D.C.: National Education Association, 1959.

Langton, Kenneth. *Political Socialization.* New York: Oxford University Press, 1969.

LaPiana, George. "Doctrinal Background of Moral Theology." In *Moral Principles of Action,* Ruth N. Anshen, ed. New York: Harper and Row, 1952.

Larsen, Otto N., ed. *Violence and the Mass Media.* New York: Harper and Row, 1968.

Larson, Lyle. "The Influence of Parents and Peers during Adolescence: The Situation Hypothesis Revisited." *Journal of Marriage and the Family* 34 (February 1972): 71.

Laski, Harold. *The American Democracy.* New York: Viking Press, 1948.

Lecky, W. E. H. *History of European Morals.* 2 vols. New York: D. Appleton and Company, 1879.

Le Havdil: To Make a Difference. 3 vols. New York: Behrman House, Inc., 1968.

Lerman, Paul. "Individual Values, Peer Values, and Subcultural Delinquency." *American Sociological Review* 33 (April 1968): 233–34.

Lewis, C. S. *The Abolition of Man.* 1943. New York: Macmillan Paperback Edition, 1965.

Lewis, Oscar. *La Vida.* New York: Vintage Books, 1965.

Lieberman, Jethro K. *How the Government Breaks the Law.* Baltimore, Md.: Penguin Books, 1972.

Life, Love, and Joy. Morristown, N.J.: Silver Burdett Company, 1971.

Lindesmith, Alfred R. *The Addict and the Law.* Bloomington, Ind.: Indiana University Press, 1965.

Linton, Ralph. "Universal Ethical Principles: An Anthropological Point of View." In *Moral Principles of Action,* Ruth N. Anshen, ed. New York: Harper and Row, 1952.

Lipman, Mark. *Stealing.* New York: Harper's Magazine Press, 1973.

Lippmann, Walter. *A Preface to Morals.* New York: Time-Life Books, 1964.

Lipset, Seymour Martin. *The First New Nation.* Reprint ed. Garden City, N.Y.: Doubleday Anchor Books, 1967.

———. *Political Man.* Garden City, N.Y.: Doubleday, 1963.

———. *Revolution and Counterrevolution.* New York: Basic Books, 1968.

Lipset, Seymour Martin, and Altbach, Philip G., eds. *Students in Revolt.* Boston: Beacon Press, 1970.

Lipset, Seymour Martin, and Lowenthal, Leo, eds. *Culture and Social Character.* Glencoe, Ill.: Free Press, 1961.

Los Angeles Times, 14 January 1973, 16 August 1973, 14 November 1974, 20 December 1974.

Lynn, Robert W., and Wright, Elliott. *The Big Little School.* New York: Harper and Row, 1971.

Maas, Peter. *Serpico.* New York: Bantam Books, 1973.

Macy, Christopher, ed. *Let's Teach Them Right.* London: Pemberton Books, 1969.

Mannen Från Nasaret. Utgivet i samarbete med, Svenska Kyrkans Centralråd, söndagsskolnämnden. Stockholm: A. B. Tryckmans, 1972.

Martineau, Harriet. *Society in America.* New York: Saunders and Otlay, 1837.

Maslow, A. H., and Diaz-Guerrero, R. "Delinquency as a Value Disturbance." In *Festschrift for Gardner Murphy,* J. G. Peatman and E. L. Hartley, eds. New York: Harper, 1960.

May, P. R. "Teachers' Attitudes to Moral Education." *Educational Research* 11 (June 1969): 215.

McCandless, Boyd. "Childhood Socialization." In *Goslin, Handbook of Socialization Theory and Research.* Chicago: Rand McNally, 1969.

McCloskey, Herbert, and Dahlgren, Harold E. "Primary Group Influence on Party Loyalty." *American Political Science Review* 53 (September 1959): 757–76.

McCluskey, Neil G. *Public Schools and Moral Education.* New York: Columbia University Press, 1958.

McCord, Joan, and McCord, William. "The Effects of Parental Role Model on Criminality." *Journal of Social Issues* 14 (1958): 66–75.

McGiffert, M., ed. *The Character of Americans.* Homewood, Ill.: Dorsey Press, 1964.

McKown, Harry C. *Character Education.* New York: McGraw-Hill Book Company, 1935.

McLoughlin, William G., and Bellah, Robert N., eds. *Religion in America.* Boston: Beacon Press, 1968.

McLuhan, Marshall. *The Medium Is the Message.* New York: Random House, 1967.

———. *Understanding Media: The Extensions of Man.* New York: McGraw-Hill Book Company, 1964.

McPhail, Peter. "Schools Council Moral Education Curriculum Project 13–16—Some Notes on the Work of the Project." Unpublished.

McPhail, Peter; Ungoed-Thomas, J. R.; Chapman, Hilary. *Moral Education in the Secondary School.* London: Longman Group Ltd., 1972.

Menninger, Karl. *Whatever Became of Sin?* New York: Hawthorn Books, 1973.

Merelman, Richard M. *Political Socialization and Educational Climates.* New York: Holt, Rinehart, and Winston, 1971.

Merton, Robert K. *Social Theory and Social Structure.* 1949. Enlarged ed. New York: Free Press, 1968.

Mesick, Jane L. *The English Traveller in America, 1785–1835.* New York: Columbia University Press, 1922.

Meyers, Marvin. *The Jacksonian Persuasion: Politics and Belief.* 1957. Reprint ed. Stanford, Cal.: Stanford University Press, 1966.

Middleton, Warren C., and Wright, Robert R. "A Comparison of a Group of Ninth and Tenth Grade Delinquent and Non-Delinquent Boys and Girls on Certain Attitude Scales." *Journal of Genetic Psychology,* no. 58 (1941).

Miller, Lebern N. "A Law Case Approach to Ethical Education." *Educational Forum* 21 (May 1967): 421–28.

Miller, Walter. "Lower Class Culture as a Generating Milieu of Gang Delinquency." *Journal of Social Issues* 14 (1959): 5–19.

Molnar, Thomas. *The Decline of the Intellectual.* New York: World Publishing Company, 1961.

Moral and Civic Education and Teaching about Religion. Sacramento, Cal.: California State Board of Education, 1973.

Moral Education: Five Lectures. Introduction by Nancy F. Sizer and Theodore R. Sizer. Cambridge, Mass.: Harvard University Press, 1970.

Morgenstern, Joseph. "The New Violence." *Newsweek,* 14 February 1972.

Morison, E. E., ed. *The American Style.* New York: Harper and Row, 1958.

Mowrer, O. Hobart. *The Crisis in Psychiatry and Religion.* New York: D. Van Nostrand Company, 1961.

Moynihan, Daniel P. *Maximum Feasible Misunderstanding.* New York: Free Press, 1969.

———. *The Negro Family: The Case for National Action.* Washington, D.C.: U.S. Department of Labor, Office of Policy Planning and Research, March 1965.

Mussen, Paul, ed. *Carmichael's Manual of Child Psychology.* 3rd ed. New York: John Wiley and Sons, 1970.

National Advisory Commission on Civil Disorders. *Supplemental Studies.* Washington, D.C.: U.S. Government Printing Office, July 1968.

National Advisory Commission on Intergovernmental Relations. *State-Local Relations in the Criminal Justice System.* Washington, D.C.: U.S. Government Printing Office, 1971.

National Commission on the Causes and Prevention of Violence. *Final Report.* Washington, D.C.: U.S. Government Printing Office, 1969.

Neumann, Henry. *Education for Moral Growth.* New York: D. Appleton and Company, 1928.

Newburg, Paula. "A Study in Deviance: Shoplifting." *International Journal of Comparative Sociology* 9 (June 1968): 132–136.

.*The New Life.* New York: William H. Sadlier, 1972.

The New York Review.

New York Times, 8 October 1972.

Nye, F. Ivan. *Family Relationships and Delinquent Behavior.* New York: John Wiley and Sons, 1958.

Nye, F. Ivan; Short, James F., Jr.; and Olson, Virgil J. "Socioeconomic Status and Delinquent Behavior." *American Journal of Sociology* 63 (January 1958): 338, 383.

Nye, J. S. "Corruption and Political Development: A Cost Benefit Analysis." *American Political Science Review* 61 (June 1967).

Official Yearbook of the Commonwealth of Australia. No. 58, 1972. Canberra: The Commonwealth Bureau of Census and Statistics, 1972.

Oliver, D. W., and Newman, Fred M., eds. *Public Issues Series.* Middletown, Conn.: American Education Publications, n.d.

Oliver, D. W., and Shaver, J. B. *Teaching Public Issues in the High School.* Boston: Houghton Mifflin, 1966.

O'Neal, W. F. "Existentialism and Education for Moral Choice." *The Phi Delta Kappan* 44 (October 1964).

Orren, Karren, and Peterson, Paul. "Presidential Assassination: A Case Study in the Dynamics of Political Assassination." *Journal of Politics* 29 (May 1967): 388–404.

Otto, Herbert A. "Sex and Violence on the American Newsstand." In *Violence and the Mass Media,* Otto N. Larsen, ed. New York: Harper and Row, 1968.

Packard, Vance. *A Nation of Strangers.* New York: David McKay, 1972.

Palmer, George Herbert. *Ethical and Moral Instruction in Schools.* Boston: Mifflin. 1908.

Parsons, Talcott, and White, Winston. "The Link between Character and Society." In *Culture and Social Character,* Seymour Martin Lipset and Leo Lowenthal, eds. Glencoe, Ill.: Free Press, 1961.

Pattison, E. Mansell. "The Development of Moral Values in Children." *Pastoral Psychology* 20 (February 1969).

Peatman, J. G., and Hartley, E. L., eds. *Festschrift for Gardner Murphy.* New York: Harper, 1960.

Peck, R. H., and Havighurst, R. J. *The Psychology of Character Development.* New York: John Wiley and Sons, 1960.

Piaget, Jean. *The Moral Judgment of the Child.* Marjorie Gabain, trans. New York: Free Press, 1965.

Pierce, Bessie Louise. *Civic Attitudes in American School Textbooks.* Chicago: University of Chicago, 1930.

The President's Commission on Campus Unrest. *Report.* Washington, D.C.: U.S. Government Printing Office, 1970.

The President's Commission on Law Enforcement and the Administration of Justice. *The Challenge of Crime in a Free Society.* Washington, D.C.: U.S. Government Printing Office, 1967.

———. *Task Force Report: Crime and Its Impact.* Washington, D.C.: U.S. Government Printing Office, 1967.

———. *Task Force Report: Juvenile Delinquency and Youth Crime.* Washington, D.C.: U.S. Government Printing Office, 1967.

———. *Task Force Report: Organized Crime.* Washington, D.C.: U.S. Government Printing Office, 1967.

———. *Task Force Report: The Police.* Washington, D.C.: U.S. Government Printing Office, 1967.

Psathas, G. "Ethnicity, Social Class, and Adolescent Independence from Parental Control." *American Sociological Review* 22 (1957): 415–23.

Rabinowitz, L. "France in the Thirteenth Century." In *The Feudal Period in Judaism and Christianity,* G. C. Coulton and A. C. Adcock, eds. New York: Ktav Publishing House, 1969.

Rainwater, Lee, and Yancey, William L. *The Moynihan Report and the Politics of Controversy.* Cambridge, Mass.: M. I. T. Press, 1967.

Ramsey, Paul. *Basic Christian Ethics.* New York: Charles Scribner's Sons, 1950.

Raths, Louis E.; Harmin, Merrill; and Simon, Sidney B. *Values and Teaching.* Columbus, Ohio: Charles E. Merrill, 1966.

Rawls, John. *A Theory of Justice*. Cambridge, Mass.: Harvard University Press, 1971.

Reichley, A. James. "Getting at the Roots of Watergate." *Fortune,* July 1973.

Reiss, Albert J. *The Police and the Public*. New Haven, Conn.: Yale University Press, 1971.

Reiss, Albert J., Jr., and Rhodes, Albert Lewis. "The Distribution of Juvenile Delinquency in the Social Class Structure." *American Sociological Review* 26 (October 1961): 720–32.

"Religious Education in a Pluralistic Society." Addresses and papers of the National Conference, Ecumenical Study Commission on Religion in Public Education, Toronto, Canada. *Religious Education* 68 (July-August 1973).

The Report of the Commission on Obscenity and Pornography. New York: Bantam Books, 1970.

Rice, Edwin Wilbur. *The Sunday School Movement and the American Sunday School Union, 1780–1917*. Philadelphia: The American Sunday School Union, 1917.

Ridley, Charles P.; Godwin, Paul H. B.; and Doolin, Dennis J. *The Making of a Model Citizen in Communist China*. Stanford, Cal.: Hoover Institution Press, 1971.

Riesman, David. *The Lonely Crowd*. Garden City, N.Y.: Doubleday Anchor, 1955.

Roazen, Paul. *Freud: Political and Social Thought*. New York: Alfred A. Knopf, 1968.

Roberts, Ben C. "On the Origins and Resolution of English Working Class Protest." In *Violence in America, Historical and Comparative Perspectives*. Staff Report to National Commission on the Causes and Prevention of Violence. Washington, D.C.: U.S. Government Printing Office, 1969.

Rodman, Hyman, and Grams, Paul. "Juvenile Delinquency and the Family." In *Task Force Report: Juvenile Delinquency and Youth Crime*. The President's Commission on Law Enforcement and the Administration of Justice. Washington, D.C.: U.S. Government Printing Office, 1967.

Rosenberg, Hans. *Bureaucracy, Aristocracy, and Autocracy*. Boston: Beacon Press, 1958.

Rougement, Denis de. *La Suisse*. Paris: Hachette, 1965.

Samuels, Charles Thomas. "Doing Violence." *American Scholar* 40 (August 1971).

Schafer, Walter E., and Polk, Kenneth. "Delinquency and the Schools." In *Task Force Report: Juvenile Delinquency and Youth Crime*. The

President's Commission on Law Enforcement and the Administration of Justice. Washington, D.C.: U.S. Government Printing Office, 1967.

Schlesinger, Arthur, Sr. *Paths to the Present.* New York: Macmillan Company, 1949.

Scholl, Mason E., and Beker, Jerome. "A Comparison of the Religious Beliefs of Delinquent and Non-Delinquent Protestant Adolescent Boys." *Religious Education* 59 (May 1964): 250–253.

Schools Council Moral Education Curriculum Project. *Lifeline Series.* London: Longman Group Ltd., 1972.

Schur, Edwin M. *Crimes Without Victims.* Englewood Cliffs, N.J.: Prentice-Hall, 1965.

––––––. *Our Criminal Society.* Englewood Cliffs, N.J.: Prentice-Hall, 1969.

Schuster, Alvin. "Graft Charges Rare in Western Europe's Judiciary." *New York Times,* 8 October 1972.

Schwartz, S. H.; Feldman, K. A.; Brown, M. E.; and Heingartner, A. "Some Personality Correlates of Conduct in Two Situations of Moral Conflict." *Journal of Personality* 37 (1969): 41–57.

Scientific Advisory Committee on Television and Social Behavior. *Television and Growing Up: The Impact of Televised Violence.* Report to the Surgeon General, U.S. Public Health Service. Washington, D.C.: U.S. Government Printing Office, 1972.

Scott, James C. "Corruption, Machine Politics, and Political Change." *American Political Science Review* 63 (December 1969).

Shanley, Fred J. "Middle Class Delinquency as a Social Problem." *Sociology and Social Research,* July 1967.

Shaw, C. R., and McKay, H. D. *Juvenile Delinquency and Urban Areas.* Chicago: University of Chicago Press, 1942.

Sherif, Muzafer, and Sherif, Carolyn W., eds. *Problems of Youth: Transition to Adulthood in a Changing World.* Chicago: Aldine Publishing Company, 1965.

Shils, Edward. *The Intellectuals and the Powers.* Chicago: University of Chicago, 1972.

Shirer, William L. *The Collapse of the Third Republic.* New York: Pocket Books, 1971.

Short, James F., Jr. "Social Structure and Group Processes in Explanations of Gang Delinquency." In *Problems of Youth: Transition to Adulthood in a Changing World,* Muzafer Sherif and Carolyn W. Sherif, eds. Chicago: Aldine Publishing Company, 1965.

Short, James F., Jr., and Strodtlick, Fred L. *Group Process and Gang Delinquency.* Chicago: University of Chicago, 1965.

Simon, Sidney B.; Howe, Leland W.; and Kirschenbaum, Howard. *Values Clarification*. New York: Hart Publishing Company, 1972.

Sizer, Theodore R., ed. *Religion and Public Education*. New York: Houghton Mifflin, 1967.

Skinner, B. F. *Beyond Freedom and Dignity*. New York: Alfred A. Knopf, 1971.

————. *Walden II*. New York: Macmillan Company, 1948.

Sneath, E. Hershey, and Hodges, George. *Moral Training in the School and Home*. New York: Macmillan, 1913.

Solzhenitsyn, Aleksandr. *The Gulag Archipelago*. New York: Harper and Row, 1973.

Spiro, Melford. "Education in a Communal Village in Israel." *American Journal of Orthopsychiatry* 23 (1955): 283–93.

Statistics Canada. *Crime and Traffic Enforcement Statistics, 1972–73*. Ottawa: Information Canada, August 1974. .

Steffens, Lincoln. *The Shame of the Cities*. 1902. Reprint ed. New York: Hill and Wang, 1966.

————. *The Struggle for Self-Government*. New York: McClure, Phillips and Company, 1906.

Stevenson, H. W., ed. *Child Psychology, 62nd Yearbook of the National Society for the Study of Education*. Chicago: University of Chicago, 1963.

Stindler, Celia. "Sixty Years of Child Training Practice." *Journal of Pediatrics* 36 (January 1950).

Stout, Hiram. *British Government*. New York: Oxford University Press, 1953.

Sutherland, Edwin H. *White Collar Crime*. New York: Holt, Rinehart and Winston, 1949.

Sutherland, Edwin H., and Cressey, Donald. *Criminology*. Philadelphia: J. B. Lippincott, 1970.

Symonds, Percival M. *The Nature of Conduct*. New York: Macmillan, 1928.

Taylor, Paul. "Social Science and Ethical Relativism." *Journal of Philosophy* 55 (1958).

Tefft, B. F. *Speeches of Daniel Webster*. New York: A. L. Burt Company, n.d.

Tilly, Charles. "Collective Violence in European Perspective." In *Violence in America, Historical and Comparative Persepctives*. Staff Report to National Commission on the Causes and Prevention of Violence. Washington, D.C.: U.S. Government Printing Office, 1969.

Toby, Jackson. "Affluence and Adolescent Crime." In *Task Force Report: Juvenile Delinquency and Youth Crime.* The President's Commission on Law Enforcement and the Administration of Justice. Washington, D.C.: U.S. Government Printing Office, 1967.

Tocqueville, Alexis de. *Democracy in America.* Phillips Bradley, trans. 2 vols. New York: Random House, Vintage Books, 1945.

————. *Democracy in America.* J. P. Mayer, ed., George Lawrence, trans. New York: Harper and Row, 1966; Doubleday Anchor Books, 1969.

Toffler, Alvin, ed. *Learning for Tomorrow.* New York: Random House, Vintage Books, 1974.

Travers, John F., and Davis, Russell G. "A Study of Religious Motivation and Delinquency." *Journal of Educational Sociology* 20 (January 1961).

Troeltsch, Ernst. *The Social Teaching of the Christian Churches.* 2 vols. New York: Macmillan Company, 1931.

Troth, Dennis C. *Selected Readings in Character Education.* Boston: Beacon Press, 1930.

Tullock, Gordon. "Does Punishment Deter Crime?" *The Public Interest,* no. 36 (1974), pp. 103–11.

Turner, Ralph H. *Family Interaction.* New York: John Wiley and Sons, 1970.

Tuttle, Harold S. *Character Education by State and Church.* New York: Abingdon Press, 1930.

Ulich, Robert. *A History of Religious Education.* New York: New York University Press, 1968.

United Nations. *Practical Results and Financial Aspects of Adult Probation in Selected Countries.* New York, 1954.

U.S. Department of Commerce. *Statistical Abstract of the United States: 1973.* Social and Economic Statistics Administration, Bureau of the Census.

U.S. Department of Justice, Law Enforcement Assistance Agency (LEAA). "Criminal Victimization in the United States—January to June 1973." *Report SD-NCP-N-1* (November 1974).

Wattenberg, William W., and Balistrieri, James. "Auto Theft: A Favored Group Delinquency." *American Journal of Sociology* 57 (May 1952): 75–79.

Weber, Max. *The Protestant Ethic and the Spirit of Capitalism.* New York: Charles Scribner's Sons, 1958.

Werner, M. R. *Tammany Hall.* Garden City, N.Y.: Doubleday, Doran, 1928.

Wertham, Frederick. "Comic Books: Blueprints for Delinquency." *Reader's Digest,* May 1954.

White, Leonard D. *The Federalists.* New York: Free Press, 1965.

————. *The Jacksonians.* New York: Free Press, 1965.

————. *The Jeffersonians.* New York: Free Press, 1965.

————. *The Republican Era.* New York: Macmillan, 1958; Free Press, 1965.

Wilson, H. H. *Congress: Corruption and Compromise.* New York: Rinehart and Company, 1951.

Wilson, James Q. "Corruption: The Shame of the States." *The Public Interest,* no. 6 (1966), pp. 30–32.

————. "Crime and Criminologists." *Commentary* 58 (1958).

————. "If Every Criminal Knew He Would Be Punished if Caught." *New York Times Magazine,* 28 January 1973.

————. *Varieties of Police Behavior.* Cambridge, Mass.: Harvard University Press, 1968.

————. "Violence, Pornography, and Social Science." *The Public Interest,* no. 22 (1971), pp. 45–61.

Wilson, James Q.; Moore, Mark H.; and Wheat, I. David, Jr. "The Problem of Heroin." *The Public Interest,* no. 29 (1972), pp. 3–28.

Wilson, John. *Moral Thinking.* London: Heineman Educational Books, 1970.

Winick, Charles. "Censor and Sensibility: A Content Analysis of the Television Censor's Comments." In *Violence and the Mass Media,* Otto N. Larsen, ed. New York: Harper and Row, 1968.

Winters, Glenn R. "What Can Be Done about Pettifoggery and Legal Delays?" *Annals of the Academy of Political and Social Science* (January 1966), p. 55.

Wittgenstein, L. "A Lecture on Ethics." *Philosophical Review* 74 (1965).

Won, George, and Yamamoto, George. "Social Structure and Deviant Behavior: A Study of Shoplifting." *Sociology and Social Research* 53 (October 1968): 44–45.

Wright, Derek, ed. *The Journal of Moral Education.* London: Pemberton Publishing Company, n.d.

————. *The Psychology of Moral Behavior.* London: Penguin Books, 1971.

Yearbook of American Churches for 1973. New York: Council Press, 1973.

Index